The Complete Ulster Way

The Ulster Way was designed to ensure comfortable access to the countryside with due consideration to landowners. Rights of way were followed where possible; however, the fact that a walk is outlined in this book is no guarantee of a recognised right of way.

Land ownership and conditions can change, and where problems do arise the author would appreciate such changes being brought to his attention so that future editions can be modified. The author and the publishers do not accept any responsibility where trespass may occur, neither do they accept any responsibility for accident or loss by the public when carrying out these walks. Common sense should prevail at all times. Take the advice of locals and heed all warning signs.

On NO account should dogs be brought on any of these walks as they cause annoyance and disturbance to livestock, wildlife and other members of the public. Show respect for the countryside, as the irresponsible actions of one person can destroy the enjoyment of so many others.

The Complete Ulster Way

Paddy Dillon

THE O'BRIEN PRESS
DUBLIN

First published 1999 by The O'Brien Press Ltd.,
20 Victoria Road, Dublin 6, Ireland.
Tel. +353 1 4923333; Fax. +353 1 4922777
email: books@obrien.ie
website: http://www.obrien.ie

ISBN: 0-86278-589-8

British Library Cataloguing-in-publication Data
Dillon, Paddy
The Ulster Way
1.Walking - Northern Ireland - Ulster Way - Guidebooks
2.Ulster Way (Northern Ireland) - Guidebooks
I.Title
914.1'6'04824

1 2 3 4 5 6 7 8 9 10
99 00 01 02 03 04 05 06 07

The O'Brien Press receives
assistance from

The Arts Council
An Chomhairle Ealaíon

Maps: Jeremy Ashcroft
General map of Ulster Way: Paddy Dillon
Layout and design: The O'Brien Press Ltd.
Illustrations: Aileen Caffrey
Photographs: Paddy Dillon
Colour separations: C&A Print Services
Printing: Cox & Wyman Ltd.

Contents

Southern Section, Counties Tyrone and Armagh

South-eastern Section, County Down

Donegal Section

INTRODUCTION

The Ulster Way is the longest waymarked trail in Britain and Ireland, and offers a real challenge to long-distance walkers. The course measures 1,070 kilometres (665 miles) in all and brings you on a journey of discovery through Ulster's most scenic countryside, with its high mountains, empty moorlands and broad forests, and fields rolling down to the cliff-lined coast. The distinct cultures of the towns and villages along the way, and the readiness of people to share their time with passing wayfarers, make this a most memorable walking route.

Ulster is one of the four ancient provinces of Ireland, along with Leinster, Munster and Connacht. The boundaries of these ancient areas were fluid and often in dispute. The 'provinces' exist today only in terms of historical and sentimental perception. Since the defining and shaping of Ireland's thirty-two counties, the name 'Ulster' has been used to cover the nine northernmost counties of Ireland: Antrim, Armagh, Cavan, Derry, Donegal, Down, Fermanagh, Monaghan and Tyrone. Since the partition of Ireland in the 1920s, the term 'Ulster' has almost become synonymous with Northern Ireland. Northern Ireland is formed of only six of Ulster's nine counties: Antrim, Armagh, Derry, Down, Fermanagh and Tyrone. More confusingly, Northern Ireland is often referred to as 'The Province', while it is common for nationalists to refer to the area as 'The North of Ireland'. Visitors are often confused by the whole thing, which is understandable! The Ulster Way spends most of its time in seven of Ulster's nine counties, visiting Cavan only briefly, while setting foot in Monaghan actually requires a short detour off-route. The provision of a tea room in the middle of nowhere in north Monaghan may entice you to take those few steps!

In brief outline, the Ulster Way makes a circuit around the six counties of Northern Ireland, while a more rugged spur extends into Co. Donegal in the Republic of Ireland. Taking Belfast as a starting point, the route crosses the Belfast Hills, then wanders over the bleak mountains and verdant glens of Antrim to the seaside resorts on the coast. The route continues through the sprawling moorlands and forests of the Sperrin Mountains stretching from Derry into Co. Tyrone, before moving into Fermanagh, where it brings you by Lower and Upper Lough Erne and into rugged limestone countryside set with extensive forests.

The gentle drumlin country of south Tyrone and north Armagh is threaded by quiet roads, until the level towpath of the Newry Canal is followed by rugged upland walking in the Mountains of Mourne. The rolling countryside and low coastline of Co. Down leads back towards Belfast, where the Castlereagh Hills and leafy Lagan Valley are explored. The spur of the Ulster Way which crosses through Co. Donegal is altogether wilder, and brings you through the county's remote mountain ranges.

For sheer variety, the Ulster Way is hard to match, and though some people might be daunted by the prospect of walking day after day, week after week, for a month or even longer, no part of the Ulster Way is particularly rigorous. In fact, taken at a steady pace, even the high mountains are easily traversed. If the Ulster Way seems like too great an undertaking, it is not because of the nature of the terrain, but simply because of its length. There are various approaches you can take to this. You can practise and train until you are fit and able for the full distance; or you can tackle the Ulster Way in a series of weekend, one-day or even shorter walks. The Ulster Way has been subdivided into six main sections, and each of these can be covered on holidays of a week or so.

Anyone can walk part of the Ulster Way, and with some encouragement most could go on to complete the whole route. Remarkably, most of the walkers who have tackled the route are retired men and women who already possess a good level of walking experience. Young people walk the route too, of course (one man even ran its entire length), and one family made the Ulster Way the subject of a series of holidays. A steady trickle of overseas walkers set off on the Ulster Way each year, some carrying full backpacking gear and camping outdoors at night. More often, walkers opt for B&B accommodation and take lifts off the route to secure lodgings if none are available along the way.

PLANNING AND PRACTICALITIES

While the Ulster Way may seem long, you can cover it if you take it one step at a time. If you have walked long distances before, then the Ulster Way should be no problem for you, but if you have not, then I would urge you to get plenty of experience before attempting a trek of this magnitude. If you generally enjoy a day or weekend in the countryside and want to cover the Ulster Way piecemeal, you should have no problem: you simply need to choose the appropriate sections and sort out how you are going to get to and from them, and where you are going to stay if you need to spend a night anywhere along the way.

ROUTE DESCRIPTIONS

Before each walk you will find **start** and **finish** details with the map references; **distance** covered; **maps** required; type of **terrain**; **waymarking**; **public transport** and **accommodation** details. Although the book contains small generalised maps for each walk, it is essential in most cases to carry the relevant Ordnance Survey maps.

The route descriptions given here offer all the information you need about each stage of the route. Feel free to alter each daily stretch, but bear in mind that walking the whole of the Ulster Way is probably going to take around forty days. The route descriptions are quite detailed as the waymarking may not always be reliable. Some indication of the nature of the terrain is also given, as this will affect the speed at which you will cover certain sections: you are likely to make slow progress through upland bog, and cover roads and forest tracks much faster.

Because of the varied nature of the terrain, it can be a good idea to carry boots for the bog or mountain and a good pair of walking shoes or trainers for the roads and forest tracks. Your clothing should be chosen to suit the prevailing weather or season; on any extended walk you are going to see a variety of weather conditions and you need to be prepared for them. Expect rain and mist at any time of the year. Winter may bring brief snow cover, while summer occasionally features a blistering heatwave. It's a good idea to monitor the weather forecast frequently.

Individual approaches will always vary, but be sure to read the route descriptions carefully before setting out, and refer them to the appropriate maps. Book accommodation in advance, especially where it may be scarce, and check the bus timetables if you need to move off-route. Shops, pubs and restaurants are noted where they are close to the Ulster Way, so you will always know where you can obtain food and drink, but remember that sometimes these places may not be open when you are passing, and your rucksack should always carry a good reserve in case of emergency.

How you complete the Ulster Way is a matter for your own imagination and experience. One thing is certain: if you do have any difficulty along the route (say the shop is closed or you miss a bus), people can be extraordinarily kind and will often go out of their way to help you. Alan Warner, the first person to walk the Ulster Way in one long trek, remarked on the many kindnesses he was shown throughout his journey. Many years later, two Dutch friends of mine who walked the Ulster Way said that the people were more friendly and helpful than in any other country where they had travelled. Perhaps one of the greatest attractions of the Ulster Way is that it brings you into the heart of the countryside where you have an opportunity to meet such people.

MAPS

The Ordnance Survey of Northern Ireland covers the main circuit of the Ulster Way at a scale of 1:50,000. The spur through Donegal is covered at the same scale by the Ordnance Survey of Ireland. At present maps do not always show the route of the Ulster Way. Ultimately, the Ordnance Survey of Northern Ireland will show the *entire* course of the Ulster Way in Northern Ireland, as they are digitising their maps over the next few years. The Ordnance Survey of Ireland does not show the actual course of the Ulster Way through Co. Donegal, and this is due to some internal ruling concerning the status of the route.

You will need as many as twenty maps to cover the whole of the Ulster Way. You might also consider using the 1:250,000 scale Holiday Map of Ireland: North as a basic outline planning map. This map once showed the entire course of the Ulster Way, which was most useful, but unfortunately the latest editions do not.

ACCOMMODATION

There are hundreds of places offering accommodation around the Ulster Way, but they are very unevenly spread: some towns and villages have abundant accommodation, while huge tracts of countryside have no lodgings at all. If you are planning to stay exclusively in hotels and B&Bs, then you will need to sort out a schedule where they can be found at manageable intervals on or near the route. There are relatively few hostels or campsites. You have a high degree of freedom if you carry a tent and pitch it along the way, but bear in mind that you will need to ask for permission wherever you camp, and that camping in forests is expressly forbidden except in designated campsites.

Details of where you can stay are found in the *Where to Stay* guide published by the Northern Ireland Tourist Board. Updated annually, it also has a specific ‘walking man’ symbol for addresses which are near the Ulster Way. Also available from the Northern Ireland Tourist Board is the *Ulster Way Accommodation Guide*, which lists hotels, guesthouses, B&Bs, hostels and campsites as they appear along the Ulster Way. It is revised less frequently, and unlike the *Where to Stay* guide does not list the range of facilities available at each address.

TRANSPORT

Bus and rail links are listed for each walk. There are frequent Ulsterbus services to many parts of the Ulster Way, and some sections are also served by Bus Éireann, but much of the route has patchy coverage or nothing at all. A few places are served by rail. You need up-to-date timetables if you are planning to join or leave the Ulster Way at intervals, and of course you need to be there to meet your bus or train at the right time. You could also call on the aid of a friend with a car to meet you at intervals, or hitch lifts to and from any accommodation you book along the way, especially where facilities are sparse.

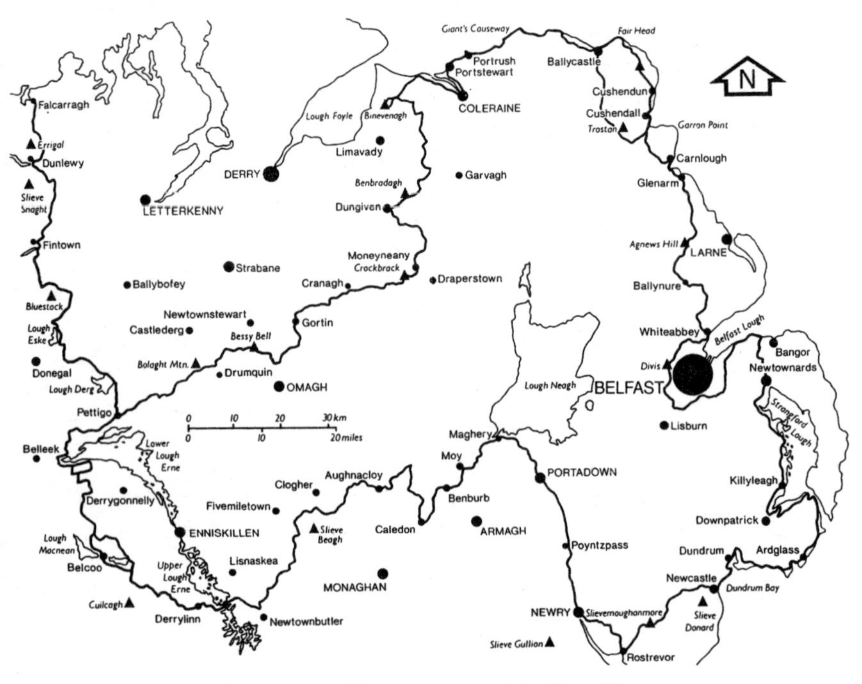

An overview of the entire route of the Ulster Way.

WILFRID CAPPER MBE - FATHER OF THE ULSTER WAY

The late Wilfrid Capper was known as the 'Father of the Ulster Way'.

Wilfrid Capper deserves all the credit for the inspiration and implementation of the Ulster Way. He is rightly remembered as the 'Father of the Ulster Way'. I enjoyed a number of meetings with the man and was amazed at the depth of his knowledge. His mind would skip eagerly through a century of great change. If you see anything good in the countryside around the Ulster Way, it is quite likely that Wilfrid's influence can be found somewhere behind it.

The Capper family came from Annalong in the Kingdom of Mourne. Wilfrid was born in 1905 and reared around Belfast and Bangor. The coast of Belfast Lough and the countryside around Annalong was explored in his early years. What most of us call the Silent Valley in the Mountains of Mourne was always known as the Happy Valley to Wilfrid, before it was flooded with reservoirs to slake the growing thirst of Belfast.

Wilfrid pursued a lifelong career in the Civil Service, in the Department of Education and Agriculture, in touch with the countryside even from his office. The 1930s were interesting times for the broader outdoor movement, and Wilfrid's travels around Europe brought him into contact with other outdoor enthusiasts. He was in the Polish Tatras and climbed over into Czechoslovakia. He walked through Finland and the Black Forest, and visited France and Spain. The outdoor movement which was developing so vigorously in Germany was influencing Ireland in the 1930s. Wilfrid was involved in youth hostelling from the start, and in Northern Ireland things began to develop differently than in the Republic of Ireland. 'An Óige was talking about having separate hostels for men and women,' he said, with a hint of disapproval. 'So we founded the Youth Hostels Association of Northern Ireland so that the men and women could stay together.'

Wilfrid was married to Evelyn in 1932 and they shared a common love of the outdoors. Wilfrid designed their house on Carney Hill above Holywood and had it surrounded with trees. They lived happily there for fifty years.

Even before the Second World War, Wilfrid was involved with a remarkable number of organisations. To name but a few, they included: the Countrywide Holiday Association, Holiday Fellowship, Youth Hostels Association, National Trust, Ulster Society for the Preservation of the Countryside, Vegetarian Society, and the Association of University Graduates. He was involved with some of these organisations for over half a century, but it's worth looking at one group in particular to see how Wilfrid expressed his deepest concerns.

In 1937 Wilfrid became so concerned at abuses in the countryside that he helped to found the Ulster Society for the Preservation of the Countryside. At first this small group could do no more than lament at the damage inflicted by insensitive planning, but they gradually developed good lobbying skills. They realised they were winning when a planner turned on them with the words: 'Look, from now on, whether we are planning a motorway or a lay-by, USPC will be the first to see the plans and will be able to comment on them and suggest changes before any work takes place.' Wilfrid was secretary of the USPC for over fifty years. When things went well, he felt a quiet pride and pleasure. When things went badly, there seemed to be no anger or bitterness, just a quiet kind of sadness.

In 1946 Tom Stephenson of the Ramblers' Association led journalists and politicians along a route which was to become the Pennine Way in England. Wilfrid was also invited, though he was unimpressed by the scenery. Returning to his beloved Ulster, 'where we have much better scenery than the Pennines', he seriously considered establishing a long-distance walk to be called the Ulster Way. It wasn't until the 1970s that the idea really began to be promoted, and 1974 was regarded as the most significant year. At that time the Sports Council for Northern Ireland showed great interest and a series of meetings were held.

Wilfrid was by this time an active, retired person. He was asked to be the Field Officer and landed the job on a six-month contract. Those six months stretched to fill the next fourteen years, during which time Wilfrid roamed the length and breadth of the Ulster countryside, checking and re-checking routes, negotiating access with farmers, lobbying and publicising the route. He had an interest in the development of the spur route through Co. Donegal, as well as a friendship with JB Malone in Dublin, who started the drive for waymarked trails in the Republic of Ireland.

'I met nothing but kindness wherever I went,' said Wilfrid, who delighted in recalling all manner of little incidents along the way. He was invited into a Co. Antrim farmhouse by a small boy one wet day, receiving a meal of boiled eggs from the boy's mother. On Bessy Bell in Co. Tyrone he was advised to drop three white stones in a holy well to obtain a wish. One farmer demanded to know, 'Are you orange or green?', as politics are never far removed from daily life. 'Neither,' was Wilfrid's reply. 'Black, white, yellow or brown – it's all the same to me!'

'I broke all the rules,' Wilfrid admitted late one night. 'I told no one where I was going and walked all alone. I wore a bright red anorak, but I knew no one would have spotted me if I'd had an accident in a remote area.' In fact, the only injury he sustained in all that time was a sprained ankle, while leaping across a ditch near his home above Holywood, and he was able to limp home. It was at his home that I used to visit him and hear tales of the Ulster Way. He wrote to me once to request a meeting, pointing out that 'the Ulster Way was only the beginning' before taking me through other plans for other routes. A walk along the length of the Lagan; a route through the Antrim Mountains; another through the Sperrin Mountains. As he worked his way through the maps, he sent one flying in my direction and gave a wry smile. 'Tell them a white-haired old man threw a map at you.' And I see that I have!

Was there anything he hadn't done? 'I climbed the highest mountains in Scotland, Wales and England,' he admitted one night. 'But I never climbed the highest mountain in Ireland!'

Meeting Wilfrid and talking to him was like travelling back to a bygone era, but the wealth of knowledge he possessed, and the way he presented it, offered a glimpse into the future – a future where things could be better, where the countryside could be cared for properly and enjoyed for ever. Wilfrid was walking with the Belfast CHA Rambling Club until almost ninety years of age. A bad fall at home resulted in a broken pelvis and subsequent residence in a nursing home. The home was on the shores of Belfast Lough, on the course of the Ulster Way, where he died at the age of ninety-three in July 1998.

The Ulster Way is Wilfrid Capper's memorial, and the preservation of the Ulster countryside through which it runs is his greatest achievement. This guidebook is respectfully dedicated to Wilfrid's life and work. Enjoy the walk and please remember the man.

NORTH-EASTERN SECTION

County Antrim

Distance: 190 kilometres (118 miles)

Most walkers who follow the Ulster Way start from Belfast, the second biggest city in Ireland. Many of the walkers live and work in the city, so it seems a natural starting point, while others choose it because of its ease of access and abundant transport links. Walking is a growing activity around Belfast, with walking routes being incorporated into most new developments and guided walks exploring the history and heritage of the city. To explore Belfast thoroughly on foot and learn more about its history, development and attractions, use a copy of *25 Walks in and around Belfast*, published by The Stationery Office.

This stretch launches walkers straight into the route, from the city of Belfast, through the hills to the celebrated Causeway coast. In the first couple of hours, the city gives way to a wooded glen and rolling, exposed hills. Be warned that access to the Belfast Hills has never been fully negotiated; they are largely pathless and unmarked and in misty weather can prove confusing to anyone not familiar with them. After a brief descent into the urban sprawl, the route once more takes to the heights and wanders through forests and farmlands as it gradually clears the city. Even when you are as far away as Ballynure, it is still possible to return to the city if accommodation proves hard to find, but after that you need to keep your wits about you as the route steers a course through the Antrim Mountains.

The bleak, boggy moorlands of the Antrim Mountains are only sparsely waymarked, and fine weather is a distinct advantage as you negotiate the route. Food, drink and accommodation are available in the villages along the way, but there is nothing along the empty moorland roads. It's a good idea to book accommodation in advance, and bear in mind that, if it proves necessary to move off-route, bus services are infrequent in some villages.

Originally, the Ulster Way was to have been routed through Waterfoot, Cushendall and Cushendun, then over the top of Carnanmore and around the cliffs of Fair Head to Ballycastle. Unfortunately, there are problems with access to Carnanmore and Fair Head, so the course of the Moyle Way is given instead from Glenariff Forest Park through to Ballycastle. This is a wild, desolate route; a fair challenge in its own right. The course has been upgraded and is free of access problems, but there are no facilities at all along the way, and without a back-up vehicle to meet you on the moorland roads, it would be difficult to break from the route early.

After leaving Ballycastle, the Ulster Way runs along the Antrim coast to the celebrated Giant's Causeway. This has to be one of the best coastal walks in Ireland, and cannot be beaten for sheer variety and interest. The National Trust is the prime mover in the drive for access, and by purchasing or leasing stretches of the coast it has provided a continuous path through its most scenic parts. Accommodation is widely available along the coast, but can also fill up quite quickly in the summer months, so it is always a good idea to book beds in advance.

WALK 1

DUNMURRY TO WHITEABBEY

Start: Dunmurry Station – 293691.

Finish: Whiteabbey Presbyterian Church – 359830.

Distance: 30 kilometres (18½ miles).

Maps: OSNI Discoverer Sheet 15. The Greater Belfast Street Map is also useful.

Terrain: Varies from urban to woodland and rugged moorland. Includes a few busy roads, some good tracks and paths, as well as pathless moorland which can be boggy.

Waymarking: The route over the Belfast Hills has never been waymarked, nor has access been fully negotiated, though there are some markers towards the end of this stretch.

Public Transport: Dunmurry has a railway station and is served by Citybus 58 and several City Stopper services. Stewartstown Rd near Colin Glen is served by several City Stopper services. Hannahstown is served by Ulsterbus 106. Citybus services run close to the route at Suffolk, Legoniel, Carr's Glen and Belfast Castle. Belfast Zoo is served by several Citybus services. Rathcoole is served by Ulsterbus 160, 161 and 167. Whiteabbey has a railway station and is also served by Ulsterbus 167.

Accommodation: A handful of hotels and B&Bs are within walking distance of the start and finish. There is no accommodation on or near the route over the Belfast Hills. Public transport services bring several accommodation options around Belfast city within easy reach.

ROUTE DESCRIPTION

Leave the railway station at Dunmurry, following Upper Dunmurry Lane as it climbs past houses and old warehouses, and cross the bridge over the busy dual carriageway. The surroundings are urban at this point and the only extensive green space is Colinvalley Golf Course off to the right. Turn left up a busy road signposted for Suffolk. The Belfast Hills rise ahead, but first you turn right at a roundabout and walk down Stewartstown Rd to reach the Colin Glen Forest Park Centre. The

Ulster Way actually runs up the Suffolk Rd, but Colin Glen offers a most delightful route to the hills. In fact, a more agreeable route from Dunmurry to Colin Glen is also likely to be created in the future.

Older residents of West Belfast still refer to Colin Glen as McCance's Glen, after a family who bought the glen in the 1770s and built a mill near by in the 1880s, drawing power from the mountain stream. The glen was also managed as a sporting reserve, which is hard to believe now that it is surrounded by housing estates. The tall trees which once graced the valley were felled for furniture manufacture by Gilpins of Sandy Row in the 1940s. Later, the development of a brick-works resulted in the area being used for tipping, but in recent years Colin Glen Forest Park grew out of a series of cross-community environmental projects. Tips were landscaped, tens of thousands of trees were planted, a network of paths and bridges was constructed, and the glen now serves as a valuable green space for the residents of West Belfast and an important educational resource for their children. The park centre contains a wealth of information about the glen and is well worth a visit.

Leave the car park beside the centre and follow a path into the woodlands. The Red Bridge on the right leads onto Suffolk Rd, so don't cross it, but keep following the well-wooded path upstream alongside Colin River to reach the Gamekeeper's Bridge. You can cross this bridge or simply keep walking upstream; you have the same choice at the next bridge, Weir Bridge, as there are paths on both sides of the river at this point. At the following bridge, the curiously shaped Tri Bridge, you must walk on the eastern bank of the river in order to continue upstream. The path passes beneath the high stone arch of the Glen Bridge, where the scene changes dramatically as tall beech trees come into view. The upper glen is owned by the National Trust and still features its ancient woodland, but paths and bridges here are not as well maintained as those in the lower glen and some parts can be muddy.

Climb uphill a short way from the Glen Bridge, then turn left and continue upstream, descending to cross a wooden bridge. Almost immediately, cross back over the river using a collapsed bridge which resembles two fallen tree trunks. If the river is running high and you don't want to get wet, then you'll have to double back to find an alternative way round. Steps climb up from the river on a steep slope, with a left turn along the top edge of the wood. After crossing a small footbridge over an inflowing stream, look out for a gravel path heading off to the right, away from the wooded glen. The path passes an old basalt quarry and heads up to the B38 road at Hannahstown. Beyond this point are the bleak Belfast Hills. There is an old firing range on the slopes of the hills, though this is unlikely to be in use. Walkers might like to check by contacting the Army Information Office on (028) 9260 9674.

Cross over the B38 road and walk up a narrow road opposite, which is signposted as private. Vehicles are barred from using the road, but walkers can follow it up to a tall transmitter mast on the rugged slopes of Black Hill. Keeping to the left of the mast, climb uphill and cross a low fence to reach the heathery summit. A trig point stands at

360m (1,180ft) and there are views of Belfast spreading from the Lagan Valley to the sea, with the Mountains of Mourne far away to the south.

Leave Black Hill and walk roughly northwards to the minor hump of Craigs, passing beneath an electricity transmission line and crossing a heathery gap to reach the top. The moorland crest is rather broad and featureless, running roughly north-east towards Black Mountain. Some parts are soft and wet, and a slight diversion down a gentle slope leads to a trig point offering another view over Belfast. The true summit of Black Mountain rises to 390m (1,280ft), from where a track can be followed to another tall transmitter mast which sits on a wide moorland gap.

Keep to the right of the mast and climb straight uphill from a gravel track to reach a narrow tarmac road on the flank of Divis. This road climbs steadily to the right, then turns sharply left to reach a military installation on the very top of the hill. The military post is a squat pyramid surmounted by twin masts and surrounded by coils of barbed wire, monitored by cameras and illuminated at night-time. You will not be able to reach the actual summit of Divis at 478m (1,568ft), but by turning your back to the summit you can still enjoy the extensive views. The Belfast Hills, Belfast and Belfast Lough stand out, while the Mountains of Mourne are seen across the lower parts of Co. Down, flanked by Slieve Croob and Slieve Gullion. The vast expanse of Lough Neagh is backed by the Sperrin Mountains, while the Antrim Mountains are ranged to the north.

Divis can be climbed easily enough in mist by following the road to the top, but in poor visibility a compass bearing may be necessary to continue. The northern slopes of Divis are very soft and wet, and it might be necessary to traverse around the southern and western sides of the security fence before descending northwards. The heathery slopes are scored by a groove and this feature should be located, then followed to the left. It leads to a boundary ditch and embankment, topped by a line of wind-blasted thorn bushes. Follow this line across a broad gap, continuing along the line of a wire fence. By crossing the fence, the crest of the hill can be followed to Ballyhill Rd on the next gap.

Cross straight over Ballyhill Rd and climb up a gently sloping field to reach a trig point at 335m (1,100ft) beside a gate on top of the hill. The line of descent is roughly north-east. After passing a gateway, keep to the left of an old quarry to reach the A52 road, also known as Ballyutoag Rd. Turn right and follow the road downhill towards Legoniel, but turn left up the minor road called Flush Rd to continue over the hills. There are houses along the right-hand side of Flush Rd, then there are broad fields. Look out for a small stile on the right and a vague path running across a field. This line leads to more stiles showing the way up the slopes of Squires Hill. The summit rises to 374m (1,227ft) and bears slender masts, but it isn't necessary to go all the way to the top. Keep well to the left of the masts, and keeping the next few stiles in line walk down through more fields. There is a horribly muddy patch to cross shortly before the B95, or Upper Hightown Rd.

There is a rather ugly landfill site across the road, but by turning right down the road, then left at a car park, the scene quickly passes from sight. Follow a farm track, continuing past a small waterfall, keeping to the left to continue gradually uphill into the Cave Hill Country Park. A clear path continues towards one of the most famous landmarks on the Belfast Hills: McArt's Fort on Cave Hill. A rocky path leads onto this Iron Age promontory fort site, which offers a splendid view over the city of Belfast. Walkers who have time to explore these surroundings will find an elaborate network of paths and tracks on the lower slopes.

The upper floors of Belfast Castle serve as the Cave Hill Heritage Centre, but this is far below in the woods and is not visited on this walk. The castle was built in the Scottish Baronial style in 1870 for the 3rd Marquis of Donegall. Cave Hill was formerly known as Ben Madigan, after a 9th-century king of Ulster, and has endured the less flattering nickname 'Napoleon's Nose', owing to its resemblance to the ill-fated emperor's nose when seen from certain parts of the city. The hill has long been woven into the history of the city. In 1795 Wolfe Tone's United Irishmen, a revolutionary society uniting 'Protestant, Catholic and Dissenter', met here in secret and swore oaths to free Ireland, setting in train a chain of events which would lead to the ill-fated rebellion of 1798.

The turrets of Belfast Castle and the distinctive prow of Cave Hill.

When leaving Cave Hill, be sure to follow the path which runs roughly northwards along the top of the cliffs. This path gradually descends and passes through fences to reach the wooded slope of the Hazelwood National Nature Reserve, though the local wildlife is rather eclipsed by the exotic residents of Belfast Zoo at the foot of the hill! A path and flight of steps leads down to the walls of the zoo and you turn left for the entrance, though after walking all the way across the Belfast Hills, it's likely that the zoo will have to be visited another day. Walkers who are worn out can catch a bus near by, as there are several services returning to the city.

To continue from the zoo to Whiteabbey, follow the access road down to the busy Antrim Rd. Turn left to follow the road over the roaring M2 motorway, then turn right along O'Neill Rd. Another right turn gives access to the Valley Park, where a broad green space is occupied by grassy areas and sports pitches, threaded by a number of paths. Follow a path gently downhill and switch to an embankment overlooking a small wildfowl pond. Keep to the right of the Valley Leisure Centre and follow its access road away to Church Rd. Cross over Church Rd near a filling station and turn left, then almost immediately turn right to follow *Glas na Bradán*, the Stream of the Silvery Trout.

A path has been created along the wooded watercourse between Whitehouse and Rathcoole, leading from Church Rd to the busy Shore Rd. Don't cross over the stream at any point, but remain on the Rathcoole bank throughout. Take care crossing Shore Rd, as visibility is limited and the traffic can be fast. Go under a nearby railway arch and walk beside a tidal lagoon. A tarmac path leads off to the right, and by keeping to the right a concrete path can be followed across Gideon's Green where a granite boulder stands as a memorial to Gideon, a diarist who recorded the landing of Williamite troops nearby in 1689.

The path runs beneath the M5 motorway and continues around Macedon Point to Hazelbank Park. Look out for an Ulster Way signpost just before the stone tower rising from the shore of Belfast Lough, then follow the most obvious path inland to reach a car park. On the way out of the park, keep to the right at a huge roundabout and continue walking along Shore Rd. The road gradually moves back towards the shore of Belfast Lough. If public transport is needed, there are Ulsterbus services, and Whiteabbey railway station is off to the left along Station Rd. The Ulster Way follows the Shore Rd, then crosses over at a pedestrian crossing shortly before the war memorial on a grassy strip overlooking the lough, and continues past a couple of shops to reach Whiteabbey Presbyterian Church near the Glenavna House Hotel.

WALK 2

WHITEABBEY TO BALLYNURE

Start: Whiteabbey Presbyterian Church – 359830.

Finish: Ballynure – 318936.

Distance: 22 kilometres (13½ miles).

Map: OSNI Discoverer Sheet 15.

Terrain: Urban at first, then parkland gives way to farming country and forest. More farming country is crossed on the way to Ballynure.

Waymarking: Metal Ulster Way signposts along the roads give way to wooden marker posts in the forest. The final stretch to Ballynure is not fully waymarked.

Public Transport: Whiteabbey has a railway station and is served by Ulsterbus 167. Ballynure is served by Ulsterbus 156 linking with Belfast and Larne.

Accommodation: Limited to a couple of B&Bs and a hotel at the start, with a few more B&Bs at the end, but there are bus services giving access to other lodgings in Belfast and Larne.

ROUTE DESCRIPTION

Start beside Whiteabbey Presbyterian Church and walk along the access road towards Glenavna House Hotel. The road runs through a small woodland and there is a narrow tarmac footpath off to the left. The path crosses a bridge over Three Mile Water and rises towards a housing estate. Pick a way through the estate to Glenville Rd, turn right and pass beneath a railway arch. Follow the road past housing and industrial estates, almost to a junction with Monkstown Avenue. Turn right just before the junction, following a track beside a row of houses. It continues as a narrow path, which runs around the perimeter fence of a bus depot. The path becomes a broad, muddy track passing Monkstown Industrial Estate and onto the busy Monkstown Rd.

Turn right along Monkstown Rd to Monkstown Community School and turn left down Bridge Rd. At the bottom, turn right along Hawthorne Rd which ends with a gate and stile. A tarmac path runs through the Three Mile Water Park, passing wooded and grassy areas.

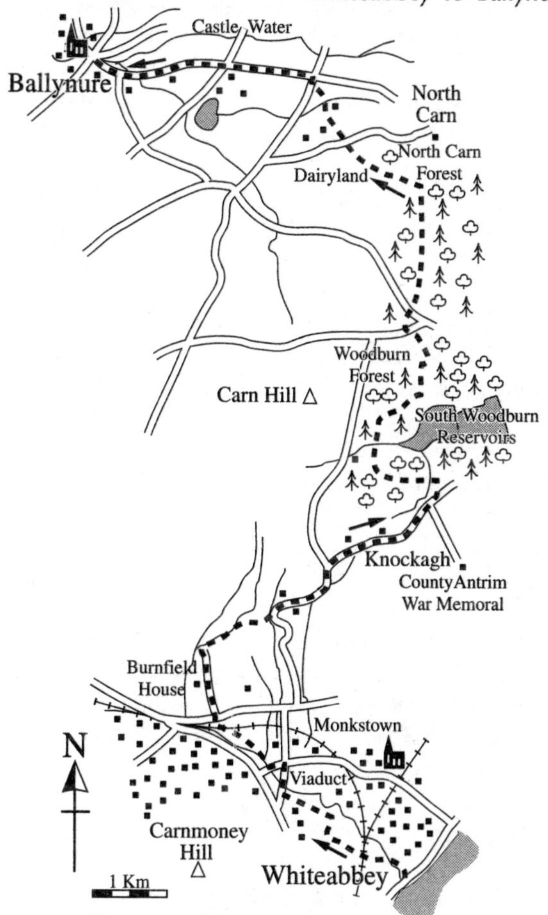

Continue along the path, passing under a concrete railway arch and rising to another busy road. Turn quickly left and right to follow Cullyburn Rd uphill, passing close to Burnfield House restaurant. The road later levels out and passes Cullyburn Lodge. Turn right up a concrete lane planted with beech trees and follow it uphill. When a white house is close to hand, turn right along a rougher track and keep right again later. The surface is quite uneven for a while and can be muddy in places. When the track reaches a minor road, turn left and follow it uphill to the junction with Knockagh Rd. Turn right into Knockagh Rd and carry on uphill to the junction with Monument Rd.

The Co. Antrim War Memorial stands off-route at the end of Monument Rd. It is a notable landmark, though more often seen from

Belfast Lough than at close quarters, and offers splendid views across Belfast Lough to the distant Mountains of Mourne; the Galloway Hills can sometimes be seen across the short stretch of water which separates Northern Ireland from Scotland. On a clear day the diversion to the memorial is well worth the extra half-hour there and back.

Knockagh Rd passes the junction with Monument Rd and reaches Woodburn Forest, where an Ulster Way marker indicates a left turn. Follow a gravel path down into the forest, then turn left along a wider, undulating track and walk to a junction. A right turn leads downhill; then, after climbing uphill again, turn right at another junction. The track bends to the left, then a right turn is made at yet another junction. Keep following the track until a narrow path is marked to the left, leading onto the Lisglass Rd. (It has to be admitted that there are more scenic ways through Woodburn Forest, and there is, for instance, a fine path alongside South Woodburn reservoir, which might have been used to good effect.)

Turn left to follow the road a few paces, then turn right onto the track into another stand of forest. The track shrinks to a path before the next minor road is reached. Turn left along the road, then right to follow another forest track which runs northwards through North Carn Forest. Eventually an Ulster Way marker indicates a left turn, uphill and away from the track. The path descends alongside the forest to reach a farm access road. Cross the track and descend through the fields using gates, following a field track which can be muddy. Cross Dairyland Rd and follow a farm access road down to Ballylagan Rd. Turn right, then left onto the B58 Carrickfergus Rd towards Ballynure; you pass by fields, farms, houses and a haulage depot before reaching the village. The Ulster Way turns right just before Ballynure Presbyterian Church and passes through a subway under the busy A8 road. There are a couple of shops, pubs, a take-away and B&Bs around Ballynure, and the village has bus services offering a link with Belfast and Larne.

WALK 3

BALLYNURE TO GLENARM

Start: Ballynure – 318936.

Finish: Glenarm – 311153.

Distance: 32 kilometres (20 miles).

Maps: OSNI Discoverer Sheets 9 and 15.

Terrain: Starts on roads, giving way to forest tracks, followed by broad and sometimes boggy moorlands. Some parts have good paths, but other parts are pathless. The final descent is on roads.

Waymarking: Metal Ulster Way signposts along roads, with wooden marker posts in the forest and over the moorlands. Markers are often widely spaced across the moorlands and could be difficult to follow in poor visibility.

Public Transport: Ulsterbus 156 serves Ballynure, linking with Belfast and Larne. Shane's Hill is served by Ulsterbus 130, linking with Larne and Ballymena. Glenarm is served by Ulsterbus 162, linking with Larne, and in summer by Ulsterbus 252, linking with Larne and Ballycastle.

Accommodation: There are a couple of B&Bs at Ballynure and a handful at Glenarm. In case of difficulty, there are many more places to stay off-route at Larne.

ROUTE DESCRIPTION

Walk through a subway, following a river beneath the busy A8 road in Ballynure. Turn left along Lismenary Rd to leave the village. Lismenary Rd rises and falls gently to a road junction, where you turn right along Lower Ballyboley Rd, as signposted for Larne, and pass by fields and farms until you turn left up Braepark Rd, just before a little garage and telephone box. The road rises past Upper Ballyboley Primary School and Ballyboley Orange Hall. Turn right along Upper Ballyboley Rd, passing a few farms and houses. Turn left up a road signposted for Ballyboley Forest to reach a car park and picnic area. A plaque on a rock here commemorates General Sam Houston of Texas, whose family was from the Ballyboley area. A brief statement records that: 'The city of

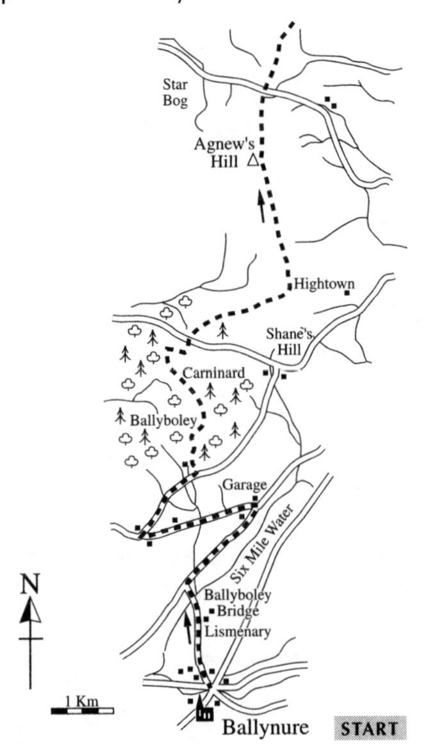

Houston is named in honour of one whose roots lay in these hills; the man the Cherokee called The Raven'.

A gate beside the commemorative stone gives way to a track which winds uphill through Ballyboley Forest. Turn right up another track, where a little bridge stands at the junction. Look out for a marker post further along, pointing up a steep, grassy forest ride to the left. This ride bears a path which is fairly clear as it climbs Carninard, but less clear as it descends the far side, so look out for other markers. Turn right along a forest track at the bottom, then left along another track, passing a concrete building before reaching a roadside car park.

Cross over the A36, Shane's Hill Rd, but bear in mind that you could reach the Ballyboley Inn by following the road to the left. A marked path leads along a forest ride and across a stile. Open moorland lies beyond, with a cairned summit straight ahead. Walk towards this summit, as marker posts become very scarce, and cross a gravel track on the way. The cairn sits on top of a hump at 412m (1,089ft), where

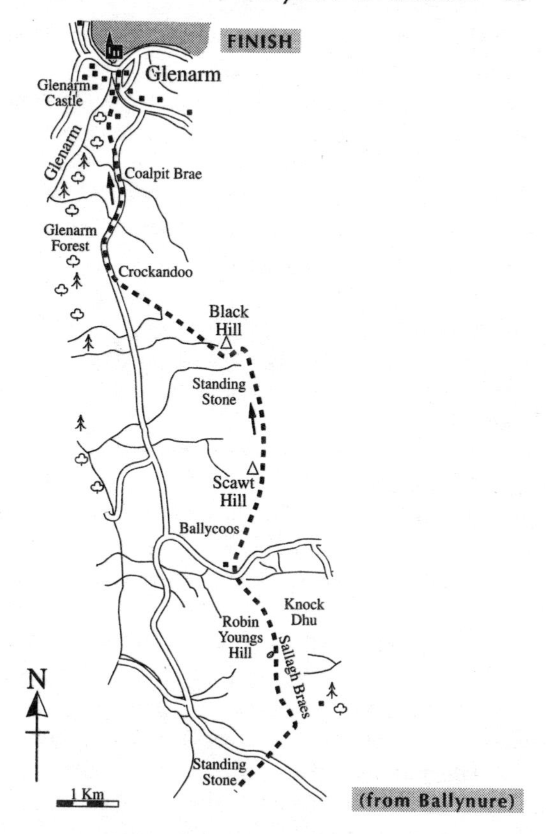

there is another post. Turn left and walk northwards along the crest of the hill. Don't follow the tumbled wall and fence near by as these lead off course. A sparsely planted line of marker posts leads over the heathery crown of Agnew's Hill. There is hardly any trace of a path and in mist it is easy to lose sight of one post before spotting the next in line. The 474m (1,563ft) summit is itself marked by a post, and in clear weather you can see the Sallagh Braes, Knock Dhu and Black Hill, which will all be crossed later in the day. Larne harbour and Islandmagee lie at the foot of the hill, while the Mull of Kintyre, the Isle of Arran and the Galloway Hills of Scotland can be seen across the sea. Slieve Croob and the Mountains of Mourne rise behind the Belfast Hills, as does Slieve Gullion, while Lough Neagh is spread across the lowlands to the south-west, with the rolling Sperrins further westwards. Slemish, Carncormick and Trostan stand out among the Antrim Mountains.

Walk northwards to leave Agnew's Hill, crossing boggy ground before climbing a stile over a fence. Keep left of a prominent cairn on the descent and cross another stile on the way down to the Star Bog Rd. Stiles flank the road. Follow a fence across a level area of bog until you have to cross another stile, then follow a series of marker posts and a sketchy path to reach a prominent standing stone close to the road. Cross the stiles beside the road to continue towards the Sallagh Braes. After crossing yet another stile, a narrow path leads through deep heather and more marker posts point the way forward. Turn left and follow the fence along the top of the cliff. A 'brae' is essentially a Scottish word for a steep slope, highlighting the links between this part of Ireland and Scotland. The Scots, in turn, have their own stories about St Patrick.

The Sallagh Braes display a perfect semicircular cliff-line falling towards a patchwork landscape of fields, leading the eye to the village of Ballygalley and the headland beyond it jutting into the sea. Ulster Way marker posts follow the fence: do not climb the fence or approach the cliff edge; stiles are provided wherever other walls or fences need to be crossed. Eventually, the path moves away from the cliffs and crosses a grassy dip between Robin Young's Hill and Knock Dhu. Although not readily appreciated from the route, Knock Dhu bears an ancient promontory fort, where the cliff-bound height was defended with a man-made embankment at its most vulnerable approach.

Other ancient earthworks can be studied on the way downhill. The heather moorland covering the basalt bedrock gives way to a lush covering of green grass where the underlying rock is chalk. Looking across the grassy gap, you can see the muddled embankments and ditches of the Linford Ancient Site. Although no one is quite sure what the earthworks represent, the area seems to have been an important meeting place from the Bronze Age to the arrival of the Normans in Ireland. When you reach the road, climb up the next slope and keep an eye peeled for stiles and marker posts, as it is easy to be drawn off course by the ditches and embankments.

A wire fence leads uphill, and at the top of the steep brow you can see Ballygalley Head and Larne. The grass is short and there is no clear path here, but the fence is a sure guide until you reach a stile near a wide gate. Continue climbing over the hump of Ballycoos, looking ahead for the widely spaced marker posts and taking special care in mist. On the way downhill, cross a stile over a wall and walk across a grassy gap. A path leads along a more obvious line of marker posts on the way across another broad, rolling gap, but take care not to be drawn off course by other tracks crossing at right angles. After crossing over another wall-stile the path leads gently uphill and you pass a rather knobbly standing stone. Crossing a stile over another wall, in clear weather the trig point on Black Hill can be seen ahead, off to the left. In mist, note that the path skirts around the perimeter of a boggy area rather than making a direct approach, so trust the marker posts. The summit of Black Hill stands at 381m (1,239ft) and offers a fine view west to the summit of Slemish. Its domed shape is caused by a geological formation known as a lacolith, where molten rock was squeezed into sedimentary layers rather like a blister. The young St Patrick worked as a swineherd on the Slemish and the hill is still an object of pilgrimage.

A standing stone passed by the Ulster Way near Sallagh Braes.

Walk roughly north-west to leave the summit of Black Hill. A wall is crossed by a stile on the descent, then you need to look ahead carefully to spot a very sparse line of marker posts leading towards the hump of Crockandoo. There is no real path at this point and the ground underfoot is quite uneven. After passing through patches of rock and bracken, join a minor road and turn right. The road runs along the eastern slopes of Glenarm, then turns down the hill at Coalpit Brae. Stay left at the junction and follow Town Brae Rd steeply downhill, past a stand of forestry, before you reach Altmore St which finally leads into the village of Glenarm. A bridge and barbican gates on the left lead to Glenarm Castle, but keep walking along the road to pass straight through the village along Toberwine St. The Presbyterian and Baptist churches are passed, along with shops and pubs, before a junction is reached with the main A2 Antrim Coast Rd. There are a few B&Bs around Glenarm, while buses offer links both ways along the coast.

Glenarm Castle has a particularly convoluted history. It was founded originally in the centre of the village by a Scotsman, John Bisset, in the 13th century. The Bissets, who later styled themselves

MacEoin, fell victim to Antrim's long-running clan feuds and lost the castle to the O'Donnells, who in their turn had it taken by the MacDonnells. The MacDonnells built the 17th-century castle which stands in the village today. It was burnt by marauding Scots, but in the 18th century the ruins were made habitable again and the surrounding buildings were removed, so that in later years the castle and village grew on opposite sides of the Glenarm River. The castle was refurbished when it became the seat of the Earls of Antrim, but it was burnt in 1929 and again in 1965. The constant rebuilding of the castle means that the kitchen is the only part which has survived from the original 17th-century structure.

WALK 4

GLENARM TO GLENARIFF FOREST PARK

Start: Glenarm – 311153.

Finish: Glenariff Forest Park – 200207.

Distance: 19 kilometres (12 miles).

Map: OSNI Discoverer Sheet 9.

Terrain: Starts on roads, then switches to a farm track and moorland paths. Upland parts can be boggy. A road and forest paths are followed later.

Waymarking: Metal Ulster Way signposts are used along roads, with wooden marker posts on the higher moorlands. Careful navigation may be needed to steer a course across the high ground as markers are widely spaced in places.

Public Transport: Glenarm, Carnlough and Glenariff are served by Ulsterbus 162, linking with Larne, and in summer by 252, linking with Larne and Ballycastle. Ulsterbus 150 links Glenariff Forest Park with Waterfoot and Ballymena.

Accommodation: Glenarm and Carnlough have a number of B&Bs, but accommodation at the head of Glenariff is limited to only a couple of B&Bs. There are more places to stay at Waterfoot. Campsites are located at Carnlough and Glenariff Forest Park.

ROUTE DESCRIPTION

Follow the A2 Antrim Coast Rd out of Glenarm, crossing the bridge and passing St Patrick's Church of Ireland. There is a little coastal green and toilet block to the right, but turn left as signposted for Ballymena, passing Glenarm Old Presbyterian Church. A datestone notes: 'This House was built in the year of our Lord 1762. The enclosed ground on which it stands With 30 Guineas Was the Bountiful DONATION of the Rt Honourable Alexander Earl of Antrim To the Dissenters of GLENARM.' At the junction with Munie Rd, keep straight on and up Straidkilly Rd, past the hazel wood on the chalk slopes which has been designated the Straidkilly National Nature Reserve. There is an old quarry at the top of

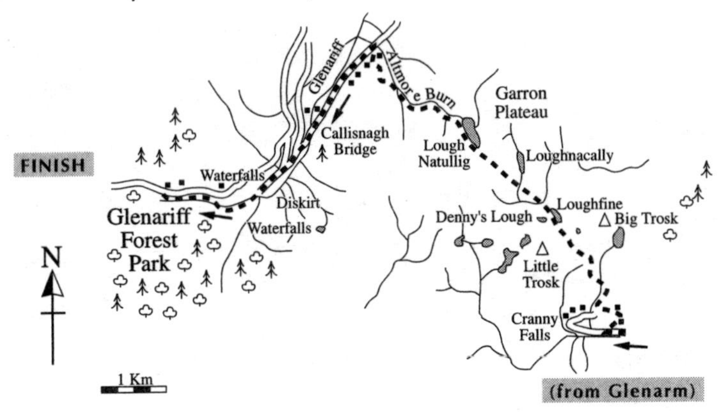

the road, then a gentle descent through the hamlet of Straidkilly leads to the Antrim Coast Rd again. Turn left to follow the road into Carnlough, passing a picnic area and crossing the Glencloy River as the houses begin to build up. Churches old and new are passed, as well as a range of shops and pubs. A prominent stone arch is part of the Carnlough railway which once linked the nearby chalk quarries to the little harbour.

Follow Bridge St, which runs between McAuley's Hotel and the Glencloy Inn, then turn left along Waterfall Rd at the Waterfall Bar. The road is narrow and rises into a wooded valley. You have a chance to make a scenic detour to the left when you see the sign for Cranny Falls. A gravel path leads across a grassy slope near the old chalk quarries, then narrows as it enters a dark, wooded ravine cut into the dark basalt bedrock and brings you to the viewing point for the Cranny Falls. After retracing your steps, continue up the road and turn sharply right along another concrete road. This bends sharply left at a farm, passing a gate and stile.

Another gate and stile on the right give access to a gravel track which climbs uphill. Turn right along a less clear grassy track as marked and go past a couple of gates as the route zig-zags uphill. When the track expires, a marker post on the left shows a path crossing stiles over a wall and a fence, then there is a left turn up another track passing through some more gates. A rugged, boulder-strewn moorland slope leads to a gap high on the moors between Big Trosk and Little Trosk. There are views back to Carnlough, Black Hill and Agnew's Hill on the way up to the gap. An Ulster Way marker post points to the right, away from the track, across the empty Garron Plateau where good navigation is required in mist.

The Ulster Way descends gently on a slope of rock, bog, grass and heather, passing between little Denny's Lough and Loughfine. After crossing a small stream and a fence, there is a vague path marked by posts which rise steadily across the moor. There are no views of the sea nor any habitations, and in poor visibility you need to keep your eyes peeled for the marker posts. These lead close to Loughnacally, then show the way along the side of Lough Natullig. A left turn leads away from the lough, down into a valley where a steep path develops after

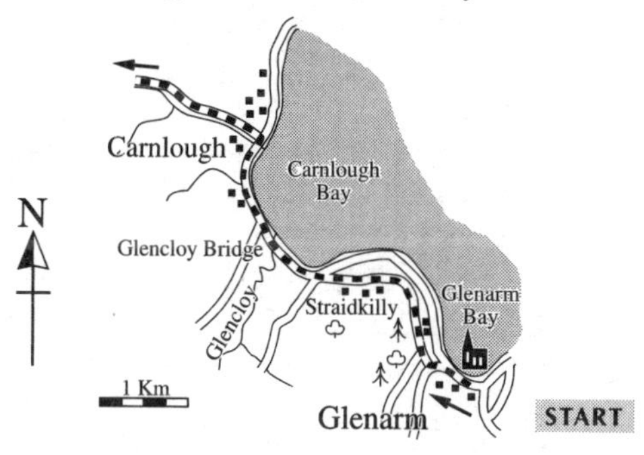

crossing a stile. Looking down into Glenariff you notice its 'ladderfield' method of cultivation, where every farm has a strip running from the barren mountain to the fertile glen. The Altmore Burn tumbles downhill, gushing over the rocks. The top of Trostan rises beyond Glenariff. Cross another stile and follow a zig-zag track down a wooded, shrubby slope to reach the minor Glen Rd at the bottom.

A sign for the Ulster Way points to the right along the road, but following it onwards will lead to a couple of areas where there are serious problems with access, because the course of the Ulster Way as it continues around Carnanmore and Fair Head was never finalised. It seems better, therefore, to turn left and establish a link with the Moyle Way, which has been completely upgraded, is free of access problems, and can be used to reach the distant town of Ballycastle.

Follow the Glen Rd right, passing a couple of B&Bs before reaching the Manor Lodge restaurant at the very end of the road. Walk between the restaurant and an adjacent craft centre, but don't cross a footbridge beyond. Instead, turn right along a path running upstream, signposted for the Glenariff Waterfalls, where payment may sometimes be required at a small kiosk. Follow gravel paths and wooden walkways, climbing up and down flights of steps to reach a viewing bridge for the largest waterfall. All around are a mixture of fine trees, as well as abundant mosses, liverworts and ferns. Zig-zag uphill on more steps and ramps, then continue upstream using any path running close to the river. There are a couple of options to exit left up to the Glenariff Forest Park Visitor Centre, or keep walking, crossing an arched wooden bridge to head further upstream where a final footbridge leads onto the access road for the visitor centre.

Many fern species will be seen along the woodland stretches, among rocks and in the boggy areas of the Way.

The visitor centre gives a good introduction to the natural characteristics of the area. The two main rock types here are basalt and chalk, and the weathering of the basalt has produced iron-rich deposits. The Glenariff Iron Ore Company mined the Inver Valley from 1872 and operated a narrow-gauge railway to bring the ore to the coast for shipment. When the company collapsed, the line was bought by the Belfast & Northern Counties Railway, who developed a station at Parkmore with a view to bringing tourists to see the Glenariff Waterfalls. Berkeley Deane Wise designed the path down through the gorge, passing by the waterfalls to reach a tea house at the bottom. A variety of trees were planted a century ago to enhance the scenic charms of the glen, and were followed by swathes of commercial forestry later, leading Thackeray to describe Glenariff as 'Switzerland in miniature'.

Walking away from the visitor centre quickly leads up to the main A43 road, which has buses linking with Waterfoot and Ballymena. To the right is a telephone box, while straight ahead is a track signposted as the Moyle Way.

Apart from the B&Bs mentioned earlier and the possibility of being able to obtain food and drink at the Manor Lodge and the visitor centre, facilities are minimal unless you move off-route.

WALK 5

GLENARIFF FOREST PARK TO BALLYCASTLE

Start: Glenariff Forest Park – 200207.

Finish: The Diamond, Ballycastle – 115407.

Distance: 32 kilometres (20 miles).

Maps: OSNI Discoverer Sheets 5 and 9.

Terrain: Forest paths and tracks, moorland paths which can be boggy in places, and some road walking. The uplands can be particularly bleak and exposed.

Waymarking: Metal Moyle Way signposts and stone plinths are used beside the roads. Wooden marker posts are used in forests and over the moorlands. Care is needed on the high moorlands in poor visibility.

Public Transport: Ulsterbus 150 links Glenariff Forest Park with Waterfoot and Ballymena. There are several Ulsterbus services out of Ballycastle to Cushendall, Ballymena, Portrush and Coleraine. Ulsterbus 252 is a summer service all around the Antrim coast.

Accommodation: Accommodation at the head of Glenariff is limited to one farmhouse B&B and a forest campsite. There are all sorts of options, from campsites and hostels to large hotels, at Ballycastle.

ROUTE DESCRIPTION

The Moyle Way starts opposite the entrance to Glenariff Forest Park, following a forest track uphill and keeping left to follow Castlegreen Burn upstream. Watch for another left turn as the route cuts through the forest to reach the Essathohan Burn at a bridge on the B14 road. Follow a path upstream to pass an impressive waterfall, crossing and recrossing the stream as more height is gained. The path can be muddy and at a higher level a narrow forest ride has to be negotiated to reach the forest fence high on the slopes of Trostan. An ascent of Trostan, the highest of the Antrim Mountains at 550m (1,817ft), is an optional extra. The Moyle Way simply carries on over the shoulder of the hill at around 500m (1,640ft).

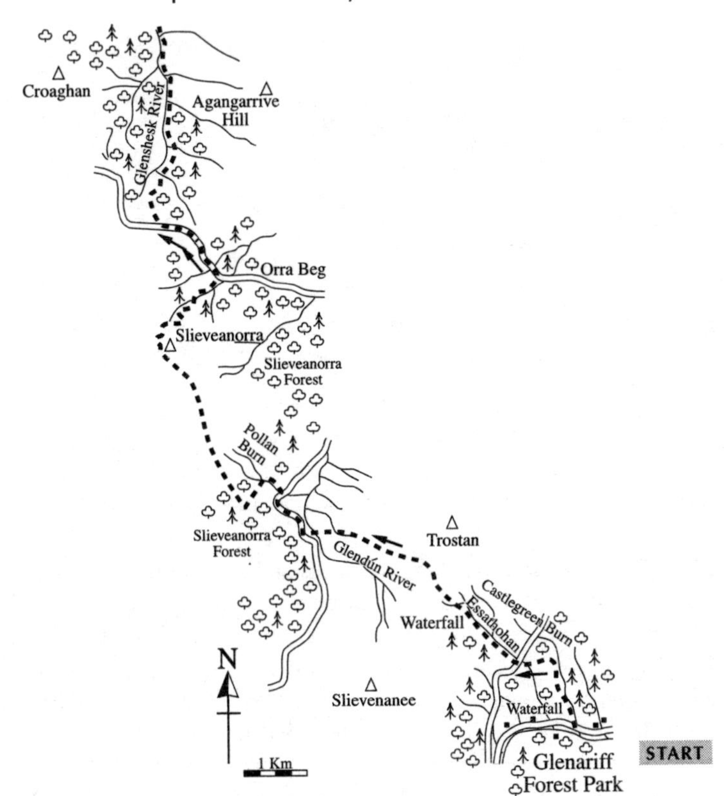

Cross a stile over the fence and look ahead carefully to pick out a line of marker posts, which lead roughly north-west down the heathery slopes of Trostan. A small stream is followed at one point, then the infant Glendun River is crossed to reach a minor road at a stone plinth. Turn right to follow the road, which bends left and right through a forest and across a bridge over Pollan Burn. Immediately after crossing the bridge, turn left along a forest track, then left again to proceed further through the forest. Towards the end of the track, turn right across a softer surface through a broad forest ride. The ground is boggy but becomes firmer as the slope steepens on the way towards Slieveanorra. Keep to the left of an isolated stand of trees on the moorland slope, following a fairly clear grassy path uphill; parallel drainage ditches ensure that the path stays fairly dry. It leads to a narrow tarmac road, where a right turn brings you past a couple of unsightly masts. There are extensive views around the Antrim Mountains and across the sea to Scotland. The summit of Slieveanorra stands at 508m (1,676ft).

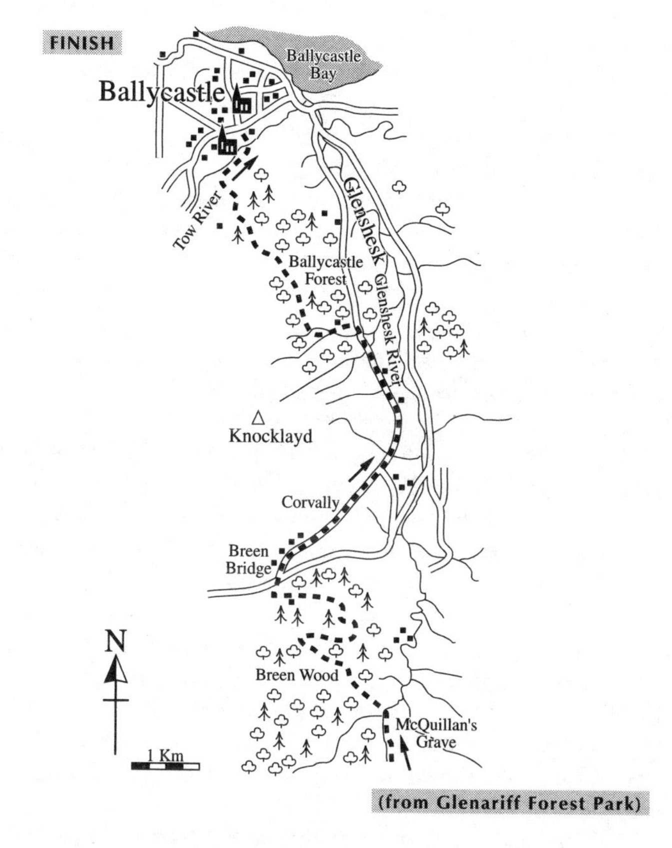

Slieveanorra National Nature Reserve consists of two areas of upland blanket bog, spread out on either side of the broad summit. At a lower level, but off the course of the Moyle Way, are two more extensive bogs, one on Orra Beg which played a crucial part in the battle fought there in 1559. When the O'Neills and McQuillans launched an attack on the MacDonnells, the MacDonnells coaxed their adversaries onto the boggy ground and counter-attacked while they floundered. The battle raged all the way down Glenshesk, where the Moyle Way leads, before the MacDonnells' victory finally consolidated their grip on this corner of Antrim. Sorley Boy MacDonnell, chief of the MacDonnell clan, raised a cairn on top of Trostan to commemorate the battle. Hugh McPhelim O'Neill was buried on the slopes of Slieveanorra, while McQuillan's Grave can be seen further down Glenshesk.

Follow a gravel track which zig-zags down the northern slopes of Slieveanorra. It drops from the moors onto the forested lower slopes, joining a minor road at another Moyle Way stone plinth. Turn left along the road, which clings precariously to the slopes. Looking off to the right, you can still see an isolated bend which suddenly detached itself from the rest of the road one night and slid downhill! Look out for a forest track on the right and follow it downhill into the head of Glenshesk, crossing a couple of small burns on the way. When the track ends, a more rugged path continues through the forest and drops down by a steep bluff to land close to the Glenshesk River. Simply follow the river downstream. It may be easier to keep to the right at first, but later it is better to cross to the left. Although it is easily missed, before leaving the riverside keep an eye peeled for McQuillan's Grave, a small pointed stone incised with the figure of a head and shoulders.

The Moyle Way climbs uphill from the river at Ardagh, following the forest fence to the left. As soon as a forest track is reached, turn right and follow it downhill. It describes huge, sweeping zig-zags on the forested slope and passes the Breen Woods, which are now a national nature reserve. The oak wood is among the few remaining from the great forests which once covered the whole of Ireland, and the forest's understorey is quite rich in species. The forest track links with a farm road, and a right turn later brings you out onto Breen Bridge on the B15 road. Cross straight over the road and continue along a minor road rising through Glenshesk. Originally, the Moyle Way climbed over the huge dome of Knocklayd, but now the route runs around the lower slopes of the hill.

Follow the minor road gradually uphill, passing a series of farms and houses, until Ballycastle Forest rises to the left. Turn left up a track, remembering to follow green waymark arrows, as there are other colour-coded walks in the forest. Climb uphill and keep to the right to reach one last viewpoint where clear-felling has opened up the forest and you can see out to the rugged prow of Fair Head. After passing the viewpoint, the forest track descends through a fairly narrow swathe of trees, turning right to leave the woods at the very bottom. The track follows the line of a tramway which once brought Belfast workers on excursions to Ballycastle. A road finally leads down into a dip and up into the Diamond in the middle of Ballycastle. There is immediate access to a range of pubs, shops, restaurants and more pubs. There is abundant accommodation, ranging from hotels, guesthouses and B&Bs to hostels and nearby campsites.

Holy Trinity Church of Ireland, or the Boyd Church, stands just off the Diamond. Built in 1756, it contains memorials to many of the Boyd family, who as landlords of Ballycastle greatly expanded the town, developing the harbour and creating industries as diverse as a glass-works, tannery, soapworks, brewery and hotels. The harbour was used by fishing boats and for the transport of coal. The ornate monument in the Diamond is not, surprisingly, in memory of the Boyds, but is a memorial to George Matthew O'Connor, who was a doctor in Ballycastle in the 18th century. One of the town's most celebrated events is the Ould Lammas Fair which is held at the end of August. While you are in the town you might try two local delicacies: the sweet toffee-like jawbreaker called 'yellow man', and dried seaweed or 'dulse' – something of an acquired taste.

Dulse or dillisk (*Palmaria*) is a local edible seaweed.

Walkers who try to follow the original course of the Ulster Way from Glenariff to Ballycastle will have no problem linking the villages of Waterfoot, Cushendall and Cushendun. However, the right to use an old moorland road, now little more than a bog road, has been challenged, and there is no negotiated route over the top of Carnanmore. While the National Trust holds a long lease on parts of Fair Head, it does not own the entire headland, and some landowners are adamant that the Ulster Way will not go all the way round the Head. There is no problem following the path and road around Colliery Bay to Ballycastle, but walkers attempting to follow the whole route as originally planned could run into problems.

WALK 6

BALLYCASTLE TO THE GIANT'S CAUSEWAY

Start: The Diamond, Ballycastle – 115407.

Finish: Giant's Causeway Centre – 944439.

Distance: 30 kilometres (18½ miles).

Map: OSNI Discoverer Sheet 5.

Terrain: Roads at first, then a variety of coastal and cliff paths. Note that some short stretches along beaches are dependent on the tides.

Waymarking: The route along roads is initially unmarked. Coastal and cliff paths are marked with hexagonal wooden posts as the Causeway Coast Path rather than the Ulster Way.

Public Transport: Ulsterbus 252 is the main summer service along the Causeway Coast. At other times of the year Ulsterbus 172 is the main link along the coast road.

Accommodation: There are all sorts of options, from campsites and hostels to large hotels at Ballycastle. The rest of the Causeway Coast features accommodation options at odd intervals based around Ballintoy, White Park Bay and Causeway Head.

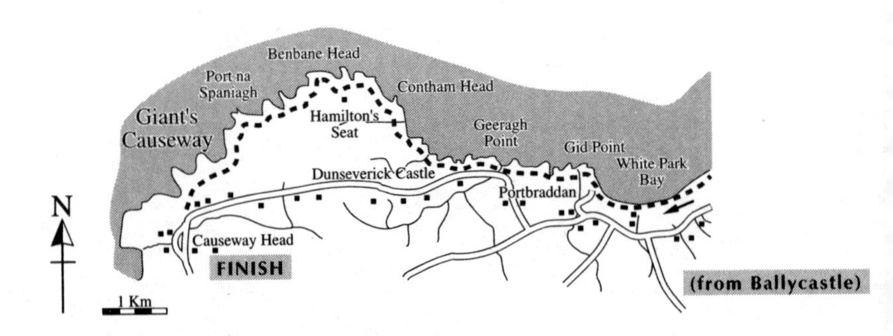

ROUTE DESCRIPTION

Leave the Diamond in Ballycastle and follow Ann St, which is signposted for Cushendun and Cushendall. There are plenty of shops, pubs and restaurants along the way, as well as other facilities. Quay Rd is lined with B&Bs facing the sports pitches, ending at the Marine Hotel, which is flanked by two hostels. Fair Head and Scotland's Mull of Kintyre are often in view across Colliery Bay and the Moyle, that narrow turbulent strait between the two countries. The Ulster Way turns left up North St, passing more shops, pubs, restaurants and accommodation. At the top of a steep section there is a Marconi Memorial overlooking Rathlin Island, commemorating the fact that in 1898 the world's first wireless message was sent from Ballycastle to Rathlin. North St runs straight on to Clare Rd, which passes the Silvercliffs holiday village and Hayes caravan park on the way out of town. The road is lined with trees, and when it suddenly turns left, continue instead straight on along a grassy track which runs between hedgerows to reach the little village of Carnduff.

Turn left along the road at Carnduff, then turn right along the B15 Whitepark Rd which climbs steeply past Gortconney Farm B&B and rolls onwards some distance from the coast. There is a road signposted off to the right for Kinbane Castle, and if you visit the castle you need to retrace your steps to bring you back to the route. On a high part of the road, Glenmore House offers teas, snacks, B&B and camping. Follow the road downhill, then when a left bend is reached, continue straight down a minor road instead. The road runs past a couple of farms in a hollow at Glenstaughey, then rises back to Whitepark Rd, where you turn right. From the Portaneevey car park you can take in fine views of

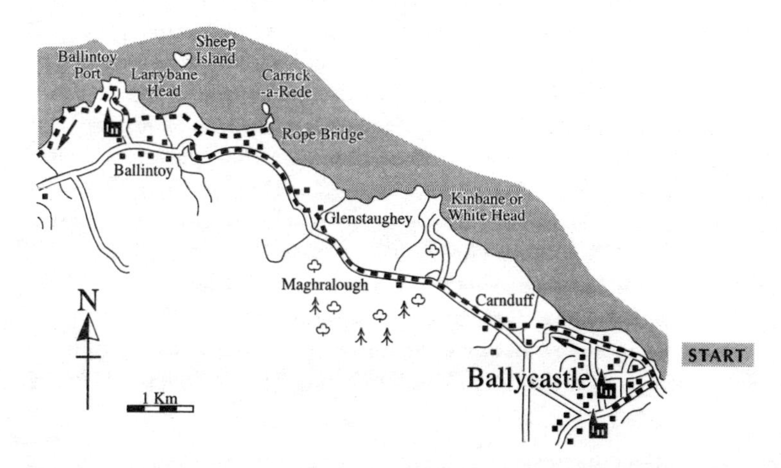

Sheep Island, Carrick-a-Rede and Rathlin, as well as the Scottish islands of Islay and Jura. The rangefinder at the car park points your eye towards Rockall, Iceland and Greenland, but you are unlikely to actually see them! The road runs onwards to the village of Ballintoy, where a couple of route options are available.

While the road zig-zags down to Ballintoy, there is a path which slices through all the loops, reaching Ballintoy at Knocksoghey Lane, where a couple of shops, pubs, B&Bs and an independent hostel are all within reach. Alternatively, turn right before the village at the signpost for Carrick-a-Rede Rope Bridge, which links the tiny island to the mainland. The cliff path is broad and clear, and stone steps bring you down to a doorway giving access to the rope bridge, which is generally open from April to September. The bridge is strung across a 20m (60ft) gulf some 25m (80ft) above the Atlantic. A good head for heights is required, as well as good balance, and as you cross with your heart in your throat spare a thought for the fishermen who have to lug boxes of salmon across in all weathers!

After visiting the Carrick-a-Rede Bridge return to Larrybane. A path continues around the cliffs above an old quarry, then runs through the fields and aims for the prominent, whitewashed Church of Ireland church you see ahead. When you reach the road beside the church, turn right and follow it downhill. A corkscrew road leads down to Ballintoy Port, where the tiny harbour is quite lovely. There are some old limekilns and caves to explore, while Roark's Kitchen serves food and drink and there are toilets available.

Follow a track away from the harbour, passing a cottage and continuing along a grassy path. The sea is full of battered chalk stacks and others are marooned on dry land. The stacks are pierced with holes and arches and take on the most curious shapes. You cross over a couple of stiles and pass by a spring spouting from beneath a large boulder. A bouldery beach lies ahead of you, and at this point a high tide could cause a short delay. White Park Bay starts with a rash of large boulders, which at a distance look rather like a flock of sheep, and levels out into a broad sweep of sand with dunes rising steeply inland, burying a former cliff-line. A few houses can be seen along the top of the cliffs, while White Park Bay Youth Hostel sits at a lower level. Rounding the chalk headland at the far side of the bay needs particular care, as the rocks can be slippery, and walkers must watch out for the tide: walkers may be delayed at this point when the tide is in. The tiny huddle of houses crouched in a rocky cleft above the shoreline is Portbraddan. One of the buildings in the village, St Gobban's, is claimed to be the smallest church in Ireland.

The path leaving Portbraddan passes by some rock stacks and continues through the cave pierced through Gid Point. After passing a small waterfall, the path crosses a series of stiles and short flights of steps which bring you along a rocky coast to a small harbour and toilets. Follow the access road up from the car park, but watch for a flight of steps on the right leading down to the next stretch of coastal path. The path leads round an attractive grassy headland and crosses a footbridge over a river and onto the rocky Geeragh Point.

The path runs close to Dunseverick Castle, whose ruins stand on a naturally fortified headland. A short diversion brings you to the site. Dunseverick may have been a stronghold as long ago as the Iron Age, the centre of the Kingdom of Dalriada and reputedly linked by road to the political powerhouse of ancient Ireland, Tara in Co. Meath. St Patrick is said to have visited here in the 5th century, but all that remains of Dunseverick's earliest times is a few earthworks; the headland was attacked by the Vikings in 871 AD and completely destroyed by them in 926. The ruins seen today are of a 16th-century tower-house, dating from a time of constant struggle between the Antrim families of MacDonnell, O'Neill and McQuillan.

The cliff path continues beyond Dunseverick, generally gaining height, along with some short downhill stretches. The headlands and bays of Contham and Bengore stretch out before you and there are some fine views back along the coast which was covered earlier in the day. The National Trust was recently able to move the fence back and allow walkers more space along the cliff edges, where the path twists and turns and eventually rounds Benbane Head to reach the dramatic viewpoint of Hamilton's Seat. From here you can look ahead to the Inishowen Peninsula in Donegal, out to the Scottish islands of Islay and Jura, and inland to Antrim. Traces of a lower path can be seen, but there is no access to it, as it was closed some years ago following a major rock-fall. While following the cliff-top path onwards, keep a lookout for fulmars and kittiwakes on the ledges, ravens and red-legged choughs, as well as merlins and sparrowhawks. The route later passes above some spiky columns of basalt known as the Chimney Tops and eventually reaches a junction above the Shepherd's Steps. A decision is needed at that point.

You can keep to the cliff-top path to head straight to the Giant's Causeway Centre, or descend the Shepherd's Steps to make more detailed explorations of the Causeway itself. The steps lead down a rugged slope to a junction with a lower path. Turning right here leads eventually to a dead end, but takes in the tall columns of basalt known as the Organ Pipes. The Port Reostan viewpoint is reached at the dead end, near where the Spanish Armada ship *Girona* came to grief on the rocks in 1588; the guns, coins and jewellery recovered here form one of the most remarkable exhibits at the Ulster Museum. Turning left at the foot of the Shepherd's Steps, or retracing your steps from the Port Reostan viewpoint, brings you past the Giant's Boot to the crazy columns of the Giant's Causeway.

The Causeway is an immensely popular place, first popularised in 1740 and easily one of the busiest outdoor sites in Ireland. Nearly 40,000 tightly packed hexagonal columns of basalt tilt towards the Atlantic. Looking inland, the cliff appears as a shapely peak, but this is an illusion as it is almost flat on top. National Trust staff handle everything from school visits to more scientific parties, mixing explanations of science, history and myth to explain the site. Was it formed by the gradual cooling of a basalt mass or was it really the work of giants? Minibuses run back and forth along a narrow road linking the Causeway with the centre, where all sorts of displays help visitors to satisfy their curiosity. Make time to explore thoroughly, and take advantage of nearby accommodation to stay overnight. Not for nothing has the Giant's Causeway been designated a World Heritage Site.

WALK 7

GIANT'S CAUSEWAY TO PORTSTEWART

Start: Giant's Causeway Centre – 944439.

Finish: Portstewart – 820372.

Distance: 25 kilometres (15½ miles).

Map: OSNI Discoverer Sheet 4.

Terrain: A series of short coastal paths, linked by roads which can be busy at times.

Waymarking: Metal Ulster Way signposts are used along the roads. Hexagonal wooden marker posts for the Port Path are used around Portrush and Portstewart.

Public Transport: Ulsterbus 177 serves most points between the Giant's Causeway and Portstewart in the summer. Ulsterbus 139 and 140 run round Portrush and Portstewart, as well as Ulsterbus 138 between Portballintrae and Portrush. Portrush and Portstewart also have railway stations.

Accommodation: There are a few places to stay around Causeway Head, with more around Portballintrae, and a choice of accommodation options around Portrush and Portstewart, including hotels, guesthouses, B&Bs, hostels and campsites.

ROUTE DESCRIPTION

A path runs in front of the Giant's Causeway Centre and follows the cliffs towards Runkerry House. The path, which is gravel at first, becoming grassy later, is forced inland around a deep chasm which the sea has carved into Runkerry Point. Runkerry House is the centre of a large building development, and the coast path keeps to its seaward side. There is a footbridge down near the Bushfoot Strand, which needs to be crossed, then a grassy path leads inland. Turn right onto the bed of the old tramway, where at present a gravel track runs along the top of an embankment, though there is a proposal to re-open the line – a hydro-electric tram ran between Portrush and the Giant's Causeway from 1883 to 1949 – and accommodate walkers alongside. Follow the track-bed until you can see a stout bridge over the Bush River, and head off to

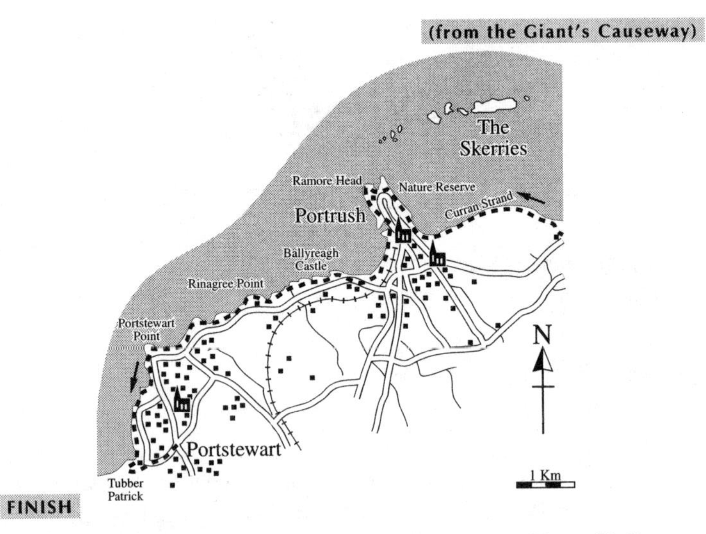

the right to follow a path through the adjacent sand dunes. You will discover a long wooden footbridge near the mouth of the river; cross over at that point and bear right up a prominent path. After crossing a low, rocky headland you reach the car park and toilets at Portballintrae. Continue along the road past the Beach House Hotel, walking above the harbour and passing by a thatched cottage to reach the Bayview Hotel.

Carry on past the Bayview Hotel and B&Bs on the Bayhead Rd, then turn left along Dunluce Park and right along Gortnee Drive. Turn right to follow the Port Hedge Public Footpath, which turns left up through fields to reach the main A2 Dunluce Rd. Turn right and walk along the footway. Follow Dunluce Rd round a headland where the road splits into two carriageways, then turn right as signposted for Dunluce Castle.

This magnificent ruin teeters on the brink of sheer cliffs. The first fortification here was built by Richard de Burgh in the 13th century. The MacDonnells later held it, apart from a spell in 1584 when clan chief Sorley Boy MacDonnell was evicted and the place was garrisoned by an English force. Not easily defeated, Sorley Boy persuaded some of his old followers inside the garrison to haul his men up the cliff in baskets and they recaptured the castle. In 1639 a peculiar accident befell Dunluce when a storm blew up during a meal and brought a whole slice of the castle – containing the kitchen, cooks, pots and pans – crashing into the sea. In later years the castle fell into decay, after Sorley Boy's descendants, the Earls of Antrim, moved their seat to the Glens of Antrim.

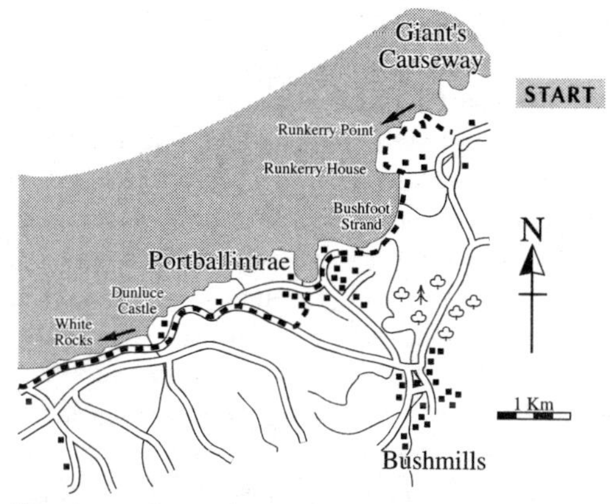

Continue along the main A2 road, using the footway, but take advantage of the viewpoint car park on the right to look back to Dunluce Castle. Follow the road onwards, bringing you by occasional cliff views where the bird life includes fulmars, kittiwakes and common guillemots. A sign points to a narrow road which zig-zags down to White Rocks beach. The white rocks are of course chalk, but with a difference: there the rock has been broken by an ancient volcanic vent, then reconsolidated. You can make a detour to the caves which lie to the right, but the Ulster Way heads left for Portrush. Walk along the broad Curran Strand, whose dunes stretch inland covered in marram grass and sprinkled with sea buckthorn, creeping thistle, harebell, red and white campion, primrose and violet.

Come ashore at East Strand and follow a promenade to the right around Portrush. Rise onto a road full of hotels and guesthouses, then follow the little paths to the next road and promenade where ranks of hotels are set back from the shore above a grassy bank. The Portrush Countryside Centre overlooks the sea, focusing on the geology and natural history of the rocky shore below. Continue on the path around the cliffs of Ramore Head, which has an unusual geology and has been designated an Area of Special Scientific Interest. The headland is a dolerite sill, with a layer of fossiliferous shale on top, notable for its content of spiral ammonites. Views stretch back to

Dunluce Castle is a well-known feature on the Antrim Coast.

the Giant's Causeway and Rathlin Island, and ahead to Portstewart, Downhill and Inishowen. Look out for hexagonal marker posts which indicate the course of the Port Path from Portrush to Portstewart.

The bustling seaside resort of Portrush has every facility to satisfy the weary wayfarer, but to continue on the Ulster Way leave Ramore Head and follow a path down steps to Water World and around the harbour. The road beyond the harbour has B&Bs stretching along its length and a promenade path can be seen curving around West Strand. There is a large green space between the promenade and railway, then a path rises uphill to join the main A2 road. Follow the road away from Portrush, passing the last few B&Bs to reach the Carrick-Dhu caravan and camping site. The Port Path is signposted along a low cliff-line, passing the Ballyreagh Castle viewpoint, and continuing beside Ballyreagh Golf Course. Pass a few houses and follow the path faithfully as it winds its way along the narrow strip of land between the road and the cliffs. A series of little car parks are passed, then the path continues beside a rocky, bouldery shore to pass The Old Course on the way to Portstewart.

Circumventing the town, and not really seeing the place to its best advantage, you walk first along a concrete sea wall, then follow a road onto a rocky point. A path around the point ends with steps leading to a small harbour and a promenade on the far side of town which is crowded with small shops, pubs and restaurants. The crenellated Dominican College can be seen on the headland further on. Follow flights of steps up and down to walk beneath the walls of the college, turning round the headland to reach a concrete path beside a bouldery shore. A few houses are arranged along the path, then steps lead down onto the broad, sandy sweep of Portstewart Strand. Don't go down onto the strand, but follow a path inland past St Patrick's Well to reach a road alongside Portstewart Golf Course.

Walking along Portstewart Strand does not lead you to the village of Castlerock and the cliff-top Mussenden Temple, though they look deceptively close. They are cut off by the deep-water mouth of the River Bann, which is hidden from view at the start of the strand. Originally, there was a plan to operate a ferry service across the Bann for the use of wayfarers, but to date this facility has not been developed. The Ulster Way detours inland from Portstewart to Castlerock entirely on roads, which is another day's walk. For the time being, Portstewart has every type of accommodation, restaurants and pubs, and bus and rail services.

NORTH-WESTERN SECTION

Counties Derry and Tyrone

Distance: 179 kilometres (111 miles)

This section of the Ulster Way creates one of the sharpest contrasts in the entire route. After passing through popular coastal resorts and the bustling town of Coleraine, the route turns inland to complete an extended traverse of the rolling Sperrin Mountains, a largely empty countryside with only the most basic facilities. This is where walkers need to start planning ahead.

The route through the Sperrin Mountains is fairly straightforward, largely running along clear forest tracks and a variety of roads. There are a few occasions where a pathless slope or moorland needs to be crossed, but these are the exceptions. Most walkers will travel in the hope of securing a place to stay each night, so it is important to check the availability of places along the way: the countryside has only a few isolated lodgings and towns have a rather limited supply of beds. And though there are plenty of shops and pubs in the towns along the way, in between times it's useful to know when you can next obtain food and drink. It is also useful to know which roads carry bus services, in case you need to leave the route in search of accommodation or sustenance. The alternative is to hitch-hike your way out of difficulty, which actually works surprisingly well on these quiet country roads!

Once you have taken care of your basic needs, you can enjoy the relative solitude of this part of the Ulster Way. The empty moors and forests are interspersed with farming country largely given over to sheep or cattle grazing. Life is lived at a leisurely pace and most of the people you meet will welcome the opportunity for a chat.

There is currently a drive for greater access in the Sperrins, which is largely coming from ordinary country folk, and it is quite likely that in due course some parts of the Ulster Way will be taken off the roads and a path waymarked through the countryside. Throughout the summer months there are several popular walking festivals in the Sperrins, most of which impinge on the Ulster Way at some point. For the most part, however, it's going to be a quiet few days on this stretch of the route.

WALK 8

PORTSTEWART TO CASTLEROCK

Start: Portstewart – 820372.

Finish: Castlerock Station – 774360.

Distance: 16 kilometres (10 miles).

Map: OSNI Discoverer Sheet 4.

Terrain: The whole day's walk is along roads, some of which are quite busy.

Waymarking: There are only a few metal Ulster Way signs along the roads, but the route is easy to follow.

Public Transport: Portstewart, Coleraine and Castlerock all have railway stations. Ulsterbus 140 and 370 run between Portstewart and Coleraine, while Ulsterbus 134 runs between Coleraine and Castlerock. Coleraine has bus and rail connections with Belfast and many other places.

Accommodation: Portstewart and Coleraine have plenty of accommodation, while Castlerock has a few B&Bs and hotels.

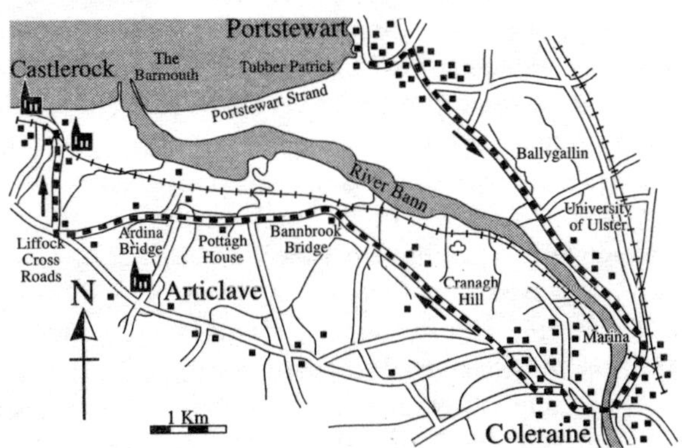

ROUTE DESCRIPTION

If you are able to arrange for a ferry service of some sort across the mouth of the River Bann, then you can save a whole day's walk between Portstewart and Castlerock. If not, then the day is spent walking along roads, some of them busy, to cross the nearest bridge over the Bann at Coleraine.

The clock tower of the Town Hall in the middle of Coleraine.

Follow Burnside Rd uphill from Portstewart and turn right to follow the busy A2 road towards Coleraine. This runs gently uphill, passing an old graveyard at a road junction near the Flowerfield Arts Centre. Nelly's Complex is the last pub and restaurant on the road out of town. There is a footway on the left-hand side of the road: don't walk on the right-hand side, as this has been designated as a cycleway. The road passes sports pitches associated with the University of Ulster and there may be a couple of glimpses of the River Bann off to the right. After passing the Theatre Riverside, which is part of the University complex, the cycleway is on the same side of the road as the footway, so keep in the appropriate pedestrian lane. Coleraine marina and a couple of B&Bs are passed on the way into town. A right turn at a junction passes a couple of shops and leads under a railway arch. Either follow the main road down to the bridge, or head left into the town centre, a pedestrian area marked by the Town Hall. There are plenty of shops, pubs and restaurants if food and drink are required. Coleraine also offers accommodation, bus and rail transport.

Coleraine was laid out in its present form by The Honourable The Irish Society in 1611, and parts of St Patrick's Church of Ireland date from 1613. Mountsandel Fort, overlooking the River Bann on the southern side of Coleraine, dates back over 9,000 years, making it one of the oldest settlement sites anywhere in Ireland, while Killowen, on the other side of the river, is an ancient settlement dating from the 5th century.

Cross over the busy bridge to leave Coleraine for Waterside, and walk straight uphill. There are a few shops, then Captain St Lower features bay-windowed houses leading up to a junction with Captain St Upper. Turn right to continue, then this road bends left to become Carthall Rd, which climbs steeply past Coleraine Secondary School until it reaches a roundabout. Turn right along Wheatsheaf Rd, crossing the main Castlerock Rd onto the minor Cranagh Rd which rises gently uphill. After a dip in the road you pass Hilltop garage and enjoy open views towards the mouth of the River Bann and Inishowen Head. Follow the road straight downhill and around the bend at the bottom. Fields stretch away on your left, and to the right there is a wilderness of bracken, brambles and gorse. Pass Pottagh House and cross Ardina Bridge over the Articlave River, then continue along Ballywoolen Rd. The main A2 Mussenden Rd is reached next to Hezlett Primary School.

Turn right along Mussenden Rd to reach Liffock crossroads. Carneety Farm B&B and the Castlerock Garden Centre stand here, along with a National Trust property, Hezlett House. A long, single-storey thatched building, it looks like a farmhouse but was actually built as a rectory in 1690. Inside, massive timber beams – or cruck-frames – stretch from floor to ceiling, all of it authentically restored after a fire in 1986.

Turn right along Sea Rd and follow it down to the railway station at Castlerock. The town is essentially a Victorian seaside resort and has a few shops, pubs, B&Bs and hotel accommodation; in fact, the last real concentration of facilities on the Ulster Way for some time.

WALK 9

CASTLEROCK TO FORMOYLE

Start: Castlerock Station – 774360.

Finish: Formoyle – 767294.

Distance: 28 kilometres (17 miles).

Map: OSNI Discoverer Sheet 4.

Terrain: Short paths giving way to longer stretches of moorland roads and forest tracks.

Waymarking: Metal Ulster Way signposts are used along roads, with wooden marker posts in the forests.

Public Transport: Castlerock has a railway station and is also served by Ulsterbus 134.

Accommodation: Castlerock has B&Bs and hotels, but there are only a couple of B&Bs near Formoyle and these may not be open all year round.

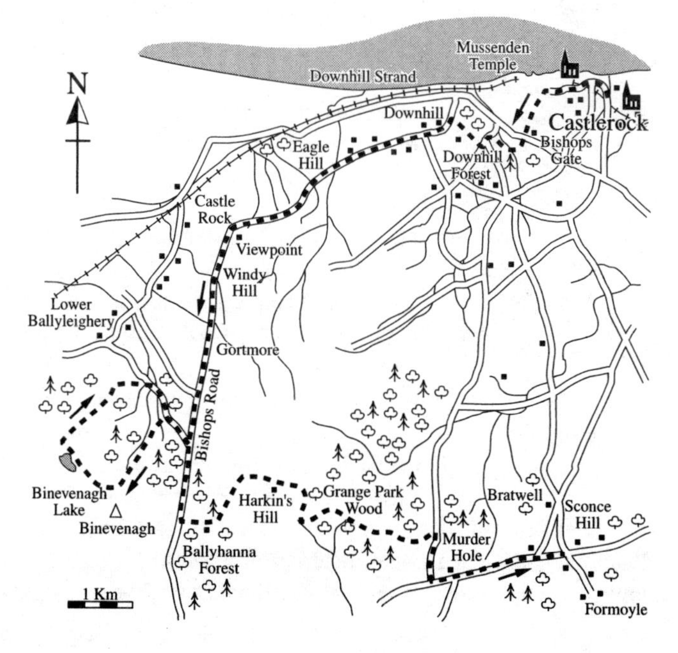

ROUTE DESCRIPTION

Leave the railway station at Castlerock and walk down towards the sea. The road swings left in front of the Golf Hotel and a belt of dunes covered in marram grass hides a broad, sandy beach from view. A grassy strip can be followed above a low, rocky shore for a short way. Follow another road uphill, swinging left in front of a caravan site as marked by a prominent Ulster Way sign. Turn right at a junction and follow a narrow road straight to a gatehouse beside the caravan park. A sign reads 'Black Glen Scenic Walks'. Go through the gate and follow a clear path flanked by rhododendrons and other trees and shrubs. These completely enclose the path for a while; then there is a view across a small dam with a peep through the Black Glen to the sea. Follow the path straight onwards, keeping left to reach Bishop's Gate and the main A2 Mussenden Rd.

Before leaving this lovely little enclave, it's worth exploring the gardens, which are threaded by a variety of short paths. There is also a path leading out of the glen to the Mausoleum, the ruins of Downhill House and the amazing Mussenden Temple perched on a high cliff above the sea. All these structures are the work of Frederick Hervey, the eccentric Earl Bishop of Bristol and Derry. Downhill House was built between 1774 and 1791, extended and altered over subsequent years, burnt in 1851, but rebuilt and modified in 1870. It was finally abandoned after being used as an RAF billet in the Second World War. Mussenden Temple, based on the Temple of Vesta at Tivoli, was built between 1783 and 1785 and used as a library and summer house. The Bishop's Gate was built in 1784, and this Classical arch stands next to a Gothic gatehouse, through which the Ulster Way passes. All these structures are in the care of the National Trust.

Mussenden Temple, built as a library by the eccentric 18th-century Bishop of Derry, Frederick Hervey, is particularly striking in the landscape at Downhill.

Cross the main road to enter Downhill Forest, following a broad path gently down and keeping to the right at any junctions. The path reaches a gateway and road at a bridge. Turn left to follow the road steeply uphill, and when it levels out turn right along a forest track. This gradually descends through mixed woodlands and joins the minor

Bishop's Rd, another of Hervey's constructions. To the right, the view through the ravine draws your eye to the sea, but you must turn left to start walking uphill along the road, passing by a few farms, the last one being derelict. Grange Park Forest is well to the left, so that views are quite open on the gradual ascent from fields to moorland.

There is a fine viewpoint at the Gortmore Picnic Area. A small knoll can be climbed, but there is also a path to a cliff-top viewpoint overlooking the dramatic vista of Lough Foyle and the hills of Inishowen. The first serious technical mapping project ever undertaken in the world started down beside Lough Foyle, when a base-line measuring nearly 13 kilometres (8 miles) was plotted from Ballykelly to Ballymulholland. All subsequent measurements and triangulations around the whole of Ireland were taken from that line, resulting ultimately in the map you now hold in your hand. The work was completed by sappers in the British Army, working under Lt Col Thomas Colby. The line was measured between 1827–8 by 70 men. While the Ordnance Survey perfected its cartographic skills during the mapping of the whole of Ireland, the survey also gathered enormous amounts of folklore and local history in many of the districts it passed through.

The Bishop's Rd bends left and runs downhill beyond Gortmore, where two roads lead off to the right. You have the option of taking the second one, Leighry Rd, running downhill from a bridge painted black and white. This way brings you to the top of Binevenagh, returning to this junction later. Alternatively, if time is pressing, you can skip the ascent, and the next two paragraphs, and continue along the road.

Walk down Leighry Rd to find a sign pointing left for Binevenagh Lake. A clear track climbs straight up the forested slope and clear felling allows open views for most of the ascent. The track bends to the right near the top, emerging on a rugged moorland with the lake to the left. The trig point on the highest part of the mountain – 385m (1,260ft) – can also be seen well to the left. The track ends at a car park and picnic site, but a grassy track continues straight onwards and suddenly reveals a sheer cliff-edge. A fine prow rises just to the left, while the waters of Lough Foyle are spread far below, with the hills of Inishowen rising beyond. You can see parts of the Causeway Coast, and on a clear day the Scottish islands of Islay and Jura off in the distance.

Turn right and follow the path along the edge of the cliff, heading gradually downhill. The path enters the forest and can be rather vague in places – and slippery. Look ahead carefully as it winds downhill, and when a track is reached at the bottom of the slope, turn right and right again to reach a gateway back onto Leighry Rd. Another right turn is made on this road, which then climbs steeply back up to Bishop's Rd.

Continue up Bishop's Rd into a stand of forest. There is a patch of moorland beyond, then when the road descends, turn left into more forest. The road passes a couple of tall masts, turning left, then right, and ends at another mast on Harkin's Hill. There is a forest track just before the abrupt road-end. Follow it along and downhill. It bends right at a junction, then a left turn is marked further along. Avoid all other turnings and let the most obvious track lead you through the forest, crossing a stretch of moorland and eventually joining a minor road. Turn right to walk down to the B201, Windy Hill Rd, and turn left uphill.

Windy Hill Rd is also known as the Murder Hole Road. In the 18th century it was the stamping ground of a highwayman called Cushy Glenn, who would murder travellers along the road and dispose of their bodies in the bog-holes on the mountain. A ruined house stands beside the road before the highest part is crossed. When the forest ends, the road is flanked on both sides by overgrown, cutaway bog. Fields flank the road further along on the descent to Formoyle. Sconce Hill rises above the countryside; the hill is associated with the mythic heroes of the Red Branch and Niall of the Nine Hostages, the progenitor of the great O'Neill clan which held sway over much of Ulster until the late 16th century.

Formoyle has a few scattered farms but no facilities of any sort. The Ulster Way turns right along Fermoyle Rd, but anyone looking for a place to stay should turn left for Bratwell Farm B&B, or continue along the B201 road to Ballinrees, to the solitary Rockmount B&B. If anything else is needed, you may have to get a lift back to Coleraine.

WALK 10

FORMOYLE TO DUNGIVEN

Start: Formoyle – 767294.

Finish: Dungiven – 695088.

Distance: 36 kilometres (22 miles).

Maps: OSNI Discoverer Sheets 7 and 8.

Terrain: Mostly forest tracks and roads over hills and moorlands. Some of the roads can be busy.

Waymarking: Metal Ulster Way signposts are used along the roads, with wooden marker posts in the forests.

Public Transport: Ulsterbus 234 on the A37 road through Springwell Forest doesn't always stop to pick up passengers. Ulsterbus 212 links Dungiven with Belfast and Derry. Ulsterbus 148 offers another link between Dungiven and Derry.

Accommodation: There are only a couple of B&Bs near Formoyle and these may not be open all year round. Dungiven has just a few B&Bs, and there are very few places to stay anywhere near the route.

ROUTE DESCRIPTION

Follow Formoyle Rd away from the B201 Windy Hill Rd. There is a forestry yard, a couple of farms and an old chapel along the road, the chapel located where the road suddenly bends right. Follow the road to a gate and continue along a track into a clear-felled and replanted area of Springwell Forest. Take the third track to the left and follow it straight onwards through the forest, ending with a couple of right turns to leave the woods. An old road alongside the forest leads to a layby on the busy A37 road; keep to the right along the grass verge. The road leaves the forest behind and crosses a stretch of moorland, with views back to Harkin's Hill and across to Inishowen. There are occasional buses along this route, but it is not usual for them to stop on the road to pick up passengers so you cannot rely on them if you need to leave the route.

On the left, a gate leads into another area of forest, with a track rising gradually uphill away from the busy road. The ascent is hampered by a succession of false summits, but the true crest features a

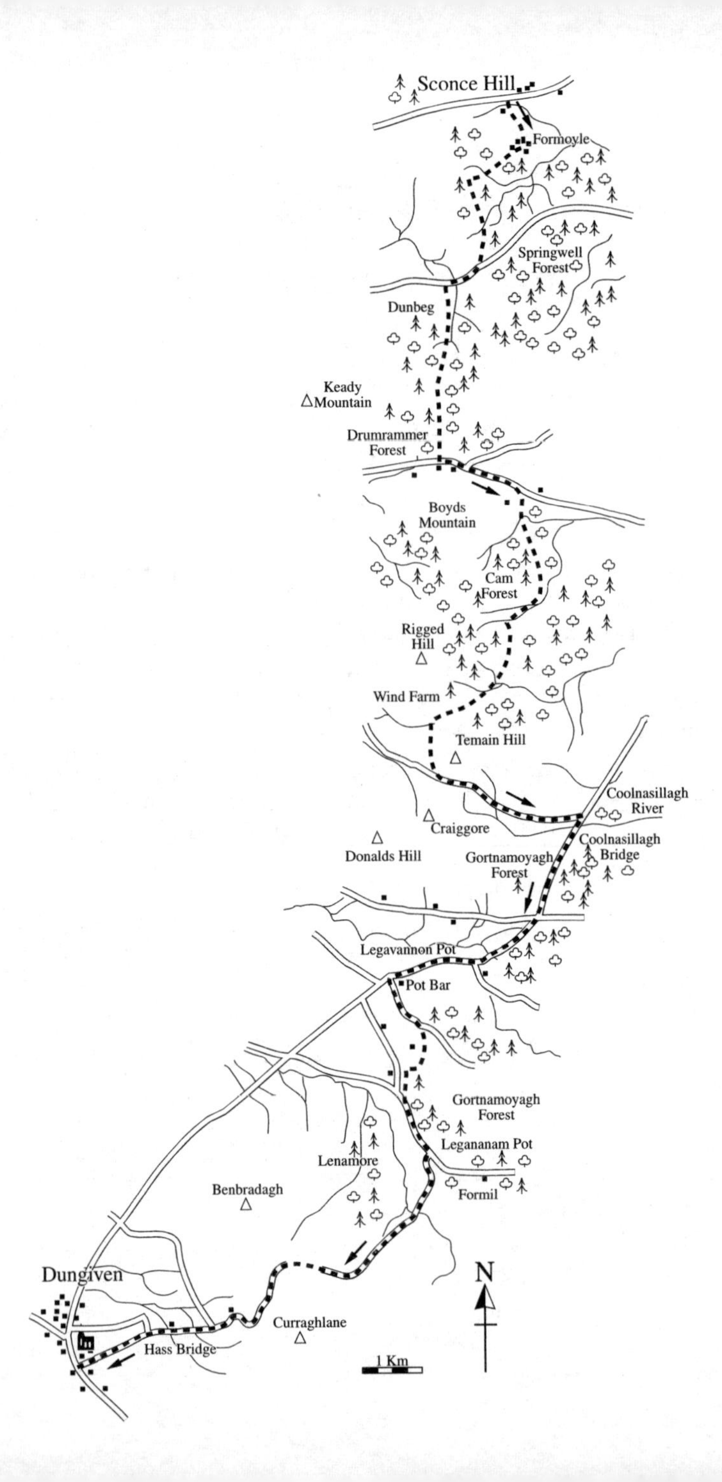

Sconce Hill
Formoyle
Springwell
Forest
Dunbeg
Keady
Mountain
Drumrammer
Forest
Boyds
Mountain
Cam
Forest
Rigged
Hill
Wind Farm
Temain Hill
Coolnasillagh
River
Craiggore
Donalds Hill
Coolnasillagh
Bridge
Gortnamoyagh
Forest
Legavannon Pot
Pot Bar
Gortnamoyagh
Forest
Legananam Pot
Lenamore
Benbradagh
Formil
Dungiven
Curraghlane
Hass Bridge
1 Km
N

brief, rugged area of unplanted moorland. A steep descent starts with a few bends, then leads straight down to the B66 road, where there is a gate and stile. Turn left along the road and leave Drumrammer Forest, enjoying open views as the road rises and falls in the direction of Ringsend.

Turn right to leave the B66 and follow a track through a gateway into Cam Forest. Turn left along a forest track and follow it until another, rougher track rises to the right. This track leads up to a crossing of tracks, where you turn left again. Follow the track over a rise and avoid other turnings. When the track suddenly turns left downhill from a junction, keep straight on and bend to the right instead. The track climbs uphill, levels out, then suddenly comes to an end. Continue along a rugged forest ride and cross a stile to reach a rough, boggy moorland gap. To the right of the gap is Rigged Hill and a wind farm, while to the left is Temain Hill and a couple of tall masts. The Ulster Way follows a fence straight onwards and gradually downhill. Look for a stile on the left, and an embankment leading gradually uphill towards the masts. A minor road on the right can be joined before the masts are reached, then this road is followed by turning left to pass the masts at around 360m (1,180ft).

Walk down from Temain Hill, following the road from the high moorlands to fenced-off fields, passing through a couple of gates on the way. Turn right along the B190 Belraugh Rd, crossing Coolnasillagh Bridge and going past a couple of houses before climbing uphill through Gortnamoyagh Forest. As the road runs downhill through a junction of five roads there are views ahead to Benbradagh. Turn right at a junction above the deep hollow of Legavannon Pot to follow the B64 Legavallon Rd. This can be a busy road, but it has a good verge and good views across the valley to Donald's Hill. A quarry clings to the slopes of Donald's Hill, with Lough Foyle and the hills of Inishowen featuring more distantly. The Pot Bar is available on the left at the bottom of the road.

Leave the Pot Bar by turning left up Temple Rd, leaving it in turn by heading off to the right at the top of the rise. Walk alongside a forest and along a high crest, then drop downhill to the right alongside another stretch of forest. All the woods in this area are detached parts of Gortnamoyagh Forest. Watch for a left turn into the forest and follow a track to a junction with a minor road. Turn left up the road, passing above the woody scrub which fills Legananam Pot. Turn right along another minor road, passing by a couple of isolated farms. The road runs up a moorland slope and passes a stout barrier and gate. Further uphill, the road appears to end at a series of ruins, but just beforehand, to the left, a more patchy road continues uphill. Follow this through another gate, then, when it bends right and aims for the summit of Benbradagh, you can either follow it for the view or exit left through a gate. The road was constructed to serve a US communications base; the summit of Benbradagh, which rises to 465m (1,525ft), once bristled with masts, of which a series of concrete anchor blocks are all that remain. Every so often the mountain is proposed as a wind-farm site.

Dungiven is noted for its lively Irish music sessions.

Follow the road downhill from Benbradagh, zig-zagging on the steep slope, with extensive views across the patchwork landscape of the Roe Valley. The road runs out onto a more level slope at the foot of Benbradagh and passes by a number of fields, hedgerows and patches of woodland, as well as farms and houses. The road dips and crosses Hass Bridge, and dips again towards the end before passing St Patrick's High School. The Ulster Way turns left along the main road, but most wayfarers will turn right and avail of the facilities offered in Dungiven. The main road runs into town, dropping downhill past shops, pubs, restaurants and a couple of B&Bs. If there is any need to move off-route, there are buses linking with Belfast and Derry. The territory around Dungiven was once controlled by the O'Cahans; the town itself was built in the 17th century by the Skinner's Company of London. Weekends in Dungiven can be quite lively, as the town is noted for its Irish music.

WALK 11

DUNGIVEN TO MONEYNEANY

Start: Dungiven – 695088.

Finish: Moneyneany – 752972.

Distance: 20 kilometres (12½ miles).

Maps: OSNI Discovery Sheets 7, 8 and 13.

Terrain: Busy and quiet roads are followed for the first half of the walk. Moorland and forest tracks and rather muddy paths are followed later, ending on the road to Moneyneany.

Waymarking: Sparsely marked from Dungiven through Glenshane Forest, but better around Moneyneany. Metal Ulster Way signs are used along roads, with wooden marker posts in the forests.

Public Transport: Ulsterbus 212 links Dungiven with Belfast and Derry. Moneyneany is occasionally served by Ulsterbus 112, which sometimes runs beyond Draperstown.

Accommodation: Dungiven has only a few B&Bs. There is no accommodation in Moneyneany, but the Rural College offers accommodation near by and there are a couple of B&Bs at Draperstown.

ROUTE DESCRIPTION

Follow the busy A6 uphill out of Dungiven in the direction of Belfast. After passing the Roman Catholic church there is a sign pointing to the right along Priory Lane where a path leads down to Dungiven Priory, which is worth a short detour. It was an Augustinian house, founded by the O'Cahans in 1100, and its most notable feature is the ornate sculptured tomb of Cooey-na-Gal, who died in 1385.

Continue along the busy A6 Glenshane Rd, using the tarmac path which exploits a good strip of greenery away from the traffic. Cross the road when a signpost indicates the way to Draperstown, walking downhill on a minor road and then uphill on Corick Rd. Turn right at a junction and walk down to cross Cluntygeeragh Bridge. Keep left on the way uphill, and keep left on the way downhill too. Only a few houses and farms are passed on the road walk, and after turning right at a whitewashed farmhouse, a fine track leads uphill and away from all

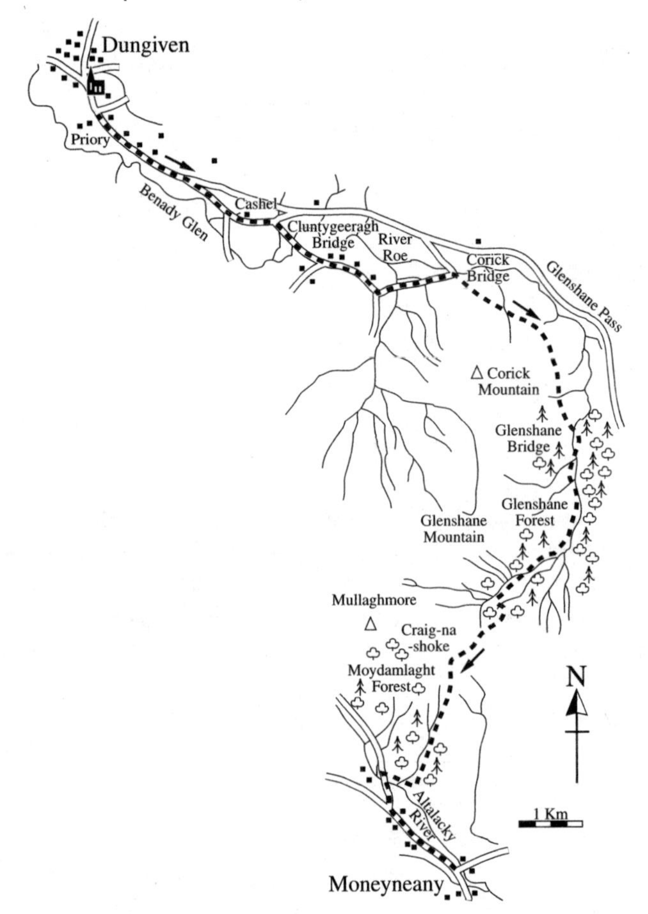

habitations. The fenced track climbs uphill and has a young forest to the right for a while. The rumbling of the Glenshane Rd is now far away across the valley. Go through gates at a sheep pen, then continue across the moors where a fairly good grassy track with a fence running alongside contours around the slopes of Corick Mountain; the track is broad enough to have been a fine highway in its day. There are some little stone culverts along the way and a stream needs to be crossed where an old stone bridge collapsed many years ago. A gate leads onto a forest track which brings you downhill into Glenshane Forest, crossing Glenshane Bridge to reach an intersection of tracks.

A left turn at the junction allows easy access to the Glenshane Rd and the Ponderosa, the highest pub in Ulster. To continue with the

Ulster Way, however, you should keep right, through a gate, and cross another bridge. Follow the track into the forest, walking upstream keeping the river to the left at first. Cross a concrete bridge and continue following the track upstream through the forest. The track finally leaves the riverside and peters out as it winds uphill. A steep, bouldery path squeezes between the trees and reaches a stile over the forest fence. Turn right and follow the fence to a far corner and cross another fence which stretches across the moors. An embankment running across a broad moorland gap offers a fairly firm surface to walk along. Descend along a track on the far side of the gap, but later drop downhill from it, keeping left of a stream to walk down a grassy slope which can be wet or stony in places.

Cross a stile to follow a waymarked path into Moydamlaght Forest. Turn left down a forest track, following it straight downhill as marked by yellow arrows. There are other colour-coded markers, but don't follow any other tracks to right or left until a right turn is made at the very bottom of the slope. The lower parts of the forest are quite mixed, with Sitka spruce and larch complemented by ash, beech and oak. Further north, off the course of the Ulster Way, is the Craig-na-Shoke Forest Nature Reserve, populated by foxes, badgers, mountain hares, red squirrels and birds of prey.

Ireland has two species of hare: Above is the reddish-brown Irish hare, whose coat may partially whiten in winter. With a completely white tail and shortish ears, it is distinguished from the speckled-coated common hare or 'thrush hare'.

The track leaves Moydamlaght Forest at a gateway beside a car park to reach a road. Turn left and follow the road across the Altalacky River and continue straight onwards down to Moneyneany. You pass by St Eoghan's Primary School and the Roman Catholic church, followed by a shop and the Hogan Stand Bar. There is no accommodation in the village, and only an occasional bus link with Draperstown, which offers a couple of B&Bs. The nearest place to stay within walking distance is the Rural College in Derrynoid Wood between Moneyneany and Draperstown. Walkers passing through Moneyneany will notice 'Hudy's Way' signposts concurrent with Ulster Way signposts. Hudy's Way, called after a local character who strapped on a pair of half-doors and made some heroic attempts at manned flight, brings you on a short circular walk around the village which can also be used to vary the route.

If you end up staying off-route at Draperstown it's worth looking around the Plantation of Ulster Visitor Centre. The centre offers an introduction to the turbulent history of 16th- and 17th-century Ulster, when the Gaelic aristocracy, led by the Great Earl, Hugh O'Neill, fled to the continent after losing its lands. The Plantation of Ulster followed, and with it the development of Draperstown as a property of the Drapers Company of London.

WALK 12

MONEYNEANY TO GORTIN

Start: Moneyneany – 752972.

Finish: Gortin – 495858.

Distance: 40 kilometres (25 miles).

Map: OSNI Discoverer Sheet 13.

Terrain: Narrow roads and tracks lead high onto Crockmore, followed by a rugged descent to the head of Glenelly. Walking through Glenelly is entirely on roads. A clear track and more roads lead finally to Gortin.

Waymarking: Metal Ulster Way markers are used over the hills and along the roads, but are sparse in places.

Public Transport: Moneyneany is occasionally served by Ulsterbus 112, which sometimes proceeds beyond Draperstown. There are no bus services through Glenelly. Ulsterbus 92 links Gortin and Omagh.

Accommodation: There is no accommodation on this stretch of the route. The only B&Bs available are off-route in the countryside around Moneyneany and Gortin. Gortin also has a hostel, but in case of difficulty it might be necessary to make a detour by bus to Omagh to secure lodgings.

ROUTE DESCRIPTION

Follow the road out of Moneyneany in the direction of Draperstown, crossing the bridge over the Douglas River and turning right up Drumderg Rd. The road zig-zags uphill and you should keep to the right at a junction. At a higher level, above all the farms, turn right again up another fenced track which leads onto slopes clad in rushes and bushes. Follow the track as it winds up through a gateway. There is a cattle grid towards the top of Crockmore, and an area of bog alongside. Turn right to descend slightly, then follow the track up to a gateway where the Ulster Way descends left from Crockbrack into Glenelly. Simply walk downhill alongside a fence, drifting left away from it towards the bottom to cross Glengomna Water. A stony track leads up to the B47 Glenelly Rd.

Turn right and follow the Glenelly Rd, which runs through the head of the valley, crossing Leaghs Bridge and descending gradually towards Goles Forest and a picnic site. There is a scattering of abandoned buildings at the head of Glenelly, and there are a few inhabited farms and houses later. After crossing Goles Bridge the road is like a switchback as it rises and falls, passing a riverside picnic site on the way to the crossroads hamlet of Sperrin.

Turn left along Corramore Rd, which is signposted as the Barnes Gap Scenic Route. This minor road runs uphill and bends to the right, offering splendid views across Glenelly to the high, rounded dome of Sawel and other Sperrin summits. The lush valley is threaded by a river and two roads, with numerous farms and fields separated by hedgerows

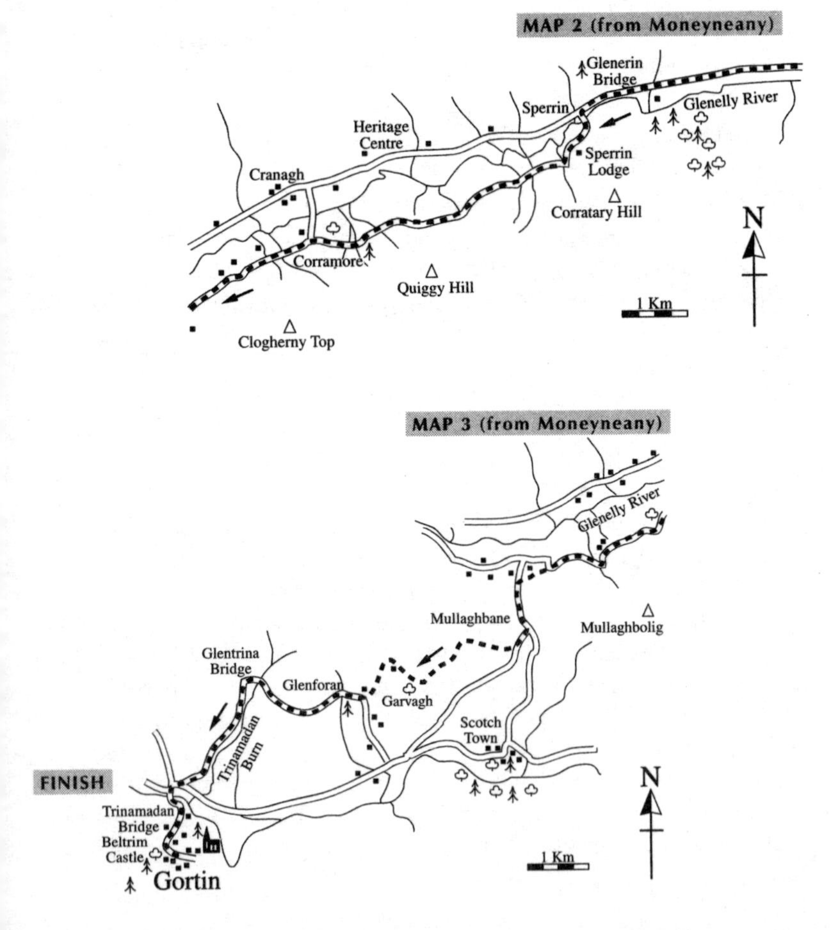

and fences: the scene is quite delightful in good weather. The road twists and turns along the side of the valley, crossing several streams and passing close to some small waterfalls. There are few buildings on the southern side of Glenelly compared with the northern side, and one stretch of the road is quite empty.

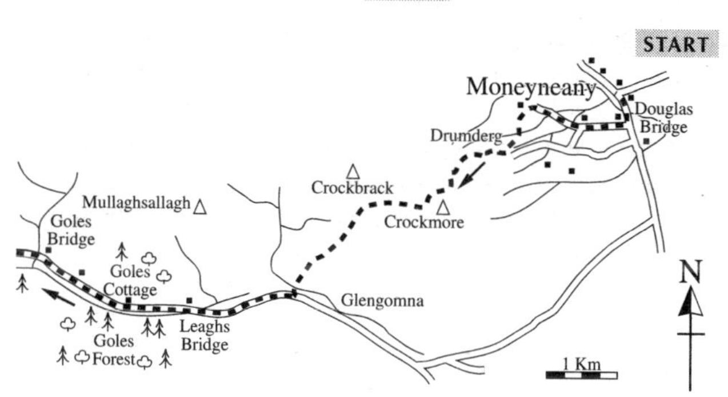

When a junction is reached, a minor road on the right can be used to reach the little village of Cranagh. This is the only sizable settlement in the upper reaches of Glenelly, but if you decide to break this long day's walk at the village be sure to make arrangements to be collected or otherwise accommodated, because there is no B&B in the village at the time of writing. A nearby feature of interest, if time can be spared, is the Sperrin Heritage Centre, which offers an insight into the Sperrin Mountains and their hidden deposits of gold. There is a small restaurant in the centre.

The Ulster Way continues along Corramore Rd, still hugging the southern side of Glenelly, leading away from Cranagh along the Barnes Gap Scenic Route. The road twists by a handful of wooded valleys and waterfalls, and when it descends to a junction, turn left to follow Magherbrack Rd uphill. This road runs at a higher level than the minor one across the Barnes Gap. Anyone carrying a tent can pitch it overnight at a basic site next to a car park. At the top of the gap, go straight through a crossroads and continue uphill for a while. Turn right along a broad, clear track, which bends round the slopes overlooking the valley of the Owenkillew River. A couple of ruined buildings are passed, and there are views across a wide area of fields, farms and woodlands, with the dome of Mullaghcarn rising beyond. When a junction is reached with another track at a stand of conifers, keep straight on to reach another junction with a minor road at Garvagh.

Turn right to follow the road, which loops its way down the valley slopes, losing height gradually. Along the way, there are four roads heading off to the left. Take the fourth one, which is found just after climbing up from Glentrina Bridge. The road is mostly well-wooded as it runs downhill beside Trinamadan Burn, past a couple of farms. Turn right at the bottom, then left, following the B48 road downhill and across Trinamadan Bridge over the broad Owenkillew River. The road climbs uphill past Beltrim Castle estate to the village of Gortin. Turn left to find the main street, which is lined with a range of shops and pubs. There is a hostel, but B&B accommodation in the surrounding countryside is sparse. A bus service links with Omagh, bringing a greater range of facilities within reach.

WALK 13

GORTIN TO MOUNTJOY

Start: Gortin – 495858.

Finish: Ulster American Folk Park – 429790.

Distance: 18 kilometres (11 miles).

Maps: OSNI Discovery Sheets 12 and 13.

Terrain: Riverside paths and forest tracks are followed by road walking through farming country.

Waymarking: Metal Ulster Way signposts are used on some of the roads. Wooden marker posts are used in the forest. The final stretches are less well marked.

Public Transport: Ulsterbus 92 serves Gortin and Gortin Glen. Ulsterbus services 97 and 273 pass the Ulster American Folk Park, linking Omagh and Strabane.

Accommodation: There is only limited B&B accommodation on or near the route around Gortin, Knockmoyle and Mountjoy, but buses offer links with the major town of Omagh.

ROUTE DESCRIPTION

Beside the bridge over Gortin Burn stands a wide street with a stockpen and toilets. On the opposite side of the street a sign announces the start of the Gortin Burn Walk. The track leads to a stile beside a gate, then a narrow concrete path links no fewer than nine footbridges as it proceeds upstream through a little valley filled with small trees and bushes. Follow the steps climbing away from the river and cross two stiles, then a right turn leads along a narrow road to join the nearby B48 road. There is a small car park and picnic area on the edge of the Boorin National Nature Reserve, a wilderness of heather and bracken with a series of small, deep pools crouched between heathery knolls and a small oak and birch woodland further on. There is free access to the reserve, but there are no trodden paths.

Follow the B48 road uphill in the direction of Omagh to reach a large sign for Gortin Glen Forest Park. Turn right down a track at this point, then keep to the left as it bends and climbs uphill. Watch carefully

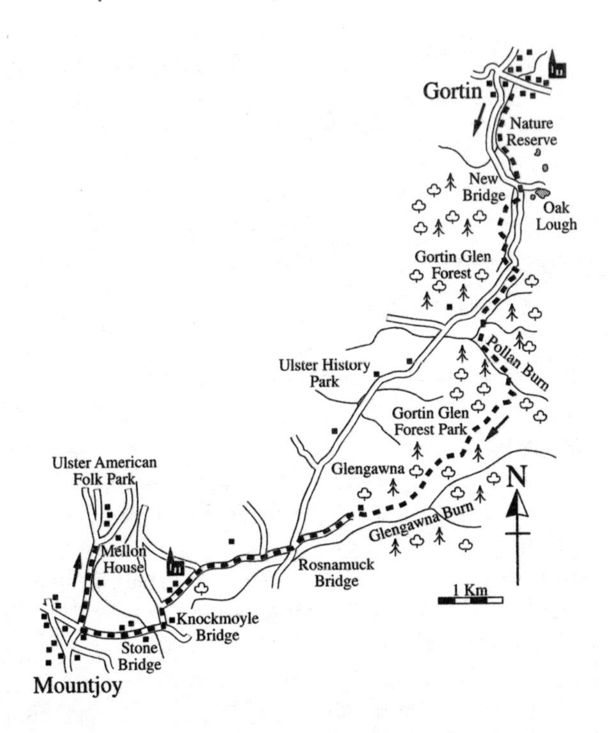

for a marker post on the left at the top of the track, where a path leads down through the forest to a bend on top of the B48 road. Cross the road to reach a gateway and cross the stile beside it. A track runs downhill between the road and a small stream. Follow the track until it joins a narrow tarmac road and descend to the right, but keep left at junctions later. It's also possible to head off to the right and avail of toilets beside a car park. Further explorations reveal an informative mapboard, nature centre, wildlife enclosure and children's play area. Gortin Glen Forest Park was established in the centre of a much larger commercial coniferous forest in 1967. There is a forest drive for motorists, as well as a series of waymarked forest trails.

The Ulster History Park is unfortunately off-route, but worth a visit. It traces man's settlement of the area from the Stone Age through early monastic times, the wars of the 16th century to the Plantation era. Authentic reconstructions of habitations and monuments are linked by delightful walkways. There is a visitor centre which is equipped with an audio-visual presentation and a restaurant. To reach it, you have to leave the forest and turn left along the B48 road.

The forest trails all commence near a barbecue site beside Pollan Burn. The Lady's View Trail is marked by red arrows and coincides with the course of the Ulster Way. Follow the clear, firm riverside path upstream through the rocky gorge, past a number of small but delightful waterfalls. These are seen to good effect from five footbridges as height is gained on the way. Don't cross a sixth footbridge, but continue upstream and cross the narrow tarmac Forest Drive. Again, don't cross the bridge at this point. As the path moves further upstream it drifts away from the Pollan Burn, twisting and turning as it climbs up the forested slope. Turn right along a track, then left up another path past a small wooden shelter. Later, the path bends to the right and reaches a road at Lady's View. Unfortunately, views are not particularly extensive or inspiring at this point.

The Ulster Way crosses the Forest Drive and passes a barrier to continue along a forest track by the edge of the forest. There is a view up to the top of Mullaghcarn later, then the track leads down into the forest; you should keep right at any junctions with other tracks. The forest has mixed margins at a lower level, then a gate is passed on the way out onto a tarmac road. The road runs down through fields and eventually joins the B48 road.

Period costume is a feature of the Ulster American Folk Park.

Turn left, then right as signposted along a minor road for Knockmoyle. Walk straight through a crossroads, and note the lovely garden to the left which is part of a residential home. The road leads up through Knockmoyle, passing St Mary's Roman Catholic church and McGrath's Bar. At the end of the road turn left, then right to cross the ten-arch Stone Bridge spanning the River Strule. The road passes Dunmore House B&B and reaches the busy A5 road. There is a shop and filling station away to the left, with Mountjoy village across the road and uphill. The Ulster Way, however, turns right to follow the busy road to the Ulster American Folk Park. Accommodation in the area is sparse, but if a wider range of lodgings or shops is needed, there are buses running to nearby Omagh.

The Ulster American Folk Park was developed alongside the home of the Mellons, a local family who left Camphill farm and emigrated to America in 1818, founding a business and banking empire, but keeping in touch with their roots. The house itself is part of the folk park and is open to the public. The folk park divides neatly into two halves. The Old World displays the buildings of 18th- and 19th-century Ulster, many of them authentic structures removed stone by stone from the surrounding countryside. The cabins, farms, houses and chapels of the area lead to rows of quaint old shops at Ulster St. Visitors then pass through an emigrant ship – the brig *Union* – and emerge on American St in the New World. This is fashioned on old Baltimore, and the trail continues past the cabins and farmsteads of western Pennsylvania. The site incorporates a Centre for Emigration Studies and a restaurant.

WALK 14

MOUNTJOY TO KILMORE

Start: Ulster American Folk Park – 429790.

Finish: Kilmore – 313784.

Distance: 21 kilometres (13 miles).

Map: OSNI Discoverer Sheet 12.

Terrain: Mostly on roads and forest tracks, but the ascent of Bessy Bell is over rugged, pathless ground which can be wet and muddy.

Waymarking: There are no markers on the ascent of Bessy Bell. Forest tracks have wooden marker posts and roads have metal Ulster Way signposts.

Public Transport: Ulsterbus services 97 and 273 pass the Ulster American Folk Park and the Mellon Country Inn. Ulsterbus 96 serves Kilmore, linking with Omagh and Castlederg.

Accommodation: Accommodation around Mountjoy, the Ulster American Folk Park and Baronscourt is quite limited, but bus services allow access to accommodation in Omagh and Castlederg.

ROUTE DESCRIPTION

Follow a minor road around the back of the Ulster American Folk Park, passing Camphill farm, to avoid walking along the busy A5 road. Later, the main road has to be followed by turning right in the direction of Strabane, and there is a cycleway alongside. Just before reaching the Mellon Country Inn, turn left up a narrow minor road, then turn right at a higher junction at Beltany. Follow the road past a few farmhouses, then turn left up a narrow farm access road which brings you to a ruined farmhouse. A track continues uphill, and you pass through gates as you make your way to the highest farm on the slopes of Bessy Bell.

A concrete lane climbs uphill through the fields above the last farm, leading through more gates onto the open hillside. It is possible to climb directly to the summit of Bessy Bell, crossing a fence on the higher slopes. You can also cut across the hillside first until you reach a holy well marked by an old telegraph pole. Look carefully for it, as a line of telegraph poles carries an electricity transmission line across the hill close to the well. The well contains numerous white stones, as it is said that anyone depositing three stones in the well will be granted a wish. Climb directly to the summit of Bessy Bell from the well, making your way over heathery tussocks and a fence to reach the top. There is a trig point at 420m (1,370ft), and unfortunately there are also a couple of unsightly masts protruding from the summit and a whirling wind farm on a lower shoulder. Despite these obstructions, the views embrace the landscape from the nearby Sperrins to the Highlands of Donegal, Truskmore, Cuilcagh and even the distant Mournes in very clear weather.

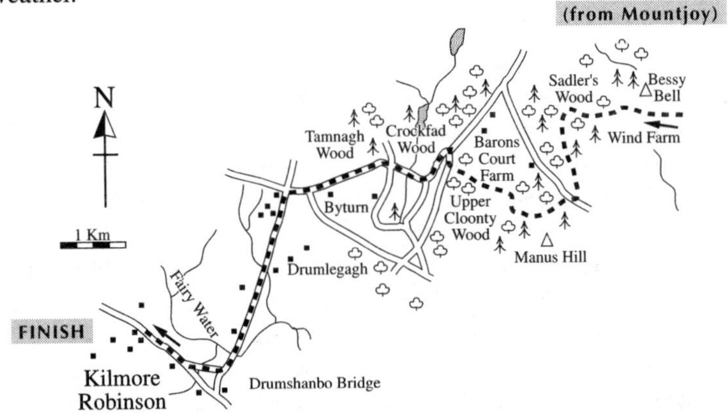

The descent is easy, using a track which serves the masts, passing the access track for the wind farm further downhill. Pass a barrier gate and walk down through the forest to an intersection of forest tracks, where you turn left and follow the track as it rises and dips across a forested shoulder. Turn right down a minor road, then left down and up another forest track. The track curves to the right, then you need to turn right and left at the next junctions to walk straight down to another minor road. Turn right along the road, then left at a stone house to follow Cloonty Rd across the forested valley floor. You are walking through the Baronscourt Estate, the seat of the Duke of Abercorn.

Walk uphill past the fine Baronscourt Church of Ireland, then turn right at the top of Cloonty Rd and left at the top of Byturn Rd. Follow the road straight uphill, then turn left downhill from a crossroads signposted for Drumlegagh. There is a useful shop beside Drumlegagh Presbyterian Church, but the nearest accommodation in this area is off-route at the Hunter's Lodge at Letterbin. Follow the road downhill, along an undulating stretch, before crossing a bridge over Fairy Water. Turn right along another minor road to reach the B50 road, where another right turn brings you to Kilmore Robinson. There is no accommodation in this area, but there is a bus service to Omagh and Castlederg. Both places offer the chance to find lodgings, food and drink, though Omagh has a greater range than Castlederg.

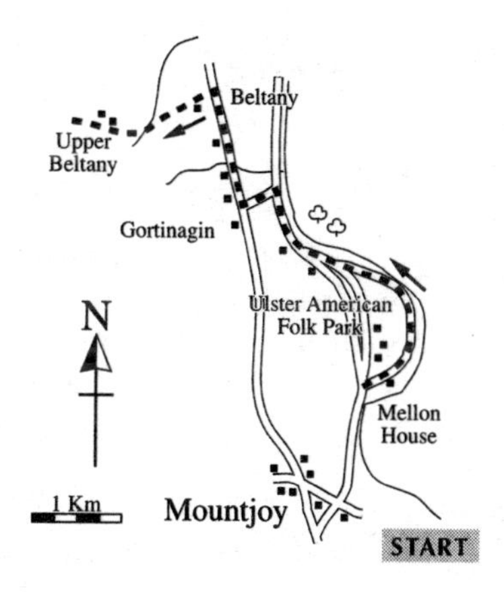

SOUTH-WESTERN SECTION

County Fermanagh

Distance: 199 kilometres (123 miles)

The south-western section of the Ulster Way is basically that part of the route which is wrapped around Co. Fermanagh. They say that Fermanagh is one-third under water, and when you see the extent of Upper and Lower Lough Erne, which completely fill the middle of the county, you may begin to believe it is true. You'll see a lot of both lake systems, as well as plenty of other varied and interesting terrain. A great amount of effort has gone into the Ulster Way in these parts, getting it off the roads and into some quite remarkable countryside. The first stretches of the Ulster Way to be marked – in fact, the first long-distance waymarked trail anywhere in Ireland – was completed in the Lough Navar and Big Dog Forests.

In order to take the Ulster Way away from the roads, the route is very intricate and involved in some places. Standing back from a map, you can see all sorts of options for taking short-cuts, but that defeats the purpose of the journey. Forest and farm tracks alternate with fields and open moorlands. Some parts can be very wet and muddy, while other areas have a foundation of dry limestone bedrock and provide a firmer footing. There are a couple of places where alternative routes have been marked, around the Cliffs of Magho and Belcoo. You need to decide in advance which line you are going to follow, depending on what facilities you need further along the way.

One of the original intentions was to take the route over the sprawling mountain moorland of Cuilcagh, but the route was taken across the lower slopes near Florence Court instead. There is a separate waymarked spur routed to the top of Cuilcagh, known as the Hiker's Trail, but anyone thinking of making the ascent is warned that it is exceedingly tough. You should allow a whole day for the climb, keeping the ascent separate from any other day's walk along the Ulster Way.

In terms of logistics, walkers need to be thinking ahead while walking round this part of the Ulster Way. There are only a few villages and no large towns, so facilities are often quite limited. There are some quite lengthy stretches without accommodation, food or drink available, and it may be necessary to move off-route in search of them. Bus services on some roads are quite sparse, while others have none at all. With judicious use of buses, however, it is possible to operate from a base in Enniskillen and commute to and from certain stretches of the Ulster Way, an option which is not available on many other parts of the route. You need to be absolutely sure of your bus times, but it means you can travel light instead of carrying all your gear along the route.

WALK 15

KILMORE TO PETTIGO

Start: Kilmore – 313784.

Finish: Pettigo – 109668.

Distance: 35 kilometres (22 miles).

Maps: OSNI Discoverer Sheets 12 and 17.

Terrain: Varies from roads to forest and farm tracks, with some moorland slopes which may be pathless and boggy. Some farm tracks are very muddy.

Waymarking: Good in some places and sparse in others. It is important to keep an eye open for wooden marker posts in complex field systems and around farms.

Public Transport: Ulsterbus 96 serves Kilmore, linking with Omagh and Castlederg. Ulsterbus 194 links Pettigo with Enniskillen, with some services extending to Belleek. Bus Éireann 31 and 68 offer summer services to Pettigo, linking with Enniskillen and Belleek respectively.

Accommodation: Apart from a few B&Bs at Pettigo, there is nothing on this long stretch, though the Montaugh Farm B&B is off-route at Drumskinny.

ROUTE DESCRIPTION

Start on the B50 road at Kilmore Robinson, where there is a bus shelter at a junction with Kirlish Rd. Follow the road uphill, passing Kilmore Gospel Hall, then continue through a crossroads and up to another road junction. Turn right along a road signposted as a scenic route, walking through a small forest. Kilmore Lodge is hidden in this forest, then the road emerges and rises gradually alongside a moorland, passing a couple of houses. Keep walking along the road and pass the Bolaght Mountain scenic viewpoint, where there are picnic tables. Turn left at the next road junction, after the picnic tables, and follow a narrow road up into a mountainy hollow where the last farm, high on the hill, is passed at the very end of the tarmac road.

Turn right to cross a stile and follow a rather squelchy bog road across the moorland slopes. Look out for a line of little wooden marker posts which show the way over the broad crest of Bolaght Mountain, which is crossed at around 330m (1,080ft). The rugged heath can be boggy in places. Descend towards Lough Lee, aiming for a clear gravel track which runs beside the water. Turn left to follow the track uphill, passing a gate and entering the extensive Lough Bradan Forest. Walk downhill and turn right, briefly leaving the plantations and passing through a few more gates at a staggered junction of tracks. Climb up into the forest again, and turn left to walk downhill. Turn right at the next junction of tracks, then keep right at a junction where there are telegraph poles, and left at the next junction. Continue straight onwards, avoiding the next junction left, continuing mostly downhill to reach a barrier gate on the way out of the forest.

Turn right along the B72 road, crossing a broad dip and a river, then rising before turning left along a narrow concrete farm road. Walk straight past a farmhouse, switching onto a grassy track to the next minor road. Turn left down the road, then right at a gateway marked as the Ulster Way. A very muddy track is followed at this point, and the only way of avoiding it is to make a wide loop around by road, passing Drumskinny Stone Circle. A solitary B&B lies off-route nearby at Montaugh Farm.

Drumskinny Stone Circle is just off-route on entering Fermanagh.

The muddy track leads into a small forest, part of the fragmented Kesh Forest, and joins onto a farm track with a firmer surface. You pass a few farm buildings before you reach the next minor road. Turn right along the road, then left along a forest track. Most of the forest on this stretch has been clear felled and replanted, so that views are quite open. Some parts of the forest track look more like a country lane, rolling along gently before descending past a couple of buildings. Another muddy stretch follows, but it is quickly over, followed by a left turn up a firmer forest track, which in turn leads to another minor road.

Turn right up the road, then follow it downhill. After passing a farmhouse on the left, turn left along a concrete farm road. Turn left again up a grassy forest track, enjoying a fine mixture of trees. After passing a ruin the track leaves this patch of forest and continues as a

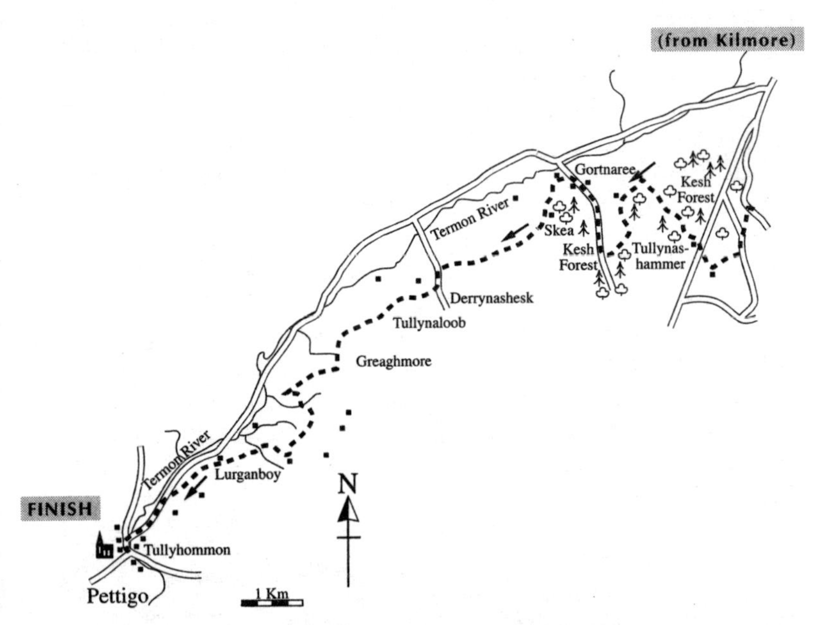

grassy, stony track through the fields. Use stiles and gates as necessary to bring you by a series of old farms at Skea, where a concrete track leads gradually downhill, gaining a tarmac surface later as it reaches a minor crossroads. Turn left along the road, then right along a forest track. The track leads downhill and out of the forest, then follows a pleasant line through fields and up past a few derelict farms. A grassy stretch of the track leads into another area of forest. Follow the track along a high crest, then walk downhill and look carefully for red marker posts off to the left which point you along a narrow path which crosses over a stream and climbs uphill on a wooded slope. When a track is reached at the top, turn right, and right again at a junction of tracks. This track wriggles and writhes along a high, forested crest at Greaghmore before descending to a farm gate at Lurganboy.

Follow the track away from the farm until you reach another farm near a minor road. Turn left between the farm and the road, following a line of trees uphill. A muddy track runs alongside, dropping down to a stile at a junction of roads. Keep straight on along the road, but note that there is also a short length of path available beside the Termon River. It

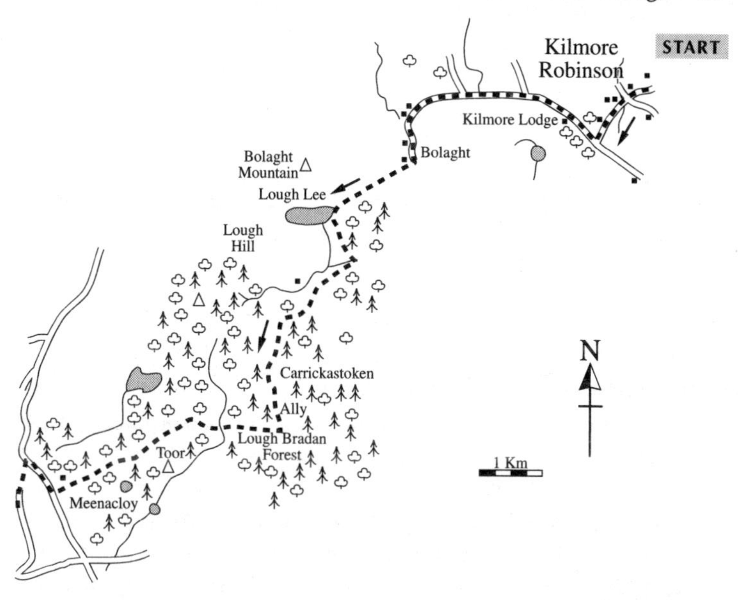

might be a good idea to get your boots cleaned of all the mud you will have picked up on the recent stretch, and enter Pettigo in an acceptable state!

Pettigo straddles the border between Northern Ireland and the Republic; the boundary is shaped by the Termon River. All three bridges across the river span the Border. Most facilities are on the Co. Donegal side, including the widest selection of shops, all the pubs and most of the accommodation. There is, however, a small shop and some accommodation on the Co. Fermanagh side, which is also known as Tullyhommon. In former times Pettigo was known as Termon-macgrath, and, lying on the boundaries of the O'Neill, O'Donnell and Maguire clans, was beyond the influence of them all! The town displays a variety of war memorials, from a tree planted 'in commemoration of the taking of Sebastopol' to a more recent 1920s Republican memorial in the centre of town. Churches include Roman Catholic, Church of Ireland, Methodist and Presbyterian, while the Lough Derg Journey Heritage Centre places an almost New Age interpretation on the traditional Lough Derg pilgrimage.

Ulster Wayfarers have a choice in Pettigo. They can either continue with the route through Co. Fermanagh or branch off along a separate spur through Co. Donegal. Amazingly, neither of these routes is signposted from the centre of Pettigo.

WALK 16

PETTIGO TO ROSSCOR

Start: Pettigo – 109668.

Finish: Rosscor – 990577.

Distance: 24 kilometres (15 miles).

Map: OSNI Discoverer Sheet 17.

Terrain: A mixture of roads, forest and farm tracks, open moorland and a few field paths. Some parts can be very wet and muddy, especially in the middle of this stretch.

Waymarking: Fairly good, but as the route is quite intricate, it is essential to keep a careful lookout for marker posts.

Public Transport: Ulsterbus 194 links Pettigo with Enniskillen, with some services extending to Belleek. Ulsterbus 99 passes Rosscor between Enniskillen and Belleek. Bus Éireann 31 and 68 offer summer services to Pettigo, linking with Enniskillen and Belleek respectively. Bus Éireann 30 also passes Rosscor.

Accommodation: A few B&Bs at Pettigo, but only a few places to stay in the countryside around Rosscor, all off-route, with the widest option available around Belleek.

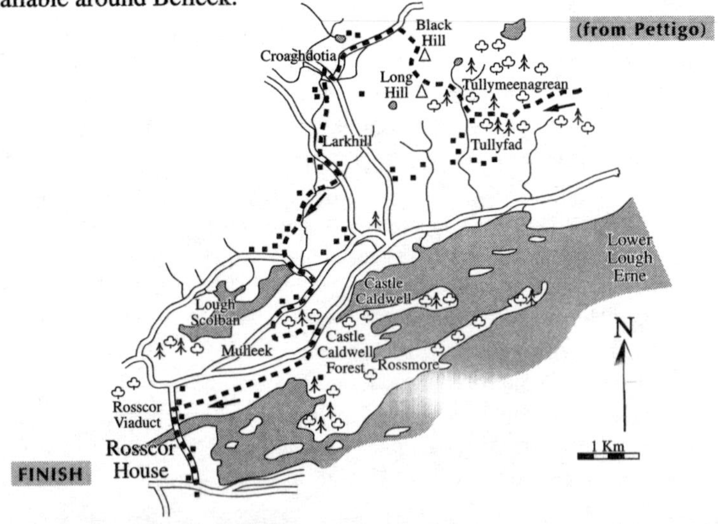

ROUTE DESCRIPTION

Pettigo offers a good selection of shops, and as shops are few and far between for the next couple of days, the opportunity to stock up should not be missed. The next place with shops en route is distant Belcoo, and if you take the route option which avoids the village the next place after that is Derrylin, 105 kilometres (65 miles) from Pettigo! There are of course shops, pubs and other places offering food and drink off-route at Derrygonnelly, and in any case a detour into the village might have to be made in search of accommodation further along the Ulster Way.

Follow the R232 road away from Pettigo in the direction of Sligo, but on the edge of town keep to the left along a narrow road which passes close to the Aughnahoo Art Studios, then a track continues straight over a little hill. This stretch is fringed by trees and can be muddy. When the next road is reached, turn left to follow it, passing the Cross Bar and a shop. Keep left to cross the Border using Letter Bridge. Before this bridge was rebuilt, the Ulster Way used to cross the old railway viaduct near the bridge to re-enter Fermanagh. Follow the road as it rises and take a right turn along a minor road at Doonella. This road runs through gentle farming country and later has wooded margins before passing a little lough in the forest at Tullyvocady. A glance at the map reveals that the placename particle 'Tully' (from the Gaelic *tulach*, meaning 'little hill') is extremely common in the area.

When the road ends, continue straight along a stony track. Enter a forest and turn left, then right. When a barrier gate is reached, turn uphill to the right, then turn left down a rather wet and muddy track.

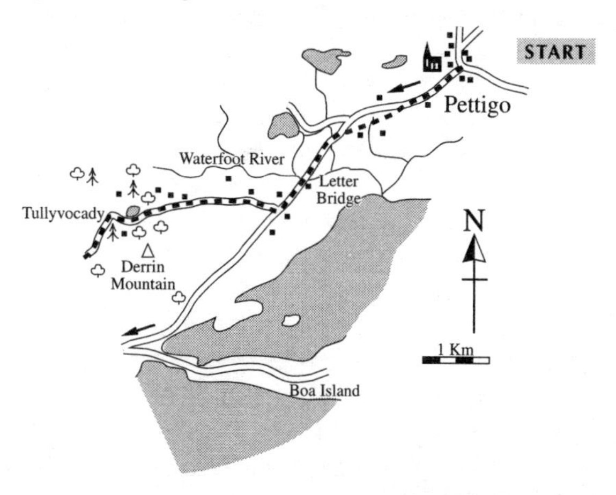

This track runs alongside a little river and leaves the forest, passing an isolated stand of trees out on the moors, where a bog road, which is also wet and muddy in places, leads to a series of turf cuttings. Look for a line of marker posts which show the way to the summit of Long Hill. Turn right to cross a broad and boggy gap to reach the adjacent rise of Black Hill. The views from here encompass the Cliffs of Magho, the hill ranges around Manorhamilton, with the prow of Benwhiskin prominent beyond Truskmore. Breezy Hill is a nearby feature, with Slieve League and the Blue Stack Mountains rising in the distance in Donegal. Follow the markers, from the summit of Black Hill, off to the left to reach a minor road, and turn left along the road. After crossing a little river you reach farmland around Croaghdotia.

Turn right at a road junction at Croaghdotia, then left down a farm access road. Don't cross the little river at the bottom, but look carefully for a way up a steep, muddy, wooded slope to the bog further up. Stay high on the bog at first, looking ahead to spot marker posts and stiles across fences, but gradually drift down towards the river again and walk roughly parallel to it. Take great care on this stretch, as there is plenty of wet ground and some really deep mud. If you sink to your knees, at least you can wash the mud off in the river before reaching the next minor road. Turn left along that road, then right along a track which leads back across the river. A few farm buildings are passed before yet another minor road is reached. Turn left to walk around by Lough Scolban and climb uphill to a junction, then turn right to reach Mulleek, where there is a small chapel.

Just before reaching the chapel, turn left through a gate and follow a muddy path through some bushes to reach a ruined church. Walk past the ruin and keep drifting to the left across a field. Cross stiles at the top and bottom of another field, then continue along a woodland track to reach a gate. Just across the A47 road, a structure which looks like a gatehouse is actually an old railway viaduct, and there is access to Castle Caldwell Forest by way of a detour. Note the Fiddle Stone memorial, which records the drowning of a drunken fiddler on Lower Lough Erne in 1770. The ruins of Castle Caldwell are off-route on the forested Rossmore Peninsula. A fortified bawn was built there in 1612 by Edward Blennerhasset and extended by subsequent owners in later years, but in the 19th century came years of decline and neglect; the castle furnishings were auctioned off in 1876 and the building fell into ruins. The surrounding forest and lakeshore is managed as a nature reserve, rich in tree species and bird-life.

The Ulster Way is supposed to follow the bed of the old railway track off to the right, running roughly parallel to the road. Unfortunately, this line is not easy to get onto and is choked with undergrowth in places; some of the old cuttings can be particularly waterlogged. It might be better to turn right and follow the main A47 road instead, turning left later to follow a leafy road to the Rosscor Viaduct. This bridge has had one of its concrete spans replaced with timber and is not used by heavy vehicles. The broad River Erne flows under the bridge on its way to the sea at Donegal Bay.

Follow the road to the junction with the main A46 road, then consider your options. There are a couple of B&Bs off the course of the Ulster Way, but the nearest concentration of accommodation, shops, pubs and restaurants is off-route at Belleek. There are only occasional buses to the town along this road, so consult up-to-date timetables. The most notable feature of this small Border town is its Belleek pottery, where a fine Parian china is woven into exquisitely intricate basketwork forms, adorned with flowers and other ornamentation, carefully hand-painted and fired. The industry was started by the Caldwell family in 1857 and flourishes to this day. The china, however, is far too delicate to carry away in your rucksack!

WALK 17

Rosscor to Doagh Glebe

Start: Rosscor – 990577.

Finish: Doagh Glebe, above Derrygonnelly – 065519.

Distance: 21 or 26 kilometres (13 or 16 miles).

Maps: OSNI Discoverer Sheet 17. Outdoor Pursuits Map of Lower Lough Erne is also useful.

Terrain: Roads and forest tracks, with some linking paths which can be wet and muddy or overgrown and brambly in places.

Waymarking: Fairly good, but because of the intricate nature of the route it is a good idea to keep a careful lookout for signposts and marker posts.

Public Transport: Ulsterbus 99 passes Rosscor between Enniskillen and Belleek. Bus Éireann 30 operates along the same route. There are no buses to or from Doagh Glebe.

Accommodation: Rather sparse around Rosscor, with a few more options around Belleek. There is nothing along the day's walk, or at the end of the walk at Doagh Glebe, but off-route Derrygonnelly has a hostel and B&Bs.

ROUTE DESCRIPTION

Leave the road junction near Rosscor and follow the main A46 road as signposted for Enniskillen. The road runs through an army checkpoint, which is most likely to be closed. The attractive little Church of Ireland building at Slawin is immediately followed by a right turn up a narrow road, then a choice of routes is available. It all depends whether you want to head straight for the heights or take in a longer stretch of road walking, though in that case you will enjoy better views later. If you want to climb straight uphill, then refer to the next paragraph, otherwise skip it and carry on from the next one.

The short-cut is available just after passing the buildings at Whealt. Turn right along a short track and aim to pass through a gate beside a shed. Climb straight uphill, looking ahead to spot a couple of widely spaced stiles which may be partially hidden. The ground is

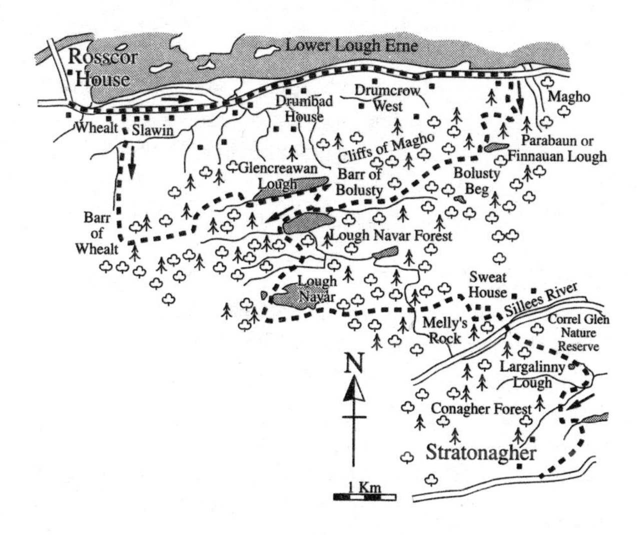

predominantly rushy and can be wet. A fence can be used as a guide to bring you up the steep ascent to the top of the slope. Continue straight over the crest known as the Barr of Whealt and cross the head of Glennalong. Follow a firebreak alongside the forest, where a channel has been cut through the boggy ground. It may be possible to walk on the excavated turf bank, otherwise walk on the heathery strip alongside. Look out for a forest track just inside the forest. Join it and turn left to follow the track. Turn left at a junction with another track, then swing right and follow the track to its end. Continue along a forest ride, then turn right along the edge of the forest. A left turn reveals a vague path, which becomes much clearer later, along the southern shore of the lovely Glencreawan Lough. A right turn along a broader track leads over the Barr of Bolusty to the shores of Meenameen Lough, rejoining the main part of the Ulster Way. If you are using this alternative, skip the next two paragraphs to continue with the route.

Walkers who opt for the longer walk continue along the minor road at Slawin, rejoining the main A46 road to continue roughly parallel to the shore of Lower Lough Erne. Apart from a few farms, houses and fields, there is nothing remarkable about the road walk, but the forested slopes falling from the Cliffs of Magho dominate the scene as you continue. A car park is reached off to the right, marked by a signpost for the Lough Navar Forest. A gate at the car park gives access to a steep path which brings you up through a thickly wooded slope carpeted in a rich variety of woodland flowers. As the path steepens it begins to zig-zag, and there are around 370 steps to climb before a viewpoint car park is reached at the top of the Cliffs of Magho. Lower Lough Erne fills the view, with ranges of hills and mountains seen beyond. They sweep around in an arc which includes Slieve League, Breezy Hill, the Blue Stack Mountains, Errigal, Muckish, the Inishowen Peninsula and the rolling Sperrin Mountains. Ranks of conifers cut out any views to the south.

Follow the cliff path westwards from the viewpoint car park. While the views are admirable, they can be enjoyed only for a short time, before the path swings left and heads towards Lough Navar Forest. A wooden fence and a waymark post indicate the turning. A narrow path leads through the forest to a small, scenic lough called Parabaun or Finnauan Lough. Keep to the right to walk around it, then follow a forest ride to reach a firmer forest track. Turn right along the track, which reaches an unplanted area of bog at Bolusty Beg. This stretch can be muddy, or even completely flooded with water. The track runs downhill and reaches a barrier gate at the bottom, where you turn right along the narrow tarmac road called the Lough Navar Drive. This rises and falls gently, then a gravel path to the left leads between the trees and becomes rather muddy. Turn right to follow a firmer path along the northern shore of Meenameen Lough, heading for a small car park where there is a link with the alternative route described earlier.

Continue walking along the shore of Meenameen Lough. Note that the path turns away from the shore, to join a forest track, before reaching a footbridge. Turn left along the forest track, where you catch an occasional glimpse between the closely planted trees of the extensive moorlands beyond. The track runs downhill to cross a bridge, then runs through a gate onto the tarmac Lough Navar Drive again. Make a quick left and right turn at this point, to leave the road and follow a rather rugged forest ride. This line leads gradually uphill, then at the edge of the forest a right turn downhill passes a fine old 'sweat house' at Melly's Rock. This small stone 'igloo' was an early Irish sauna, where people would go to sweat out a fever or just to keep in general good health. There are numerous examples in the north-west of Ireland. Continue downhill to join the Lough Navar Drive and turn left into a dark patch of forest. A right turn along a grassy ride leads onto a minor road.

A quick left and right on the minor road leads ac[illegible] through a gate onto another forest track. Follow this track until it expires, then pick a way along a muddy path leading out of the trees and into a rugged glen. The ground is wet in places, and carries a great many small trees and shrubs, as well as awkward, tussocky grass. Bog myrtle grows profusely. Look carefully for markers as the path is braided in places, passing the little Largalinny Lough before joining a stony track. Follow the track uphill through a valley where a forest has been clear-felled and replanted. Turn left at a junction of tracks and cross a river, then turn left up a grassy, muddy track between the trees. The path is narrower as it emerges onto a heathery crest, heading towards the little Lough Fadd. Follow the markers carefully as they loop to the right, wandering through bracken and brambles alongside a fence. This stretch needs more walkers to keep the path clear of vegetation. Gradually, a squelchy slope is climbed, with the markers arranged alongside another fence. Bear to the right to descend a wooded slope and join a minor road near Doagh Glebe.

Bog myrtle (*Myrica gale*), with its yellow catkin-like flowers and aromatic leaves, grows abundantly along the shores of lakes and other boggy wetlands on this section of the Way.

There is nowhere to stay on this part of the Ulster Way, and no bus service either. Most walkers will agree that Belcoo, 26 kilometres (16 miles) away, is another day's walk and will be ready to call a halt for today. The only real option, unless a handy lift can be arranged, is to walk 5 kilometres (3 miles) off-route to Derrygonnelly. This attractive little village offers a small amount of accommodation, as well as shops, pubs and restaurants.

WALK 18

DOAGH GLEBE TO BELCOO

Start: Doagh Glebe, above Derrygonnelly – 065519.

Finish: Belcoo – 084386.

Distance: 26 kilometres (16 miles).

Maps: OSNI Discoverer Sheets 17 and 26.

Terrain: Mostly forest paths, though there are a few roads and paths too. Some of the paths can be muddy or boggy.

Waymarking: Fairly good, but because of the intricate nature of the route it is a good idea to keep a careful lookout for signposts and marker posts.

Public Transport: There are no buses to or from Doagh Glebe. Ulsterbus 64 serves Belcoo, linking with Enniskillen, with an occasional extension to Belleek. Bus Éireann 66 and 69 also serve Belcoo, linking with Enniskillen and Sligo.

Accommodation: Derrygonnelly is the closest place to Doagh Glebe offering accommodation. There are a few B&Bs available in and around Belcoo.

ROUTE DESCRIPTION

The minor road at Doagh Glebe rises gently westwards, passing a number of farms and houses. Just before reaching the Big Dog Forest, there is a left turn down through a farmyard, where a track continues across a river to enter the forest. The track runs uphill, passing a junction, then descends, and at that point you should look out for a path off to the left. The path leads to the little Lough Doo, then cuts across a rugged slope to reach Lough Nabrickboy. A track forms a sort of causeway across the second lough, then a right turn is made to climb away from the track, following a path towards Little Dog. There are a series of steps leading to the top of Little Dog, which is a fine viewpoint, but if these are followed, then walk back down them to continue along a lower path afterwards. The view from the top takes in Cuilcagh, Slieve Anierin, the hills around Manorhamilton, Truskmore and the brow of Benwhiskin, continuing around Slieve League, the Blue Stack Mountains and other ranges in Co. Donegal and back to the distant Sperrin Mountains.

The path away from Little Dog is very soft and squelchy, crossing

a stream and passing through a patch of forest before climbing Big Dog. There is a prominent block of rock known as the Giant's Stone on this summit; it is said to have been carried there by a giant, who left the imprint of his back on the surface! The path wanders along the rough crest, becoming quite muddy as it curves to the left around the lower slopes. Look out for some old stone buildings, then follow a cobbly old track uphill away from them. This leads onto a forest track which continues onto a minor road. Turn left along the road, taking a break from the forest as you pass a few fields. A track on the right leads across the Roogagh River, then up through a barrier gate into Ballintempo Forest.

Follow the forest track uphill, then downhill to cross a stream, and carry on up and over to Lough Formal. The track curves around the shore to the far side, then a left turn is marked which leads along a grassy ride. Follow the ride uphill and turn left along another ride which is also marked. The route runs out onto a broad stretch of moorland bog where it is best to drift slightly to the right. You should aim for the Shaking Stone, a prominent boulder passed by a line of marker posts. The route leads back into the forest, where a left turn is made along another track. This track is as much on the moor as it is in the forest, so views along the way keep changing. Turn left at a junction of tracks to pass Lough Namanfin. The track later crosses a river, climbs uphill a short way and bends to the right. After reaching a strip of moorland, the track descends to a junction at Tullynagapple where you can turn either left or right. Turning left leads towards Belmore Mountain, while turning right leads to Belcoo. Both routes pursue separate courses until the Cladagh Glen is reached near the Marble Arch Caves.

Turning right for Belcoo, follow the track downhill, twisting and turning to reach a building at another junction. Turn left uphill, passing little Lough Martincrossagh and a dip in the track. Continue on the uphill slope to reach a point where tracks cross each other, and turn right down a fairly muddy track. When you exit from the forest you enjoy fine views across the countryside ahead, with the huge sprawling shape of Cuilcagh dominating the scene. The track nips back into and out of the forest, then a green ribbon of track is followed by a more stony surface. You pass through gates on the way downhill, when the landscape opens out before you. Holywell Church is reached where the track joins a minor road. Turn left to follow the road down towards Holywell and onwards to Belcoo.

The holy well at Holywell lies just to the right at a road junction. An astonishing amount of water gushes from the well; the flow has been calculated at a rate of 2,500 litres (600 gallons) per minute. The well is dedicated to St Patrick and is supposed to have curative properties. Near by lie the ruins of Templerushen Church, which dates from the 9th or 10th century. Belcoo is a much later settlement, its real development stemming from the arrival of the railway in 1878. The station site and a level crossing are nicely preserved in the village, even though the railway has long been closed. There are a few B&Bs in and around Belcoo, as well as shops and pubs offering food and drink. As Holywell Church is so distant from Belcoo, a tiny oratory has been built in the village, and a splendid park known as the Cottage Lawn stretches towards Lower Lough Macnean.

Holywell Church and a view across Lough Macnean Upper.

Belmore Mountain Alternative

As the route over Belmore Mountain is such a major alternative, it deserves a decent amount of space. Any walkers who choose to follow it will of course have to forgo all the facilities offered by Belcoo, though they can catch a bus to the town on the main A4 road. Otherwise the only place to stay near this stretch is a solitary farmhouse B&B at Abocurragh.

Starting from the junction with the route of the Ulster Way at Tullynagapple, turn left to follow the track through Ballintempo Forest, with occasional views out across unplanted areas. The track turns right at a junction to cross a cattle grid and leave the forest. (A left turn at this point could be used to detour to the Aghanaglack Dual Court Grave.) The narrow road leaving the forest crosses some rugged fields and reaches a junction with a minor road. A detour to the right could be made for a glimpse of Margaret Gallagher's quaint little cottage at Mullylusty, otherwise turn left on the road to continue along the Ulster Way.

Leave the road by turning right along a forest track. There is a dip, then the track climbs uphill, passing a junction, with the gradient gradually easing. Take a right turn across a stream and continue climbing, gaining a view of Belmore Mountain through the trees, though the route does not climb to the summit. Walk downhill along the track and turn left at a junction. Continue downhill to reach a pronounced bend, then make an exit left from the forest. Leaving the forest can be awkward: the idea is to cross the forest fence, forge across a rugged slope and link with a muddy track beyond. Follow this track downhill; it gains a firm concrete surface when it reaches some old buildings. Carry on to further buildings lower down, with views over Lough Macnean Lower and Cuilcagh. Turn quickly left and right along a minor road and continue down a very narrow road past a huddle of renovated buildings. Turn left along the main A4 road, but look out for a stile beside a gate on the right.

Cross the stile and follow a concrete track to a bridge. Cross another stile and keep left along the embankment of an old railway track. Look out for waymark posts, stiles and gates to gain access to the shore of Lough Macnean Lower, passing at first through an area of bushes and wild iris. Looking across the water, a hump known as Cushrush Island, or Rabbit Island, was settled as long as 6,500 years ago. Even a cursory glance at the map reveals a host of ancient standing stones and raths in this area. Raths were basically fortified farmsteads occupied by extended families, and thousands of them are scattered across Ireland. There is a crannóg in Lough Macnean Lower – an island fortification rather like a rath in water. This area has a very long history of settlement and the area bounded by West Fermanagh, West Cavan and North Leitrim was once known as Breffni. The lake shore can be very muddy, especially when the outflowing river is reached in a small area of wet woodland. Cross over a metal sluice footbridge and turn left. A track can then be followed off to the right, away from the river and through a series of fields. Look for marker posts, gates and stiles which will lead you towards the Cladagh River, and follow it upstream. Cross the road, then the riverside path becomes rather more difficult to follow for a short while to the next road. At that point, the 'main' course of the Ulster Way is regained at the Cladagh Bridge.

There is no real difference in distance between the main and alternative routes between Tullynagapple and Cladagh Bridge.

Fair Head and the distant Mull of Kintyre seen at dawn.

Carrick-a-Rede and its famous Rope Bridge on the coast.

Portbraddan is a little fishing village on the Causeway Coast Path.

Nearly 40,000 hexagonal columns make up the Giant's Causeway.

The Sperrins begin to build up towards the rugged Binevenagh.

The Bishop's Gate at Downhill near the seaside resort of Castlerock.

Benbradagh's proud profile above the countryside near Dungiven.

Looking along Glenelly to Cranagh and Dart Mountain.

A cluster of farm buildings on the slopes of Slieve Beagh.

Broad and barren moorland slopes are a feature of Slieve Beagh.

Benaughlin rises high above the gardens at Florence Court.

Looking along the River Blackwater near Milltown.

Just off-route, Peatlands Country Park is worth exploring.

WALK 19

BELCOO TO KINAWLEY

Start: Belcoo – 084386.

Finish: Drumroosk, Kinawley – 236295.

Distance: 28 kilometres (17½ miles).

Maps: OSNI Discoverer Sheets 26 and 27.

Terrain: Road walking at first, followed by woodland paths and forest tracks, with some pathless, boggy hillsides. Some lowland roads, tracks and bogs feature at the end.

Waymarking: Fairly good, but because of the intricate nature of the route it's a good idea to keep a careful lookout for signposts and marker posts.

Public Transport: Ulsterbus 64 serves Belcoo, linking with Enniskillen, with an occasional extension to Belleek. Bus Éireann 66 and 69 also serve Belcoo, linking with Enniskillen and Sligo. Ulsterbus 58 serves Kinawley from Enniskillen. There are also Ulsterbus 194 and Bus Éireann 30 and 77 services along the main road near by.

Accommodation: There are a few B&Bs available in and around Belcoo. Only a couple of places offer accommodation in the countryside around Florence Court and Kinawley.

ROUTE DESCRIPTION

Leave Belcoo by following the road across the Border which brings you to the village of Blacklion in Co. Cavan. By continuing straight onwards you could follow the Cavan Way for the day, linking up with the Leitrim Way afterwards, but the Ulster Way is followed off to the left. The road leaves Blacklion and crosses the Border again to re-enter Co. Fermanagh. Continue through Mullaghbane, passing farms and houses, and keep left at Mucklagh, despite the offer of a scenic road to Marlbank and the Marble Arch Caves. Gortatole Outdoor Education Centre is off to the left, while you should keep right at the next road junction. The road passes close to St Lasser's Well and a ruined church, then crosses the Cladagh Bridge to rejoin the route of the Ulster Way as it crosses Belmore Mountain.

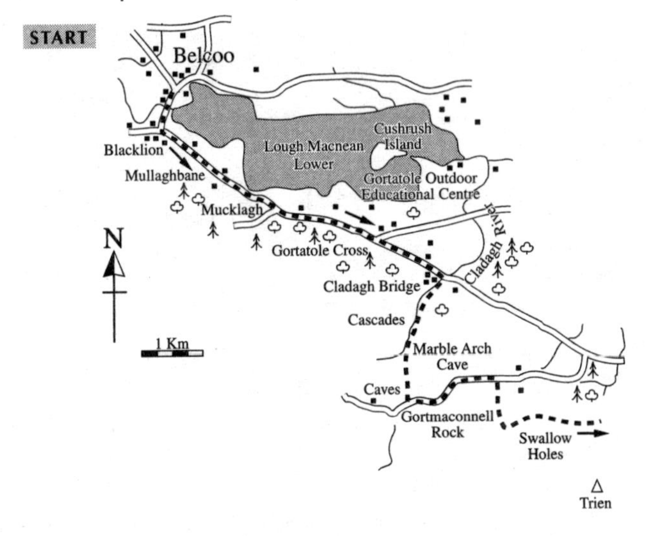

Turn right to cross a stile beside a gate at the Cladagh Bridge and follow a delightfully wooded riverside track. Pass a building and a sign for Marble Arch and the Marlbank National Nature Reserve. The track becomes a narrow path clinging to the rocky, wooded slope, surrounded by a damp ash wood which is rich in other tree species and has a good understorey. Always there is the sight and sound of rushing water. A powerful resurgence is seen to the left, where the water is immediately drawn off along a concrete duct. The path leads to a wonderfully wild, rocky area, where time should be taken to observe the intricacies of the Marble Arch. The arch is a massive natural span of limestone, and flights of steps actually rise across it. Information boards explain about the area, using diagrams to illustrate the formation of the cave systems which are hidden from view. When the path reaches a level stance, the main entrance to the Marble Arch Caves is off to the right, where steps appear to lead down into a pit. Prospective visitors must first continue up through the woodlands and obtain tickets from the visitor centre above, before they can enter the caves on one of the guided tours which run through the summer months.

The Marble Arch Caves Visitor Centre is packed with information about the formation of the caves, including plenty of displays and an audio-visual presentation. Life-size models hanging from the ceiling illustrate the difference between modern-day cave exploration and the 19th-century methods, when the noted speleologist Edouard Martel plumbed the depths in 1895. There is also a shop, restaurant and toilets

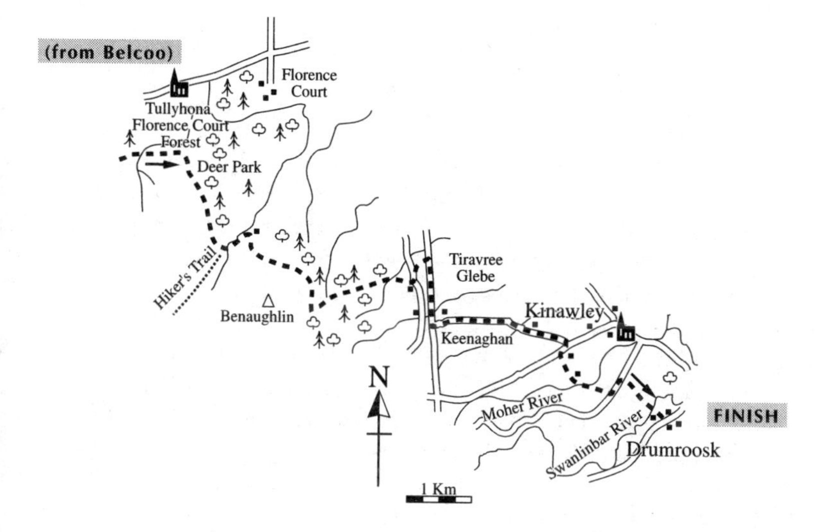

on site. A visit to the caves is of course highly recommended. The tour begins with a short boat ride across an underground pool and brings you further into the caves along concrete walkways and steps. At the end of the underground route, visitors are taken up flights of steps to emerge quite close to the visitor centre. If an exploration of the caves is included in your day's walk, be sure to leave plenty of time to reach your ultimate destination. If you are unlikely to reach Kinawley, there is a farmhouse B&B at Tullyhona down the road in the direction of Florence Court.

Follow the road uphill from the visitor centre, turn left over a rise, then walk downhill to pass an entrance for the Gortmaconnell Rock scenic viewpoint. Cars can drive part of the way up this limestone knoll, while walkers can reach the very top. The Ulster Way continues further down the road, however, then crosses a stile on the right and climbs uphill on the eastern side of Gortmaconnell Rock. The ground is quite rough, and after making a left turn it is sometimes quite difficult to spot the way ahead. There are some extensive wet and muddy areas and the limestone bedrock here is punctuated with swallow holes. The Ulster Way heads roughly eastwards through a little rocky gap. After passing through the gap, allow yourself to be drawn down into the valley sloping towards Florence Court Forest. A path leads into the forest and links with a broader track, which is followed further downhill to a junction.

Turn right at the junction; then, at the next junction of tracks, look carefully for a grassy path climbing steeply to the right. This path leads through a ride and heads for the top part of the forest. Turn left along a path which eventually reaches the birch wood margins along the top edge of the forest. Cross a stile and keep following the edge of the forest, sometimes drifting along braided muddy paths through bracken and heather. The path begins to pull away from the edge of the forest and passes through a rugged little gap. Watch carefully for another path which suddenly drops down to the left. This reaches a stile at a corner of the forest where a sign indicates the Hiker's Trail to Cuilcagh.

The Hiker's Trail would be a commendable option to include on a fine day, but it really does take all day to climb the slopes of Cuilcagh, and the ascent is purgatorial during foul weather. Another feature of note is downhill, off-route at Florence Court House. Built in 1770, Florence Court was the seat of the Earls of Enniskillen. The interior is lavishly furnished and has some exceptional plasterwork, while outside are the rich and varied Pleasure Grounds and a tea room. Incidentally, the Florence Court Yew in the grounds was one of two specimens found on Aghatirourke Mountain in the 1740s, from which all Irish yews worldwide are descended.

Follow the path down into the forest, keeping close to the edge until a gate and stile on the right allow an exit to be made. A grassy track leads to a ford across a stream, quite close to a farm hidden in a patch of woodland. Keep to the right after crossing the stream, climbing carefully up through some wet and rushy fields, looking carefully for marker posts and stiles. If in doubt about the course to take, it is best to drift uphill rather than downhill, gradually making height on the steep slopes of Benaughlin. You should aim to reach the top side of the forest, which rises to 250m (820ft) on the slopes of the hill. There is a path along the top edge of the forest, just inside the forest fence. Later, the path drops downhill and a right turn is made along a wider track. This joins another track under the frowning, rocky face of the hill, where a left turn leads downhill and eventually leaves the forest. After crossing one rushy field the track joins the main A32 road. There are occasional buses along this road.

Turn left along the road, passing only one house, then turn right along a concrete lane which bends between the hedgerows. Turn right at the end of the concrete lane up a minor road, then, after crossing a rise, turn left along another concrete lane. This becomes a gravel track, then another concrete lane leads onto a narrow tarmac road. Follow this to a junction with the B108 road, turning right and left to go up and down another concrete lane. A series of stiles lead to the Moher River, which is crossed to reach yet another concrete lane. Follow this to a minor road and turn left, passing Kinawley Health Centre and a couple of houses. You can follow this road straight to Kinawley, which offers the prospect of food and drink, or continue a while longer with the Ulster Way. Turn left across some rugged fields, looking carefully for stiles and markers on an area of bogland sprouting a variety of young trees. Aim to descend near a house and cross a bridge over the Swanlinbar River, then walk up one last concrete lane to reach a minor road. The Ulster Way turns right along this road, but there is a single B&B near Drumroosk and Kinawley is still within easy walking distance. There are buses linking Kinawley with Enniskillen and Derrylin.

WALK 20

KINAWLEY TO NEWTOWNBUTLER

Start: Drumroosk, Kinawley – 236295.

Finish: Newtownbutler – 417261.

Distance: 30 kilometres (18½ miles).

Maps: OSNI Discoverer Sheet 27. Outdoor Pursuits Map of Upper Lough Erne is also useful.

Terrain: The whole of this day's walk is along roads, which vary from quiet, scenic minor roads to short stretches along busier main roads.

Waymarking: The roads are mostly marked with metal signs for the Kingfisher Trail cycleway, rather than the Ulster Way.

Public Transport: Ulsterbus 58 serves Kinawley and Derrylin from Enniskillen. Ulsterbus 95 serves Newtownbutler from Enniskillen.

Accommodation: Limited to only one or two places around Kinawley, Derrylin, the Share Centre and Newtownbutler.

MAP 1

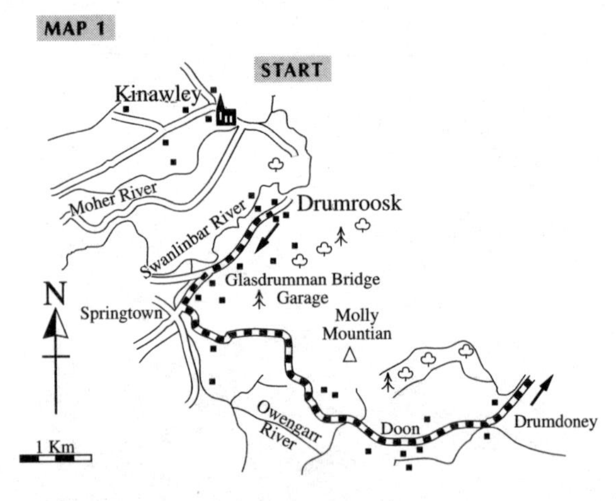

ROUTE DESCRIPTION

Leaving Drumroosk, near Kinawley, follow the minor road to Springtown, which means walking downhill, uphill, then down again. Turn left before a telephone box and bridge, following a road signposted as the Doon Scenic Route. The road rises and falls but generally climbs uphill, passing fields and a few farms, as well as a quarry. At the top of the gap between Molly Mountain and Slieve Rushen, the Doon scenic view is signposted off to the right, but the Ulster Way continues straight onwards. A whirling wind farm can be seen on the slopes of Slieve Rushen, while ahead is the broad, island-studded expanse of Upper Lough Erne. Follow the road downhill to reach Derrylin, avoiding any other roads to right and left. As soon as Derrylin is reached, the Mountview offers food and drink, while a couple of shops can be found off to the left on the main A509 road.

The Ulster Way actually turns right along the A509, then passes a telephone box and turns left along a rolling minor road through drumlin country. Make a right turn later to join the B127 road, then a left turn to walk to Lady Brooke Bridge. The bridge leads onto Trasna Island, in the middle of the complex Upper Lough Erne, where you can turn left at a gate and follow the shore of the island, rejoining the road later. Cross Lady Craigavon Bridge to leave the island, reaching a car park and toilets.

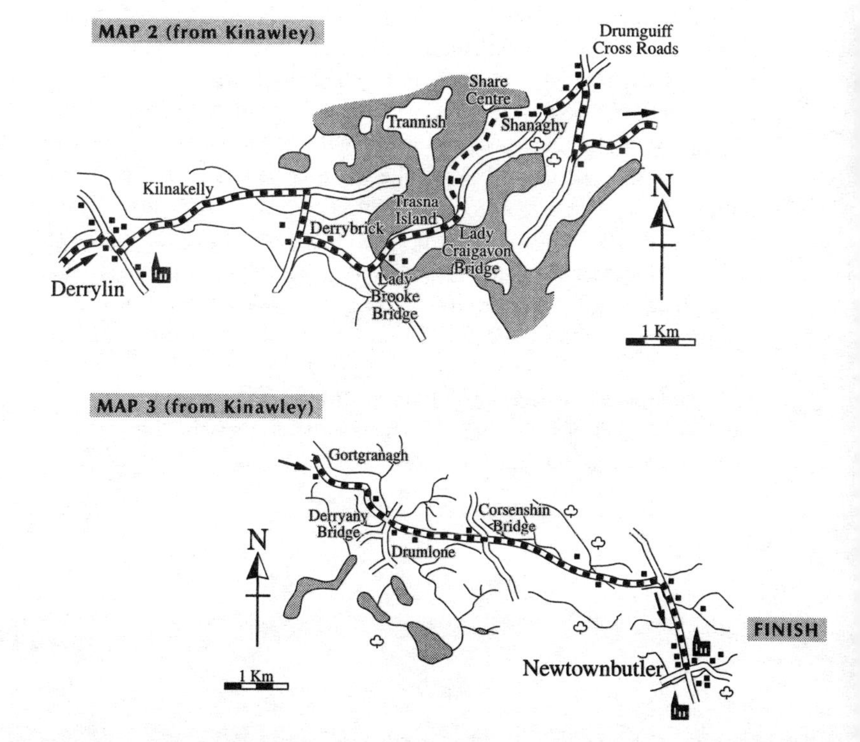

A stile gives access to another lakeshore walk, heading to Corradillar Quay, where timber and stone jetties jut out into the lake. A shop can be found up a narrow, wooded road, if food or drink is needed. The shore walk continues and rejoins the B127 road further along. A feature of note here is the Share Centre, where disabled and able-bodied people can share a multitude of sports, especially watersports. The Share Centre is often busy and has its own restaurant and accommodation. Alongside is Smith's Strand, which gives access to the lake, and a car park, picnic benches and toilets.

Follow the B127 further along to reach a crossroads. Turn sharply right as signposted for Derryadd Quay, following a tree-lined minor road. Turn left when you come to a little chapel and follow a road which winds along a leafy drumlin crest. When a more open stretch is reached, walk downhill and turn right to follow another road leading uphill. Keep left at a junction further along, then go straight through a cross-roads to pass Drumlone Gospel Hall and a telephone box. (There is a B&B well off-route to the right at Ports Lough.) Continue along the road, then go through another crossroads and along another leafy stretch of road to reach the busy A34 main road. Turn right along the road, then there is a decision to make. The Ulster Way turns sharp left up the next minor road, and there are no more facilities actually on the route until distant Aughnacloy is reached. Following the road into Newtownbutler, however, brings a range of shops, pubs and restaurants within reach. The Lanesborough Arms in the centre of town is the only place offering accommodation. The town is named after the Butler family, Earls of Lanesborough. In 1689 a force of 2,000 Enniskilleners led by Colonel Wolsey attacked a Jacobite force of twice that size, defeating them roundly at Newtownbutler. Soldiers fleeing to Roslea were dispatched the following morning. Black Preceptories from Fermanagh march on 12 July in commemoration of the Battle of Newtownbutler.

Aughnacloy is over 60 kilometres (40 miles) away. If you need anything at all in that distance, you have either to carry it with you or to make lengthy detours for it.

WALK 21

NEWTOWNBUTLER TO GLENOO

Start: Newtownbutler – 417261.

Finish: Glenoo Bridge – 495423.

Distance: 30 kilometres (18½ miles).

Maps: OSNI Discoverer Sheets 18 and 27.

Terrain: Mostly minor roads and forest tracks, with some rugged paths in the forest or across high moorlands.

Waymarking: Metal Ulster Way signposts along the roads, with wooden marker posts in the forests. Some early parts are only sparsely marked.

Public Transport: Ulsterbus 95 serves Newtownbutler from Enniskillen. There are no other services to any part of the day's walk.

Accommodation: Apart from limited accommodation at Newtownbutler, there are no places offering lodgings along this day's walk. The nearest place with accommodation is off-route at Fivemiletown.

ROUTE DESCRIPTION

Leaving Newtownbutler, which is technically off-route, retrace your steps along the busy A34 and branch to the right up an unsignposted minor road. There is a dip where the road crosses a river, then a climb up to a junction where you turn right. The road-walk becomes a switchback as it crosses drumlins, passing fields and houses on the way. Turn quickly right and left at a staggered junction, following the road downhill, along and uphill again. When it bends right at the top, go straight on along a concrete farm road instead; the way is marked with a marker post. Walk down past a house and along a wooded riverside track below. Join the B36 road and turn right to walk through Ballagh crossroads. Although an old marker post here may show a left turn, continue straight onwards and turn left along another minor road instead. This road rolls past farms, fields and wooded patches, parallel with the B36 road, with views over some small loughs. The largest is Mill Lough, and when you see it, watch for an Ulster Way signpost pointing left.

The left turn leads up a concrete farm lane, over a rise and away from a handful of buildings, then bends to the right. Turn left through a gate and walk up through a field to reach a gate into a woodland. Follow a grassy, muddy track uphill into the woods. A broader, clearer, firmer track leads onwards, generally uphill through coniferous forest. Eventually it leads across a patch of unplanted moorland and into a further patch of forest, then a right turn leads out of the forest onto a minor road. Turn left and follow the road downhill, then turn right down a short forest track and cross a rugged, wooded patch to reach a footbridge and another minor road. Turn right and follow the road over a rise, then turn left along a track marked for Doon Forest.

The track runs into Doon Forest and passes a hollow holding Eshcleagh Lough. Follow the track uphill and turn left at a junction. Keep right as marked at other junctions, downhill through a clear-felled and replanted area. Follow the track uphill later to pass around Lough Corry and eventually leave the forest, close to a solitary farm. When a minor road is reached, a right turn will bring you to the Carnmore viewpoint, but the Ulster Way turns left, down into a dip, leaving the road by turning right at a gate. A muddy track leads towards a rugged, heathery moorland, where a detour could include the summit of Doocarn at 315m (1,043ft).

Noah's grandson, Bith, is said to have landed here in his ark forty days before the biblical flood which was sent by God to punish a sinful world. As Ireland was uninhabited at the time, no sin had been committed here, so the land was spared the deluge. Bith travelled with Fintan, Ladra, Princess Cesair and fifty of the fairest women ever seen. The three men shared the fifty women between them, but Ladra complained at only getting sixteen. He was the first person to die in Ireland. The women buried him on Doocarn.

Forge onwards along this rugged crest, drifting roughly to the left and looking ahead to spot a ruined house near a patch of forest. There is a grassy track leading down from the house to the next minor road. Turn left along the road, then right up a concrete farm lane. When the lane bends left, continue straight on along a gravel track and enter a forest. The trees are delightfully mixed at first, and you should follow the clearest and most obvious track uphill, avoiding all others. The track bends left to pass Lough Nadarra, which is just to the left. Later, Lough Jenkin lies off to the right. The top of Jenkin Hill is largely unplanted moorland, offering wide-ranging views in clear weather, though the immediate prospects are unremarkable.

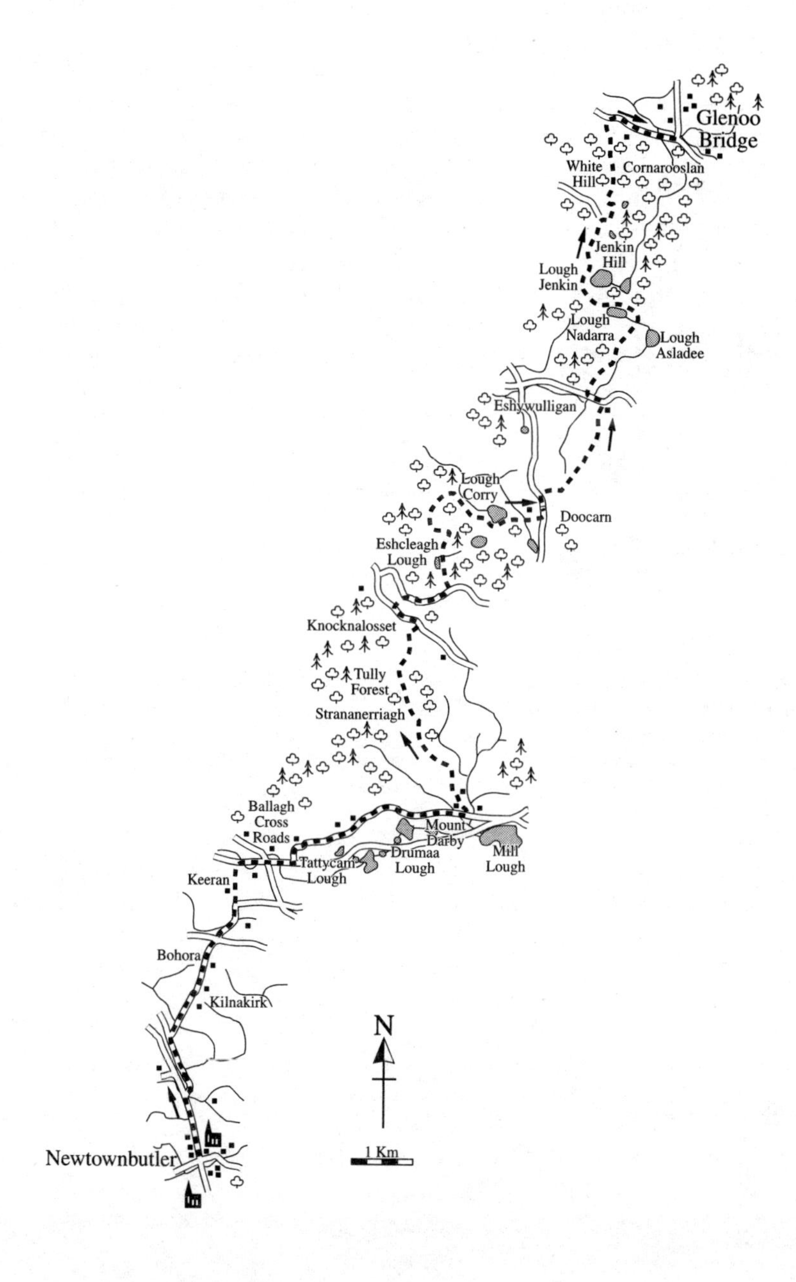
Glenoo
Bridge
White
Hill
Cornarooslan
Jenkin
Hill
Lough
Jenkin
Lough
Nadarra
Lough
Asladee
Eshywulligan
Lough
Corry
Doocarn
Eshcleagh
Lough
Knocknalosset
Tully
Forest
Strananerriagh
Ballagh
Cross
Roads
Mount
Darby
Mill
Lough
Drumaa
Lough
Tattycam
Lough
Keeran
Bohora
Kilnakirk
Newtownbutler
N
1 Km

The track descends into forest again, and as soon as a tarmac road-end is reached, you should turn sharply right down another forest track. Turn left at a junction and follow the track down through a point where tracks cross each other near a barrier gate. An ascent and descent through a largely clear-felled area is followed by a right bend to reach a minor road. Turn right and follow the road as it rolls towards a junction. Turn left at this point and walk downhill to cross Glenoo Bridge. Admittedly, this stretch ends in the middle of nowhere, with no nearby facilities. If you can't arrange to be collected by anyone, then you'll have to continue along the road and consider detouring off-route to Fivemiletown in search of lodgings, food and drink. It could turn out to be a long day's walk.

Beech (*Fagus sylvatica*) was first introduced into demesnes in the 17th century. Beech trees can seen along roadsides and in the woodlands along the Way.

SOUTHERN SECTION

Counties Tyrone and Armagh

Distance: 158 kilometres (99 miles)

As the Ulster Way crosses into Co. Tyrone, this section is initially devoid of facilities, with no shops, pubs, buses or accommodation close to the route. Apart from a weekend tea room in the middle of the rolling moors and forests of Slieve Beagh, all other facilities are well off-route. Generally, you will need to head to places like Fivemiletown and Clogher to find food, drink and a bed for the night so that, although the initial daily stretches are fairly short, the detours in search of lodgings can make them much longer. It is a good idea to plan well ahead and if possible to be collected from the route at intervals.

A recent re-routing of the Ulster Way between Aughnacloy and Caledon has cut out one of the worst road-walking sections of the entire route, leading instead through pleasant, rolling, drumlin country sprinkled with a string of small loughs. Further improvements are planned around Caledon. Waymarking is rather sparse between Caledon and Portadown and most of the way is along roads, with only a few off-road opportunities. According to the late Wilfrid Capper, the initial idea in these parts was to walk alongside the River Blackwater, but it is unlikely that this will ever be realised throughout its length, so nearby roads are followed instead. There are opportunities to explore interesting patches of countryside off-road at Benburb, The Argory, Peatlands and Maghery Country Park. Apple orchards are a particular feature of this part of the Ulster Way.

A long-term plan to take the Ulster Way alongside the River Bann near Lough Neagh has been proposed, but seems slow to progress. The remains of the old Ulster Canal can be seen from time to time, and there has been some talk about restoring the waterway. If this were to happen the Ulster Way could be re-routed along the towpath, assuming a towpath was provided. Between Portadown and Newry lies one of the best low-level stretches of the whole route. The old Newry Canal has a continuous towpath, or towpad as it is known in these parts, running straight through the lowlands on a course largely free of roads and bringing you past the locks, wharfs, basins and mills of the old canal. There are ongoing plans to revitalise this waterway, and in the future it might well again be open for cruising, with a cycleway and walkway alongside.

Basically, the Southern Section of the Ulster Way is easy, but for much of the way facilities are quite limited. You need to plan your route with the available facilities in mind, being aware of bus timetables if it proves necessary to move off-route for any reason.

WALK 22

GLENOO TO BORDER TEA ROOM

Start: Glenoo Bridge – 495423.
Finish: Border Tea Room – 582469.
Distance: 19 kilometres (12 miles).
Map: OSNI Discoverer Sheet 18.
Terrain: Minor roads and forest tracks through low farmland and higher moorlands.
Waymarking: Wooden Ulster Way marker posts, both along the roads and in the forests, with some Carleton Trail signposts too.
Public Transport: No part of this day's walk is served by public transport.
Accommodation: There is no accommodation along this day's walk. The nearest places offering accommodation are off-route around Fivemiletown and Clogher.

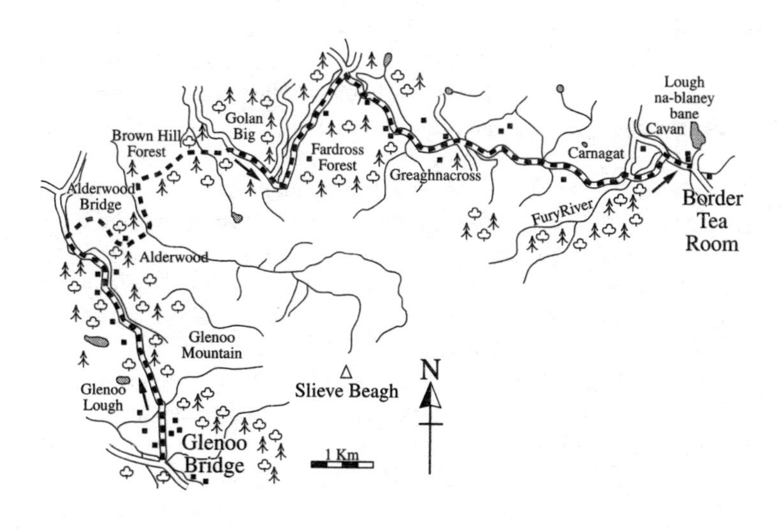

ROUTE DESCRIPTION

This stretch is quite without any sort of facilities, apart from the possibility of the Border Tea Room being open at weekends. The day's walk is fairly short, as it is quite possible that wayfarers will start from somewhere off-route, and finish somewhere off-route – even to the extent of having to walk from Fivemiletown to Clogher, unless transport to and from the course of the Ulster Way can be arranged. An obvious improvement which could be made to the route in these parts would take the Ulster Way up from Glenoo Bridge, over the moorlands of Slieve Beagh and down to the Border Tea Room. The route as it currently stands is quite convoluted, but at least it shows off the varied nature of this particular tract of countryside.

Leave Glenoo Bridge and pass the entrance to a forest office at Mullaghfad. A couple of isolated farms are passed as the road rolls uphill, then there is a forested descent. A series of marker posts stand beside the road, leading almost to Alderwood Bridge. At this point, a Carleton Trail sign will be seen, and it is important to remember that the Ulster Way and Carleton Trail routes diverge at times. The Carleton Trail is named after William Carleton, a noted poet, novelist and journalist, who was born in the Clogher valley in 1794. This area featured in much of Carleton's writing.

Do not cross Alderwood Bridge, which leads off-route to Fivemiletown, but instead turn right up a concrete farm lane. The lane later bends right and becomes a forest track, which in turn bends left as it climbs. The forest has been largely clear-felled and replanted. The track descends, crossing a bridge and running alongside a little river. When another bridge is reached, don't cross it, but turn right up another forest track. The track rises and has only a couple of level or downhill stretches, and there is one rugged, mossy area too. When the track emerges from the forest at a barrier gate it lands on a minor road running through the moors. There is a Carleton Trail information board at this point. The Carleton Trail turns left here, but the Ulster Way turns right.

Follow the minor road across a dip, then climb uphill through part of Fardross Forest. Emerging from the forest, take the second turning left, down from the moorland slopes, through another stand of Fardross Forest, until you reach a few houses at a crossroads. Turn right and follow another minor road gradually uphill, passing fields, wooded areas and a couple of farms and houses. When you reach the moors, note the Brackenridge Monument far away to the left – a prominent, three-tiered folly and mausoleum belonging to a former landlord.

While crossing Rocky Water there is a view of Hen Mountain.

Slieve Donard rises high above the seaside resort of Newcastle.

The beach walk around Murlough in the shadow of Slieve Donard.

Sunset over the Mountains of Mourne seen across Dundrum Bay.

The ruined east window of Ardtole Church near Ardglass.

Strangford village beside the narrows of Strangford Lough.

Old Castle Ward is a National Trust property near Strangford.

The stately beeches of Killynether Wood on the slopes of Scrabo Hill.

A view from the bouldery shoulder of Glascarns Hill above Crolack.

The rugged recesses of the Poisoned Glen seen from Dunlewy.

A little waterfall before the Doonan waterfall in the Blue Stack Mountains.

The conical profile of Errigal as seen from the village of Dunlewy.

A tower-house beside Altan Lough at the foot of Aghla More.

Follow the road to a junction and go straight onwards, passing some particularly rugged heather-filled moorland.

At the next junction, go straight onwards again, passing a bus shelter in the middle of nowhere. This is a pick-up point for the school bus; there are no public bus services. The road continues downhill past a house, with a view of an isolated farm, a few fields, some forest and plenty of bleak moorland. The road runs over a rise and downhill, passing a junction, then you turn right at the next junction. A marker post suggests you should go straight on, which appears to be wrong, but there is an interesting chambered grave at Carnagat worth inspecting in that direction. There are a handful of these graves in the area. Walk downhill alongside a forest and a stream, turning right at a junction at the bottom. The road leads onwards, then bends to the left. The Border Tea Room is straight on, though it is usually only open in the afternoon at weekends. It stands just across the Border in Co. Monaghan, which is the only opportunity you will get to set foot in this county. While this stretch of the Ulster Way ends hereabouts, there are no lodgings. Clogher is down the B83 road, passing the Furey House B&B at Lisbane on the way to the village.

WALK 23

BORDER TEA ROOM TO AUGHNACLOY

Start: Border Tea Room – 582469.

Finish: Aughnacloy – 665523.

Distance: 19 kilometres (12 miles).

Maps: OSNI Discoverer Sheets 18 and 19.

Terrain: Mostly roads through farming country, but a few paths and tracks too.

Waymarking: Metal Ulster Way signposts are used along some of the roads, with wooden marker posts also used.

Public Transport: Ulsterbus 73 links Aughnacloy with Enniskillen and Caledon, while Ulsterbus 76 links Aughnacloy with Dungannon.

Accommodation: There are only a couple of B&Bs in the countryside around Aughnacloy.

ROUTE DESCRIPTION

Leaving the road junction near the Border Tea Room, follow the road past Lough na Blaney Bane, locally known as Lough Cavan. The road rises to a minor crossroads, then runs downhill. A right turn uphill is signposted as the Carleton Trail and Scenic Drive, running alongside a forest and passing close to Lough More. After passing Lough More, follow the road over another rise, then continue downhill past a few houses to reach a car park on the left, signposted for St Patrick's Chair and Well.

Follow a fine path down into a forested valley, keeping to the right. A flight of stone steps to the left leads to St Patrick's Chair and Well after crossing a rocky, forested ridge clothed in mosses, ferns, bilberry, wood sorrel and brambles. St Patrick's Chair is a huge block of sandstone shaped like a seat, and apparently anyone sitting in it and making a wish is sure to have their wish granted, provided they don't tell anyone else about it! A short flight of steps leads down to a boulder containing a little round hollow of water, St Patrick's Well, which is credited with

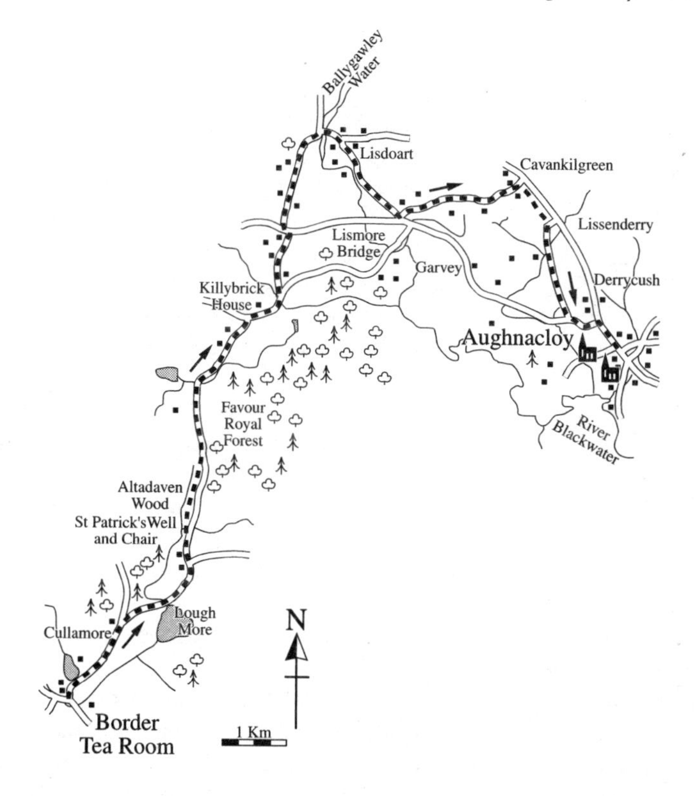

curative properties and is said never to run dry. A small tree alongside is festooned in strips of cloth and other everyday items, where supplicants have left a memento of the ailment they wish to be cured of. Follow the steps back up to the chair and continue along the ridge, descending back on the main forest path and continuing through the valley. The path is coated with pine needles at first, then becomes more rough and grassy as it traverses the floor of the valley. You may see fallow deer grazing in the valley before the path reaches a gateway and joins a minor road.

Turn left and follow the road onwards, rolling through drumlin country, passing fields, farms and houses. Avoid other turnings to left and right, and notice the stout walls and gateways of the old Favour Royal estate along the way. A gardener's boy called John Joseph Hughes once worked on the estate, then emigrated to America where he became the first Archbishop of New York. After passing through a crossroads, the main A28 road is reached, which can be rather busy. Turn right, as signposted for the Carleton Trail and Scenic Drive, in the direction of Aughnacloy. There is a gateway on the right leading to St Mary's Church of Ireland, which is a curious building, then the main road crosses the River Blackwater and the Ulster Way turns left onto minor roads signposted for Lisdoart. Pass an Orange Hall rejoicing in the name Mountforrest Anketell Moutray Memorial Hall and continue along the road until it rises to a junction. Turn quickly left and right at a staggered junction signposted for Lisdoart. The road rises and falls, passing Ballynanny Methodist Church and the Rev. Dr Moutray Memorial Orange Hall. The road bends right, and then you turn right at Lisdoart Post Office and cross Ballygawley Water. (There is a B&B off-route at The Grange, by the Ballygawley roundabout.)

Deer can be sighted on the stretches of forest walking. Many are fallow deer brought to Ireland by the Normans in the 12th century.

Follow the road uphill and turn right, then the road rolls on before a left turn is made at another junction. (Another B&B can be reached by detouring to Garvey Lodge.) Follow the road along, uphill and down, almost reaching a busy main road. Watch for a farm track marked on the right, which climbs gently and is lined with trees, pursuing a parallel course to the main road. It descends to another minor road, but walk straight onwards and when the A28 road is reached, turn left, then right to enter Aughnacloy following Moore St up into town. The street was named after Acheson Moore, who founded Aughnacloy in its present form. You pass St Mary's Roman Catholic Church, with its striking tower, while St James's Church of Ireland has a spire further along the street. Dozens of numbered spaces have been marked out for market stalls which line the streets at weekends. While there are plenty of shops, pubs and restaurants, the few B&Bs in this area are all out of town. There are bus services if facilities near by need to be reached.

WALK 24

Aughnacloy to Caledon

Start: Aughnacloy – 665523.
Finish: Caledon – 756454.
Distance: 31 kilometres (19 miles).
Map: OSNI Discoverer Sheet 19.
Terrain: Mostly roads through farming country, but some short paths too.
Waymarking: Wooden marker posts are used at road junctions.
Public Transport: Ulsterbus 73 links Aughnacloy with Enniskillen and Caledon, while Ulsterbus 76 links with Dungannon. Ulsterbus 74 and 379A also link Caledon with Dungannon.
Accommodation: There are only a couple of B&Bs in the countryside around Aughnacloy and Caledon.

ROUTE DESCRIPTION

This day's walk is one of the most significantly re-routed parts of the Ulster Way. Originally, the main A28 road was followed for much of the way between Aughnacloy and Caledon, but now a loop extending northwards into rolling drumlin country, taking in a string of scenic loughs, links the two places. Furthermore, a couple of link paths are still to be negotiated and marked, which will lead to further improvements in access and the overall quality of the scenery en route.

Start by following the busy A28 road as if leaving Aughnacloy for Armagh. When the road almost reaches a river, the recently restored McCready's Mill stands to the left. It's worth having a look at it, then turn left again to pass Aughnacloy Presbyterian Church. Turn right and walk past the police station, then turn right along the B128 as sign-posted for Benburb to leave Aughnacloy. A track on the right is quickly followed by a left turn onto the bed of an old railway track which is flanked by trees and leads straight across an area of fields. When an access road is marked to the right, follow it to a minor road and turn left. Follow the road and turn left again at a junction, later passing straight through a crossroads set in a dip in the landscape. Rehaghy Lodge B&B is just off to the right, which might be worth bearing in mind. Follow the road up to a junction, turning right to reach a small chapel, then turning left up another road. Follow the road downhill and turn left, then climb steeply uphill to the hamlet of Carnteel. There is a small shop and a ruined church, where a right turn is made downhill.

After passing Carnteel Lough, follow the road up to a crossroads

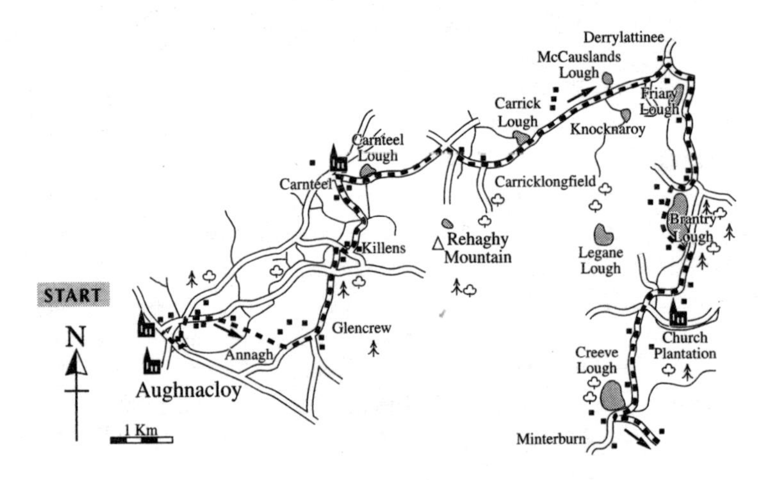

and turn right, then follow the road downhill and turn left at the next road junction. While passing Carrick Lough, there is a chance to enjoy a very short, wooded, lakeshore path, then you follow the road uphill to continue. After a downhill stretch, go straight through a crossroads and follow a rolling road to Derrylatinee Primary School. Turn right at the school down another road, then climb uphill past farms and farm ruins. Keep right at road junctions to descend to a parking space close to Brantry Lough. A sign indicates the Brantry Lough Woodland Walk, which follows a path through delightfully mixed woodlands and takes in parts of the lakeshore. When the path reaches a track, turn left to reach a road and another car park, then turn right to follow the road. A right bend leads past a small church, then you turn left at the next junction. Walk through a crossroads where there is a bus shelter and follow the road signposted for Creeve Lough. When this is later signposted to the right, turn sharply left instead, uphill, then through rolling countryside where gradients can be steep at times.

The restored Dredge Bridge over the Blackwater at Caledon.

There are some fine old stone buildings along the way, some of them sadly derelict.

Turn left to walk through the straggling settlement of Dyan, noting Dyan Orange Hall and some of the village's solid old buildings. Pass a bus shelter and turn right, then follow the road gently up and downhill, turning right later. The road rises and falls again to reach another right turn. (There may be a route marked through the fields bringing you past Glenarb, otherwise continue as directed.) Follow the road up and over to a junction, then turn left along a wider road. Another left turn at the next junction reveals the road which finally runs to Caledon, climbing over one last rise. On the way down into the village, pass St John's Church of Ireland and the Elim Pentecostal Church, turning left along the main road. There are a few shops and pubs, with some attractive old buildings and a row of estate houses with yellow doors. Accommodation is quite limited, with only a couple of B&Bs scattered through the surrounding countryside.

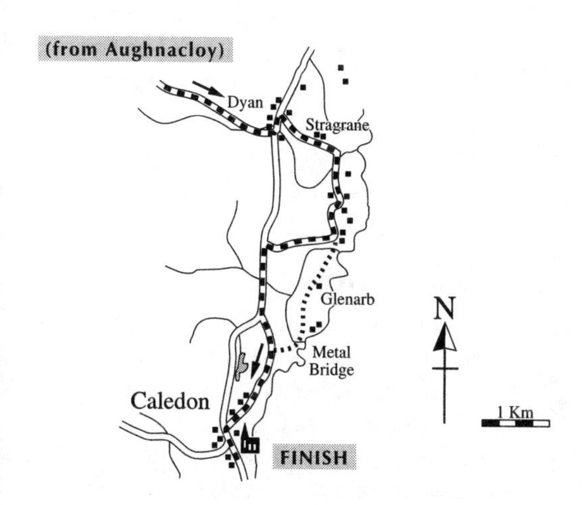

WALK 25

CALEDON TO CHARLEMONT

Start: Caledon – 756454.

Finish: Charlemont – 854557.

Distance: 25 kilometres (15½ miles).

Map: OSNI Discoverer Sheet 19.

Terrain: Mostly along roads through farming country, with a couple of short paths.

Waymarking: Very sparse, with only a few wooden marker posts along the roads.

Public Transport: Ulsterbus 73 links Caledon with Aughnacloy. Ulsterbus 74 and 379A link Caledon with Dungannon. Ulsterbus 72 serves Benburb, Blackwatertown, Charlemont and Moy from Armagh. Ulsterbus 379B serves Benburb from Dungannon. Ulsterbus 67 serves Charlemont and Moy from Portadown.

Accommodation: A couple of B&Bs are located around Caledon and Moy, while a hostel is available at Milltown.

ROUTE DESCRIPTION

Follow the main A28 road out of Caledon, walking along the footway beside the tall wall which surrounds the grounds of Caledon House, the seat of Lord Caledon. A glimpse of the grounds is available at one of the estate's imposing gateways. The Caledon estate in Co. Tyrone abuts the Tynan Abbey estate in Co. Armagh and the Leslie estate at Glaslough in Co. Monaghan. Watch for a marker post on the other side of the road and cross with care to find a short path leading across Dredge Bridge. There will one day be a riverside path from Caledon to the bridge, cutting out part of the main road. A fine little suspension bridge over the River Blackwater, Dredge Bridge was restored from a derelict condition and the land around it made into a picnic area. After crossing the bridge, you still need to follow the main road onwards, using the footway provided to travel safely. When a bus shelter is reached, turn left along Ballymacully Rd.

While the map indicates that a network of minor roads run through the countryside near the River Blackwater, the Ulster Way tends to follow the most obvious road ahead at all times. Generally, keep left at road junctions, passing farms, houses and fields, and crossing two old bridges over the dry bed of the Ulster Canal. At the end of Ballymacully Rd, turn left onto Lisnafeedy Rd and later continue along Wilsonstown Rd. This last road is quite narrow and grass-grown in places, with very little traffic. When it reaches a junction with the busy B115 Battleford Rd, go straight across and follow Milltown Rd uphill, keeping left at the Castle Mushroom Farm. The road runs down to Milltown, where an old mill building now serves as the Benburb Heritage Centre, reached by crossing an old lock on the Ulster Canal.

The Benburb Heritage Centre displays two steam-engines and a range of linen-making machines dating from 1850 to 1950, while the Ulster Canal lock alongside dates from 1840. The centre incorporates a hostel. Continue along the track from the old mill, walking along a

The Benburb Heritage Centre
is in an old mill at Milltown.

wooded embankment between the Ulster Canal and the River Blackwater. The track leads uphill later, then a road runs down to a stile leading back onto a woodland path. Tall beech and pine trees tower overhead, then a white footbridge leads over the River Blackwater. A choice needs to be made at this point. Either follow a zig-zag path uphill to visit the village of Benburb, or continue downstream alongside the Blackwater to reach the next road.

Benburb has only a couple of shops, a limited bus service and no accommodation. Benburb Castle stands between the village and the Blackwater, on the site of a 16th-century castle built by Shane O'Neill. In 1610 Richard Wingfield, High Marshal of Ireland, obtained the estate and built a defensive bawn around it, though he had his main residence at Powerscourt in Co. Wicklow. In 1641 the O'Neills sacked Benburb; Owen Roe O'Neill later camped in the castle during the Battle of Benburb in 1646 – a scale model of the battlefield can be studied at the Benburb Heritage Centre. The castle lay semi-derelict through the 18th century and a cottage was later built within its walls. In 1886 James Bruce bought the estate and built the fine red-brick mansion near by, which was used as a hospital by American troops during the Second World War. In 1949 the estate changed hands again and the mansion has been used as a Servite Priory ever since, while the bawn is in the care of the State.

Follow the riverside path to the bridge and turn left up the road. Turn right at the top, walking downhill before turning right again along a narrow road. The road bends left and rolls past fields and farms to reach Blackwatertown. An attractive Roman Catholic church is passed at Clonfeacle, then the road crosses a bridge over the River Blackwater to Blackwatertown. A couple of shops and pubs are available along the main street, Quay Mount. Towards the top of the street, before the school and Hibernian Hall are reached, turn left along a narrow road, which itself turns right and rolls through the countryside towards Charlemont. There are occasional views of the Blackwater to the left. Charlemont has a few shops and pubs, but the nearest B&Bs, as well as more shops, pubs and restaurants, are found across the bridge in neighbouring Moy.

Moy is worth visiting to see its fine, tree-lined greens surrounded by houses from the 1760s. The layout of the greens is credited to James Caulfield, Earl of Charlemont, who is said to have drawn his inspiration from the square at Marengo in Lombardy, which he admired greatly while on a grand tour of Europe. Many of the houses have old stable-yard features: Moy once had stabling for 2,500 horses and was the location of one of the most important horse fairs in the North.

WALK 26

Charlemont to Portadown

Start: Charlemont – 854557.

Finish: Bridge St, Portadown – 013540.

Distance: 32 kilometres (20 miles).

Maps: OSNI Discoverer Sheets 19 and 20.

Terrain: Road-walking through gentle farming country.

Waymarking: Very sparse, with only a few wooden markers and metal Ulster Way signposts along the roads.

Public Transport: Portadown railway station offers connections to Belfast and Newry. Ulsterbus 67 links Moy and Portadown. Ulsterbus 75 serves Verner's Inn and Maghery from Portadown, while 67A links Derryanvil and Portadown on schooldays. Portadown has several more Ulsterbus services.

Accommodation: There are a handful of B&Bs in Moy and Portadown, but hardly anything in between.

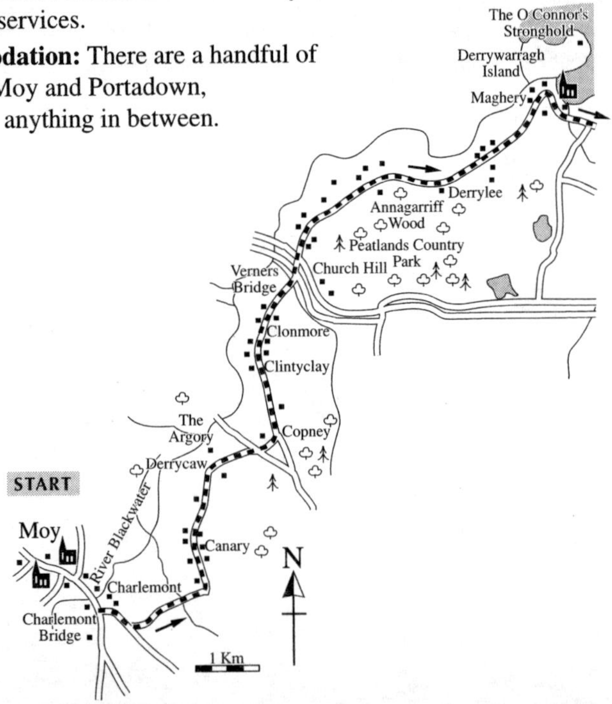

ROUTE DESCRIPTION

Leave Charlemont by following the B28 College Lands Rd, signposted for Portadown from Millars Hill Orange Hall. The road crosses the dry Ulster Canal and passes Collegeland O'Rahilly's Gaelic Football Club. Turn left along a minor road signposted for The Argory. Follow the road, then later turn left along Derrycaw Rd to pass some farms, houses, Canary Orange Hall and a small shop. The Argory, a neo-Classical house built in 1824 and now owned by the National Trust, is later found off to the left. Set in woodlands beside the River Blackwater, The Argory's contents and furnishings are incredibly varied and the only form of lighting comes from an acetylene gas plant which was installed in 1906. A variety of paths can be used to explore the surrounding grounds, riverside and woodlands.

If the house and grounds are visited, you have to return to the road later to continue. At the end of the road, turn quickly right and left through a staggered junction to follow another road signposted for Clonmore and Maghery. Turn left at the next road junction, where there is a bus shelter, to pass Clintyclay Primary School. The road crosses an

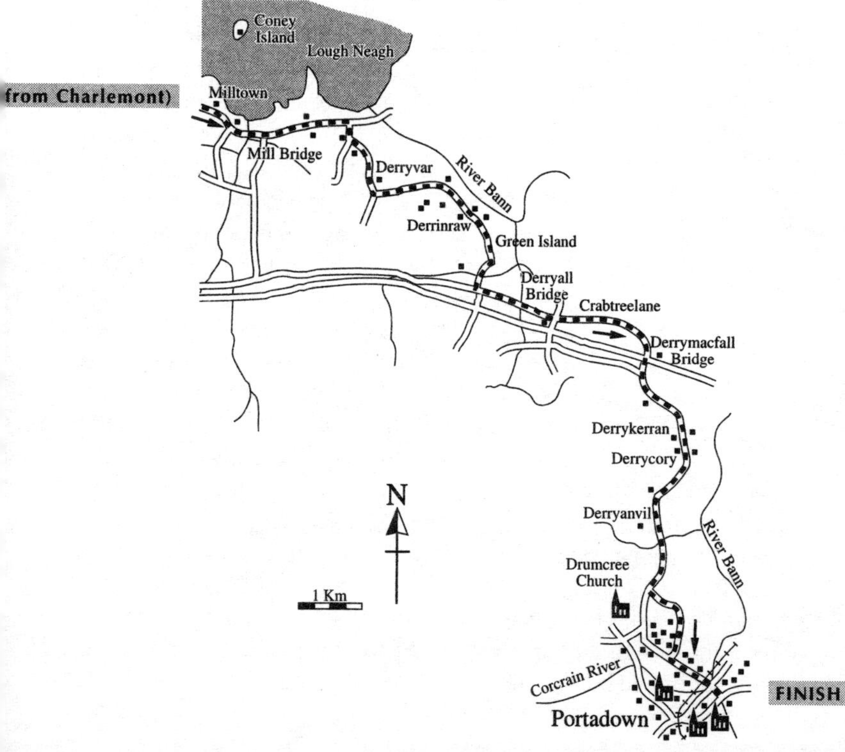

old railway line and passes by apple orchards and a small chapel. When the next road junction is reached at Verner's Inn, turn quickly left and right and follow the B196 road over the busy M1 motorway. Verner's Inn Orange Hall and a shop lie off to the left. The road is signposted for Derrylee and Maghery. If time allows for a detour, then try to include a visit to the nearby Peatlands Park, an area of wooded, cutaway bog which has grown wonderfully wild, with a visitor centre dedicated to the development and conservation of bogland.

The road leads through the settlement of Derrylee, passing Derrylee Orange Hall and post office. Derrylee Methodist Church stands alone in the countryside further along the road. Maghery is the next little village; the Lough Neagh Lodge restaurant and Fisherman's Bar lie off to the left, with access to the wooded and grassy areas of the Maghery Country Park, which includes a stretch of the Lough Neagh shoreline. Features of interest in this area include O'Connor's, or Derryvarragh, Castle, on a low island; Coney Island, which was once linked to the shore by St Patrick's Rd; and Lough Neagh itself, which is the largest expanse of fresh water in Britain or Ireland, measuring 400 square kilometres (155 square miles). According to local legend, Fionn Mac Cumhail scooped up a handful of earth to throw at a visiting giant, creating Lough Neagh in Ireland and, missing the giant altogether, forming the Isle of Man in the Irish Sea! The lough is notable for eel fishing, and for strange, encrusted stone nodules, which local people call 'petrified potatoes'.

Lough Neagh is the largest expanse of fresh water in Britain and Ireland and is noted for its eel fishing.

The Ulster Way turns right along the road at Maghery, passing the old stone St Mary's Church and the more modern Roman Catholic chapel. St Mary's Primary School is also passed on the way out of the village, and the footway is screened from the road by a hedgerow on the way to St Andrew's Church of Ireland. Maghery Rd passes the Lough Neagh Private Nursing Home, where there are further glimpses of the lake. Towards the end of the road turn right onto Greenisland Rd, though you could first make a diversion to see where the River Bann flows into Lough Neagh. Greenisland Rd bends left and winds past fields, farms and houses and continues past a couple of little orchards and the tiny Derrinraw Orange Hall further on. Turn left along Farlough Rd at a junction where there is a bus shelter. The road passes the lovely, thatched Crabtree Cottage, then rises to a crossroads at Crabtreelane. Continue along Derrycarne Rd, passing a little chapel and another orchard. When the road crosses the M1 motorway, there are surprisingly extensive views from the bridge. The distant Slieve Gullion and Mountains of Mourne may be seen ahead, as well as the Belfast Hills and Antrim Mountains, while Slieve Gallion and the Sperrin Mountains are often in view back along the road.

The road runs onwards, passing a whitewashed school and a more extensive area of apple orchards. Apples have been cultivated in north Armagh since 1150. Armagh Apples are often sold from roadside stalls and big Bramleys are used for juice or cider, and for cooking. Apples have supplanted native oaks, which are now relegated to hedgerows, but are remembered with numerous Derry (*doire* – oak) placenames. Continue to Derryanville Methodist Church, where the Redbrick Country Guesthouse is signposted right along Corbracky Rd. The Ulster Way, however, continues along Derryanvil Rd, coming quite close to the landmark spire of Drumcree Parish Church.

Images of Drumcree Parish Church have been flashed around the world following recent impasses between Orangemen and nationalists over the route of the Orangemen's annual march. The Ulster Way neatly sidesteps the problem by turning left up Ashgrove Rd, passing Drumcree House B&B on the way down to an estate. When a junction is reached at a row of shops, you turn left along the Garvaghy Rd, passing a shop and pub, then the Ulster Carpet Mills. The road passes Park Rd, then goes under rail and road bridges. Head off to the left, where a short stretch of path can be followed alongside the River Bann. Heading off to the right leads into the centre of town. Ultimately, it might be possible to follow the banks of the River Bann from the countryside into town, but at present a large gate blocks access.

Portadown is associated with the ancient and powerful McCann family, who were among the area's first settlers; their former castle controlled the passage across the river. The construction of the Newry Canal in 1740 and the arrival of the railway in 1842 ensured that Portadown remained at the hub of transport routes in this area. Linen manufacture was once an important industry, though the mills have since been turned over to other uses. There are plenty of places offering food and drink, but only a limited number of hotels and B&Bs actually within the town.

WALK 27

PORTADOWN TO NEWRY

Start: Bridge St, Portadown – 013540.

Finish: Newry Town Hall – 086267.

Distance: 32 kilometres (20 miles).

Maps: OSNI Discoverer Sheets 20 and 29.

Terrain: The towpath is a clear track or gravel path, but may be grassy for long stretches. Some parts of the towpath are regularly mown but other short stretches may be muddy or overgrown.

Waymarking: The towpath is signposted as the Newry Canal or Newry Canal Footpath, rather than the Ulster Way.

Public Transport: There are railway stations at Portadown and Newry, linking with Belfast and Dublin. Ulsterbus 63 also links Portadown and Newry. Both towns have plenty of Ulsterbus links with other parts of the Ulster Way.

Accommodation: There are a few B&Bs and hotels in Portadown and Newry, along with other accommodation options in the surrounding countryside.

ROUTE DESCRIPTION

Leave the busy Bridge St over the River Bann and walk upstream along the path known as the Upper Bann Boulevard. A sign at the start reads 'River Bann – Newry Canal Footpath'. Another sign explains that 'The inland section of the Newry Canal, constructed between 1731 and 1742, ranks as the earliest summit level canal in the British Isles. It extended from Newry some 18 miles north-westwards to the Upper Bann at Whitecoat Point, just south of Portadown. The Ship Canal, south of Newry, was completed in 1850 and this created a continuous navigable waterway between Lough Neagh, through the port of Newry, to Carlingford Lough and the Irish Sea.'

The Meadows Shopping Centre stands at the edge of town, and the riverside path continues past it, lined with poplars and with the views across fields leading the eye to the distant Slieve Gullion and Camlough Mountain. Note the position of Camlough Mountain, as Newry sits

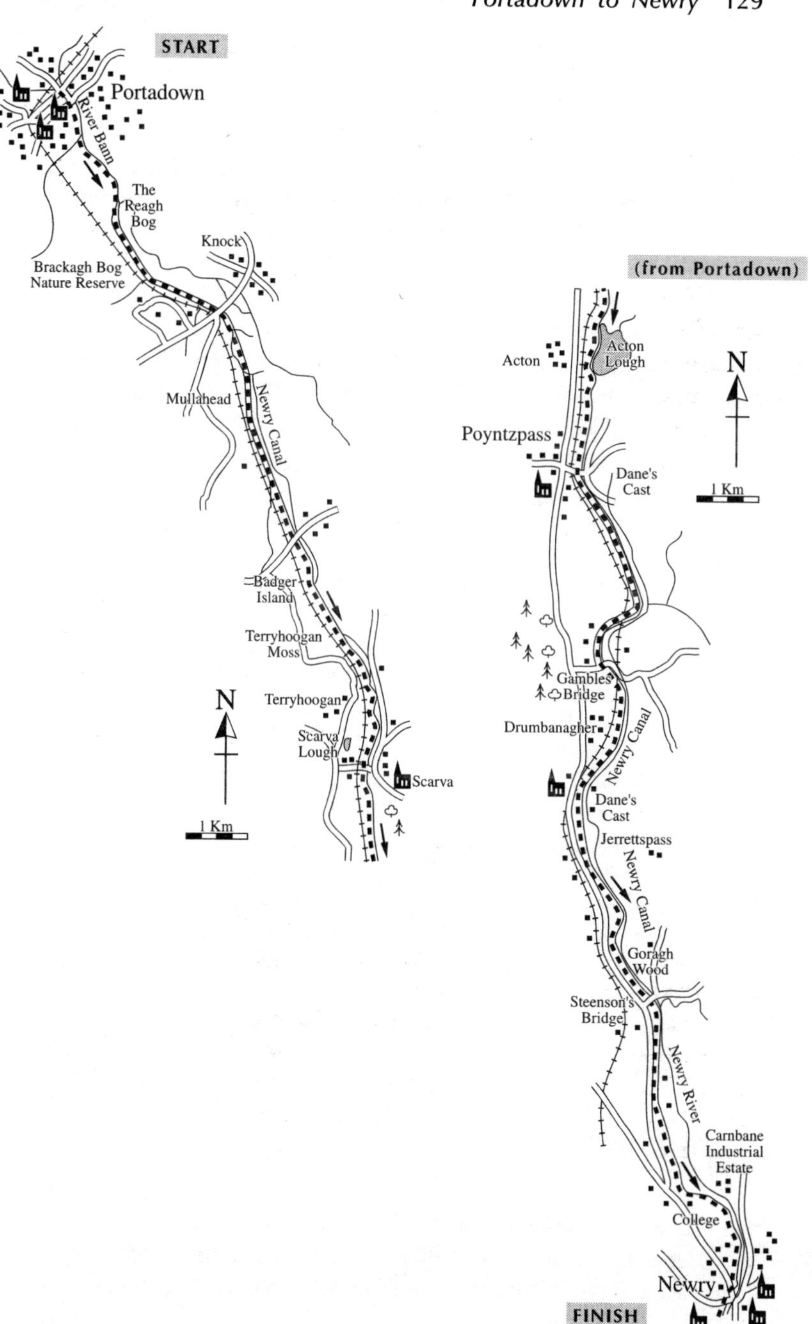

START
Portadown
River Bann
The Reagh Bog
Brackagh Bog Nature Reserve
Knock
Mullahead
Newry Canal
Badger Island
Terryhoogan Moss
Terryhoogan
Scarva Lough
Scarva
N
1 Km
(from Portadown)
Acton
Acton Lough
Poyntzpass
Dane's Cast
N
1 Km
Gambles Bridge
Drumbanagher
Newry Canal
Dane's Cast
Jerrettspass
Newry Canal
Goragh Wood
Steenson's Bridge
Newry River
Carnbane Industrial Estate
College
Newry
FINISH

beneath it at the end of today's walk. Cross the striking tubular structure of Whitecoat Bridge which spans the Newry Canal as it meets the Bann. The canal is followed faithfully all the way to Newry. It is an outstanding wildlife corridor, alder and willow trees gracing the waterside, with nettles, reeds and bulrushes alongside the banks and waterlilies and Canadian pondweed floating on the water. A gateway leads the towpath onto a track passing Moneypenny's Lock, which is surrounded by trees. Signposts point to the Lock House and Museum, Stables and Bothy, which offer information about the Newry Canal and a chance to experience the life and times of a lock-keeping family.

The track is lined with trees to Knock Bridge, where a busy road is crossed, after which the track continues along the line of the canal. Cross a stile beside a gate to walk along a rough strip of grass on top of the embankment between the canal and the channel of the Cusher River. Views extend across the fields and woodlands, then a footbridge is crossed at a point where there is a link between the canal and the Cusher. The next stretch, running along another embankment between the two waterways, is often overgrown with tall grass and nettles, and shorts are not recommended in summer when the nettles are at their worst! More walkers along this stretch would of course keep the nettles down! A stile later leads onto a lower embankment where the grass is shorter. There is a gate to pass through as hedgerows close in on either side. Some old warehouses which stand on the far side of the canal are now used for farm storage. Pass through gates and cross the A51 road between Tandragee and Gilford to continue.

The towpath continues along a low, grassy embankment, bending to the right, then bending left. Cross a stile and walk along a broad strip of grassland, rather like a long field. The canal lies on the left and a swampy channel runs parallel to it on the right. The track eventually runs past heaps of wood and scrap metal to join a minor road at Terryhoogan. Keep left to follow the road alongside the canal until you reach Campbell's Lock, where a fine track and path can be followed past fields towards Scarva. You pass an old railway bridge buttress and the Cusher River aqueduct, then trees flank the waterway on the last stretch to Scarva. On the opposite bank is the Scarva Visitor Centre, which is reached by doubling back after crossing the next road bridge over the canal.

Scarva House dates from 1717 and is said to have been built by John Reilly, who offered hospitality to King William and his army as they camped beneath the trees on their way to meet the Catholic King James at the Battle of the Boyne in 1690. King William's famous white charger is said to have been tethered to a particular Spanish chestnut tree which still stands in the grounds. Reilly was subsequently given as much land as he could walk in a day, and this became the Scarva demesne. Every 13 July a 'sham fight' is staged here between King William and King James: no prizes for guessing who wins, and the losers seem only too eager to throw themselves at the feet of the victors! The event commemorates the Battle of the Boyne (which actually took place on 12 July 1690) and is very much a family day out. The village of Scarva is quite small, but it was an important place on the canal and had its own basin and landing quay, constructed as part of a series of improvements to the waterway between 1801 and 1811. Scarva has a couple of shops and a pub, as well as bus and rail services. Scarva Parish Hall is seen on the approach to the village from the canal bridge, while the spire of the parish church, built on a bank behind, truly dominates the village.

Newry Canal Footpath signs flank the bridge at Scarva, and a fine path continues away from the village. Note the old buildings which seem to rise from the swampy cut of the canal, and later look out for a sign which explains about the Dane's Cast, or Black Pig's Dyke. Historical data on this earthwork is scant, but myths and legends are numerous. The one favoured locally, and raised on a stout metal sign, runs as follows: 'In 350 AD three brothers fought in the Battle of Aghaderg. Euchaidh was slain but Conal and Eoin survived, won the battle and afterwards divided Ulster between them. They decided to mark out their newly won territory and constructed what has been called the Dane's Cast or Black Pig's Dyke. This ran from Lisnagade Fort to Donegal Bay. The ditch was some ten yards wide. Originally the banks were five yards high but time and weather have reduced them to two or three yards high. It was Geraldus Cambrensis who gave it the name Dane's Cast, but it had nothing to do with the Danes.' There are dozens of variations on the 'Black Pig's Dyke' story all over Ulster.

The gravel path is often flanked by trees, but there are always views of nearby fields. As Acton Lake, or Lough Shark, comes into view, you pass Acton Lake Visitor Centre, which is built on the site of a former sluice-keeper's cottage and offers plenty of information about the canal and its surroundings. The Newry Canal was watered from Acton Lake and reaches its summit level here at 24m (78ft). The canal was the first in Ireland or Britain to cross a watershed. The path continues by the rampant hedgerows alongside Acton Lake until it reaches a gateway at Poyntzpass.

The crossroads village of Poyntzpass was formerly called Fenwick's Pass, but the land was given to Lieutenant Charles Poyntz who fought a battle in the area in 1603. He was from Acton in Gloucestershire, and gave that name to the new village as well as the lake. The streets in Poyntzpass are named along denominational lines – Church St, Chapel St and Meeting St – while the secular Railway St crosses both the railway and Newry Canal. There are bus and rail services, as well as a handful of shops and pubs.

Leaving Poyntzpass, note the old warehouses beside the canal, pass a lock and follow the road alongside the old cut. The railway line and a few houses are off to the right. The road runs under a railway bridge, makes a broad curve, then reaches a road junction at Gamble's Bridge. Continue straight past the bridge, following a broad track under another railway bridge. The canal curves through a valley, and by now Camlough Mountain looks much closer. After passing an old lock and cottage, a fine track leads onwards to Jerrettspass. Although the view takes in cultivated fields, the margins of the canal are rampant with vegetation. A lovely old stone bridge carries Carrickrovaddy Rd over the Newry Canal at Jerrettspass, while another fine arch carries the railway over Knockduff Rd on the other side of the main road. Jerrettspass is no more than a row of houses with a small shop, and there are bus and rail services linking with Newry and Portadown.

The heron is a large bird often seen standing motionless on one leg, or gathered in noisy treetop heronries.

The towpath is a gravel track at this point, turning round a right bend and passing an old lock and cottage, becoming grassier as it bends to the left. At Steenson's Bridge the towpath passes under the same arch as the canal; there is also a smaller arch for an adjacent channel. A narrow gravel path leads to Forsythe's Lock and another old cottage.

After passing beneath a concrete bridge which carries a farm track over the Newry Canal, the grassy towpath becomes lined with trees which later screen the factories and chimneys of the Carnbane Industrial Estate. As another lock and cottage are passed, great growths of giant hogweed may be noticed, especially along a channel running parallel to the canal. After passing beneath a bridge which carries the main Belfast to Dublin road over the canal, the towpath becomes narrower, then broadens into a fine track. You reach lock-gates near St Colman's College, and there is another pair of lock-gates near the end of the tow-path.

Go through the gate at the end of the towpath and walk along the road past the Win Business Park. Look out for the Linenhall Arch to the right, which was built in 1783 as the entrance to a barracks, but now stands at the entrance to a housing estate. When the canalside road reaches a busy road-bridge beside a tall brick mill, cross over and continue alongside the Newry River, passing the Riverside Reformed Presbyterian Church. Cross another busy road to reach Newry Town Hall on the Armaghdown Bridge. The Tourist Information Office is located in the Town Hall, and the Newry Museum and Arts Centre is just to one side. There are places to stay in and around town, as well as a full range of shops, pubs and restaurants.

SOUTH-EASTERN SECTION

County Down

Distance: 234 kilometres (145 miles)

This part of the Ulster Way sees us return to the coast, though at first the sea is only glimpsed from time to time as the route makes its way around the Mountains of Mourne. The Mourne Trail itself is a popular part of the Ulster Way which can be covered in a weekend. The highest parts of the Ulster Way are traversed over the peaks of Slievemoughanmore and Pigeon Rock Mountain, but once Newcastle is reached, the sea returns as a companion all the way back to Belfast.

Coastal walking along this section of the Ulster Way varies from strolls along sandy beaches to walks along specific coastal paths and stretches of low cliff coast. Gradually, the route works its way around headlands and bays to reach Killough and Ardglass, then Ballyhornan and Strangford. The Ulster Way links with a network of paths known as St Patrick's Way, and runs through St Patrick's Country, the region round Lecale closely linked with the life and work of Ireland's patron saint. After spending years as a slave in Antrim, St Patrick began his Irish mission here and founded his first church at Saul. He is said to be buried at Downpatrick.

The National Trust owns many stretches of the coast, as well as other properties in Co. Down, and operates a wildlife scheme to manage the varied habitats of Strangford Lough. In the future there may be improvements made to the course of the Ulster Way alongside Strangford Lough, but for most of the time the route weaves through a network of roads rolling through the drumlin-filled countryside. Scrabo Hill, beyond the head of Strangford Lough, offers a particularly fine viewpoint before the Ulster Way reaches Newtownards.

A series of paths and tracks leave Newtownards, crossing rolling hills and passing through lovely woodlands before finally reaching the shores of Belfast Lough. The North Down Coastal Path is covered by the Ulster Way between Helen's Bay and Holywood. As the route approaches Belfast, it takes a quite scenic course through the suburbs, linking places such as Stormont, the Castlereagh Hills and Cregagh Glen. The final stretches are through the wooded Lagan valley, mostly along the Lagan Canal towpath, finally leaving the river to return to Dunmurry.

Apart from the stretch across the Mountains of Mourne, there are plenty of places offering food, drink and accommodation along this part of the Ulster Way. Most of the facilities are located in the small towns and villages en route, but there is ready access to bus services to reach a greater range of facilities. As the route turns towards Belfast, there are opportunities to make detours into the city with its wide range of services.

WALK 28

NEWRY TO ROSTREVOR

Start: Newry Town Hall – 086267.

Finish: Rostrevor – 179184.

Distance: 18 kilometres (11 miles).

Map: OSNI Discovery Sheet 29.

Terrain: Practically all this section is on hilly minor roads, though there is a short stretch through fields which can be muddy.

Waymarking: Once clear of Newry, most of this section is marked with metal plates along the roads reading 'Ulster Way: Mourne Trail'.

Public Transport: Newry has a railway station, linking with Belfast and Portadown on the Ulster Way, as well as Dublin. Ulsterbus services offer further links with the Ulster Way, including 63 to Portadown, 39 to Rostrevor, and 240 to Newcastle, Dundrum and Downpatrick. There are also Ulsterbus and Bus Éireann services to and from Belfast and Dublin.

Accommodation: Newry and Rostrevor have hotel and B&B accommodation. There is also a campsite in Kilbroney Park near Rostrevor.

ROUTE DESCRIPTION

Newry Town Hall is an obvious starting point and a walk along Hill St offers an interesting way through town, though you can also leave town via The Mall, which runs beside the Clanrye River. Hill St is the town's main shopping street and most of it is pedestrianised. It has two squares, Margaret Sq and Marcus Sq, after which you reach the imposing granite Cathedral of St Patrick and St Colman. It dates from 1829 and was the first Roman Catholic cathedral to be built after Emancipation, when civil and religious freedoms were restored to Catholics. The interior is especially ornate. Further along the street is St Mary's Church of Ireland, which was begun in 1810 as a replacement for the older St Patrick's, whose tower can be seen rising above town. The tiny St Colman's Park is opposite. At the end of Hill St is the First Presbyterian Church, dating from 1853. Newry has a wealth of history spread through its streets. The character of the town used to be proclaimed in the rhyme: 'High church, low steeple, dirty streets and proud people.'

Turn left at the end of Hill St and walk up a busy main road. Use a subway to cross to the other side, then walk through the Abbey Yard. Although no trace remains, a Cistercian abbey was built in this area by St Malachi in the 12th century. According to tradition, however, Newry was founded when St Patrick planted a yew tree at the head of Carlingford Lough. Walk along Boat St, passing the Schooner Lounge, bearing in mind that this part of town was once the quayside of the old port of Newry.

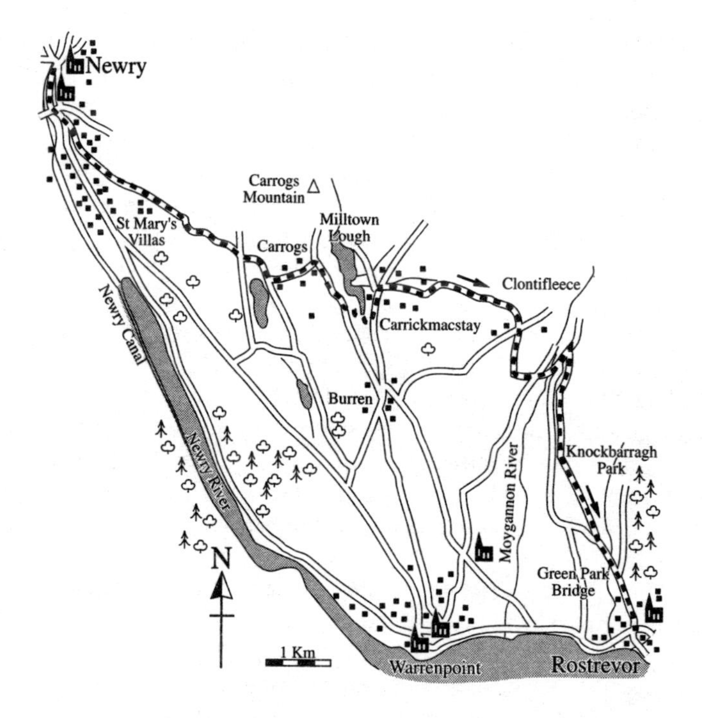

Start climbing in earnest up Chapel St, passing a Roman Catholic chapel dated 1790, as well as a small shop. There are no other shops along the way until Rostrevor. The road climbs past a recycling centre and the gradient eases at a staggered crossroads near a row of houses called St Mary's Villas. The road continues on a gently undulating course through fields, passing scattered houses, then drops down through a crossroads to follow Lower Carrogs Rd. A pig farm sits in the bottom of the valley, and from here there is a view of the crest of Slieve

Foye. The road bends right and left as it climbs, with a view across the reedy Greenan Lough. Note that the road is marked as 'Corrags Rd' as it climbs, which is surely a misspelling. After it rolls past a few houses at Carrogs, a right turn is marked as Carrogs Rd.

A track on the left leads down towards a farm overlooking the little pool of Milltown Lough, but don't follow it. Instead, continue further down Carrogs Rd and take the next farm track on the left. After passing through the farmyard, turn right along an old track bounded by trees, crossing ground which can be muddy when wet. A left turn later leads up to another road, the B7, where a left turn is made uphill. It's worth noting at this point that the little village of Burren is just to the south. It has a shop and a heritage centre, as well as a cottage where Jim Larkin, fiery leader of the Irish labour movement in the early 19th century, spent his boyhood.

Keep to the right at a fork when following the B7 road uphill, passing Treanor's, where furniture and garden ornaments are stored and sold. Take the next road to the right, which climbs uphill past a few buildings, then bends left and right before crossing the hill. There is a car park with picnic benches on top, at nearly 230m (750ft), on the shoulder of Craignamona. Your view as you walk extends from Camlough Mountain to Slieve Gullion, the Cooley Hills and Slieve Foye, ending with Slieve Martin. Follow the road down past a farm and on through a crossroads on the valley side. Continue along the road, which drops down past Clontifleece National School, where a plaque records that it was 'Erected by Narcissus Batt Esq. 1839'. Turn quickly right and left down Lugancanty Rd onto another road and cross over the Moygannon River.

Follow the road uphill, turning right at the second junction, which is Upper Knockbarragh Rd. The road climbs past a small covered reservoir and descends past a few farms, and there are good views along the way across to the Cooley Hills. After passing a belt of oak, beech and sycamore trees, you can see down to Rostrevor on the shores of Carlingford Lough. The road runs down past a huddle of houses at Drumreagh Park and crosses Park Bridge. Continue past a Gaelic football ground and pass by the houses at St Rita's Park. At the end of Greenpark Rd, turn left to reach the middle of Rostrevor. Many of the buildings sport a colourful lick of paint, while there is seating and car parking under a handful of fine oak trees. The broad Church St narrows as it runs beside the Church of Ireland and continues uphill to the Roman Catholic church, but the Ulster Way continues to the right along Bridge St. For the time being, there are a handful of shops and pubs, places to eat and places to stay. The nearby Kilbroney Park provides a campsite.

Kilbroney's name is derived from St Bronach's Church, though this is off the course of the Ulster Way. The ruins of a 6th-century church remain, surrounded by an ancient graveyard. An artefact known as St Bronach's Bell resides in the Roman Catholic church. It is said that the bell used to hang in a tree, then was forgotten about until the tree was felled and the bell was rediscovered.

WALK 29

ROSTREVOR TO NEWCASTLE

Start: Rostrevor – 179184.

Finish: Newcastle Youth Hostel – 379314.

Distance: 37 kilometres (23 miles).

Maps: OSNI Discoverer Sheet 29. Outdoor Pursuits Map of Mourne Country is also useful.

Terrain: Forest tracks give way to rugged mountain paths where care is needed with navigation. After a road-walk in the middle of this stretch, where walkers can leave the route if they have arranged a lift, hillside paths and forest tracks give way to short road-walks and parkland paths at Newcastle.

Waymarking: Wooden marker posts are used in Rostrevor Forest, but waymarking over the mountains is sparse. Wooden marker posts are used in Tollymore Forest, with metal Ulster Way signposts along the roads.

Public Transport: Ulsterbus 39 links Rostrevor with Newry. There are no bus services over the Deer's Meadow. Ulsterbus 240 links Newcastle with Newry, Dundrum and Downpatrick.

Accommodation: Rostrevor has a number of B&Bs, while a campsite is located in nearby Kilbroney Park. A B&B is located well off-route at Attical. Newcastle has every type of accommodation from campsites to large hotels.

ROUTE DESCRIPTION

Leave Rostrevor by following Bridge St, crossing the river at the entrance to the Fairy Glen. While the Ulster Way technically runs to the main road before turning left into Kilbroney Park, it's also possible to cut through the park at a gateway on the left, which bears the park's name, and follow a path across a broad, grassy slope dotted with fine trees. Keep to the left to follow the path up to the Forest Restaurant, then keep left on narrow tarmac roads to pass the campsite and reach a triangular road junction and a barrier gate flanked by 'no entry' signs.

Walk past the barrier, cross a river and follow the tarmac road into Rostrevor Forest.

When the road turns left to leave the forest, turn right along a track, which climbs rather steeply uphill. As the gradient eases, there are two stretches of track running alongside the edge of the forest overlooking the fields. Keep straight on at a track junction, crossing the slope on an undulating course but generally heading uphill. Keep straight on at a junction where there are good views across the valley over the tops of young trees. Go through two barrier gates and continue along the track, passing a Water Service building. Continue on the track, turning left down a gravel path to reach a footbridge where waterfalls gush into the Yellow Water River. Cross over the footbridge and then turn quickly left and right along tracks.

There has been some clear felling and replanting around the head of the valley. Cross a stile at the edge of the forest, but don't walk out onto the road. To the right follow a path which can be muddy, running up and down across a bracken slope which is sparsely wooded. Cross a stream and turn up a path which takes you around the edge of a stand of forest. Look out for a Mass Rock on the right, made from a large boulder of Mourne granite at Altataggart. When many Catholic practices were banned under the Penal Laws of the 18th century, Mass was often held in remote places using a suitable stone as an altar. Follow the track onwards as it runs across another thinly wooded slope and note how many fine Scots pines grow here. A grassy, stony path cuts through the bracken and begins to descend. Walk through a gate in the wall and cross a river at a ford made of granite slabs. Turn right up a bending track, passing a water intake high on the hillside. Don't cross a bridge over the river, but turn left upstream and follow a narrow, stony, often muddy path up to a broad gap.

The path leads down to a confluence of two mountain streams, Rocky Water and the Windy Gap River. From here you can see straight up to the Windy Gap, which you will reach higher up. Cross the Rocky Water – there may be a forlorn Ulster Way marker post on the far side – and, looking downstream, note the rocky peak called Hen Mountain, as well as the more distant Slieve Croob. Follow the other watercourse upstream and locate a scanty path through tussocky grass and heather, reaching a boggy gap. Don't cross the stiles over the wall junction at the top, but simply turn left and follow Batt's Wall up a steep slope of rock, grass and heather. Narcissus Batt was a 19th-century Belfast merchant. He had the wall built and was responsible for planting most of the Scots pines you saw earlier. As you come near the top, drift to the left to reach the summit cairns. The second cairn marks the true summit of Slieve-moughanmore, the highest point gained by the Ulster Way at 559m (1,837ft).

From here you can see the dome of Eagle Mountain close at hand, followed by the Cooley Hills, Slieve Gullion, Camlough Mountain and the distant Sperrins. Lough Neagh fills the lowlands, followed by the Antrim Mountains, Divis and Slieve Croob. In the distance, little Scrabo Hill is identified by its tower. All the hills around the Spelga Dam are close to hand, then Meelmore, Slieve Bearnagh and Slieve Commedagh are among the higher mountains in view. Slieve Muck and Slieve Binnian lead the eye into the Kingdom of Mourne, which is dominated by the forested hill of Knockchree. In the distance, Lambay Island, Howth and the Wicklow Mountains may be seen on a clear day.

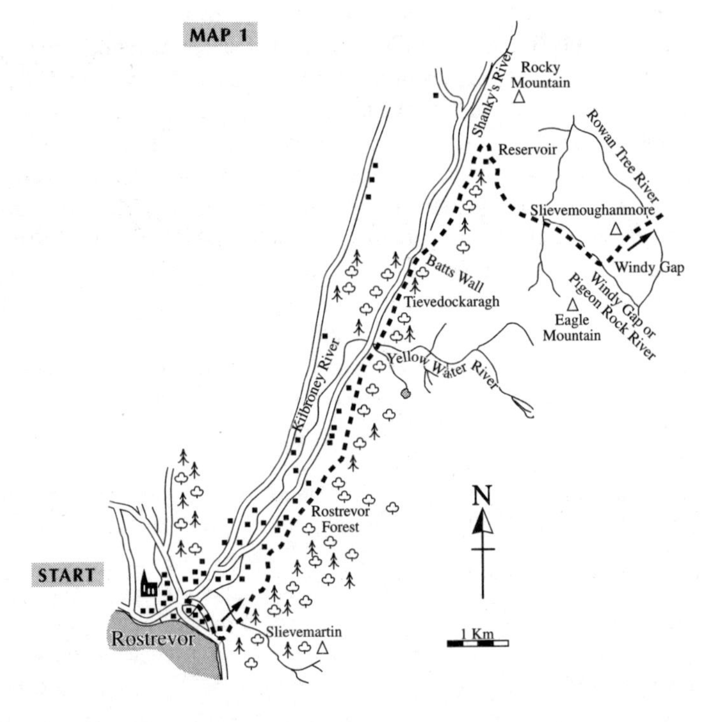

Join the course of Batt's Wall again to continue downhill. The wall drops steeply and there are a couple of rock-steps where you need to take care on the descent to the next gap. A less steep, grassy slope rises

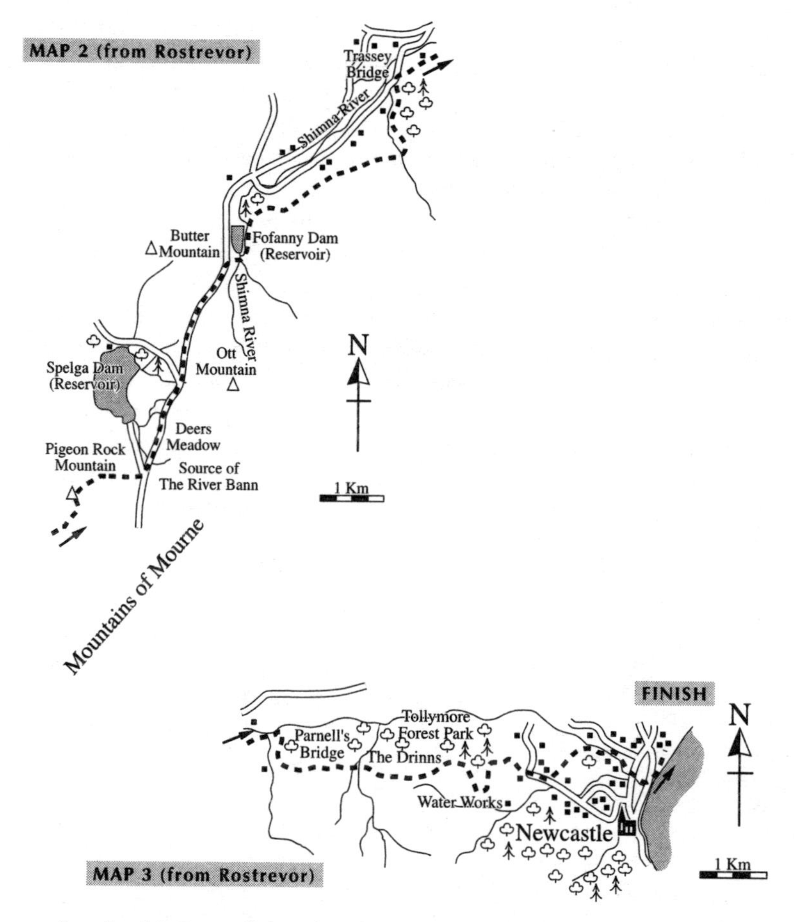

ahead, with the wall running through it in a prominent line. The wall turns left and right as it passes the summit cairn on Pigeon Rock Mountain, the second highest point gained on the Ulster Way at 534m (1,755ft). Follow Batt's Wall downhill again, which is as straight as can be on the final run down to the Deer's Meadow. Cross a stile and a narrow road at the bottom, then cut across a strip of ground to reach the B27 road on the Deer's Meadow.

Walkers who have had enough at this point are reminded that there is no accommodation close to hand, but if a lift can be obtained off-route to Attical, there is a farmhouse B&B located there. The day's walk is barely half-completed at the Deer's Meadow and Newcastle is still a long way away.

Turn left to follow the B27 road roughly northwards over the Deer's Meadow, looking down on the Spelga Dam where the headwaters of the mighty River Bann are impounded. Branch right along a minor road signposted for Newcastle. There is a parking space to the right of this road, and as the road descends there is another car park off to the left, near the start of the Ott Track. Continue down the road until a small forest is reached on the right. A gate and stile give access to a slope which can be followed down alongside the forest. Cut through a small corner of the forest, then follow a grassy embankment on the far side of the Fofanny Dam Reservoir. Cross a little footbridge over a channel at the end of the embankment, but don't cross the dam.

A stile reveals a track leading away from the dam. Cross the stile and follow the track around the hillside. Turn right along a narrower path marked by occasional concrete posts. The path in fact marks the line of a water pipeline, which is exposed from time to time along the way. Cut off down into a little valley and cross a stream, climbing up a flight of stone steps to cross a stile at the top. A path can be followed across the lower slopes of Slieve Meelmore, running roughly parallel to a drystone wall, but generally keeping well above it. The slope is mostly grassy, but has some stony patches along the way. Cross over the Trassey River, which tumbles down from the Hare's Gap, then turn left to follow the Trassey Track through a gateway. A path known as the Brandy Pad runs this way, along which smugglers once brought illicit spirits across the mountains from the small harbours on the coast. The track is quite stony as it runs downhill, passing two more gates before reaching a road near a car park.

The pine marten, Ireland's rarest mammal, is the size of a cat, with a bushy tail. The fur is chocolate brown with a creamy patch on the throat.

Turn right on the road, then right again to pass above the car park. A gravel track leads to a junction of three tracks. Take the middle one, then cross three stiles beside three gates on the way to Tollymore Forest Park. A gentle rise on the track passes the Salmon Leap viewpoint, then there is a slight descent to cross Maria's Bridge, where there is a waterfall off to the right. Turn right up a track after crossing the bridge, and keep right at a higher junction, following a path uphill roughly parallel to the inside edge of the forest. Another track is joined at a bend, so keep climbing uphill, still on the inside edge of the forest, crossing a sort of a gap. Walk downhill on the track, keeping right at a couple of junctions signposted for The Drinns, where there has been some clear felling.

Cross over Hore's Bridge, which bears a datemark of 1824.

After crossing Hore's Bridge, keep straight on along a broad track. A narrow, muddy path is followed uphill to the right, cutting out a bend in the track. Turn right, then left, then rise gradually alongside the inside edge of the forest again. Turn right at a junction of tracks where a rock is inscribed with the words 'To the Mountain Top 1826' with a red hand giving the direction. If you choose to go that way, note that the height of the trees cuts out any chance of a view! The forest track descends gently at first, with a view across a rugged mountain gap to the right, and later zig-zags, allowing you to take in fine views over Newcastle, Murlough, St John's Point and St Patrick's Country. Take the track to the right at a junction, zig-zagging down to some gates. Go straight through, then continue down a narrow tarmac road passing a few houses.

When a bend in the road is reached, keep walking downhill a short way, then turn left along a gravelly lane signposted as a public footpath. This leads down past a handful of houses, the last one being the large Tipperary House. Follow the Shimna River downstream and note the fine mixture of tree species along the way, as well as gorse, broom and bracken. Turn left and cross a road bridge over the Shimna River, then turn right to follow a tarmac path further downstream, passing manicured grassy areas and benches. Cross a broad footbridge and let the path lead you to another footbridge over another river, then cross the busy Bryansford Rd. Walk past the play areas and boating pool in Castle Park, then join a busy road into Newcastle. The Tourist Information Centre is off to the right, while further away, also to the right, is the Mourne Countryside Centre. Newcastle's main shopping street is off to the left.

Cross over the road, turning left to cross the bridge over the Shimna River, then follow the broad path along the promenade. Towards the end of the promenade you see the funnel-shaped Roman Catholic church and the Slieve Donard Hotel; the youth hostel is located between the two. This side of Newcastle is essentially a seaside resort, with a full range of accommodation options, as well as plenty of shops, pubs and restaurants. It is quite separate from the older harbour area on the southern side of town. The huge dome of Slieve Donard, the highest mountain in Ulster at 850m (2,796ft), completely dominates the town. An ascent, which on a fine day might well be the crowning glory of a walk round the Ulster Way, is an optional extra you might like to consider.

WALK 30

NEWCASTLE TO BALLYKINLER

Start: Newcastle Youth Hostel – 379314.

Finish: Ballykinler – 435366.

Distance: 18 kilometres (11 miles).

Maps: OSNI Discoverer Sheets 21 and 29.

Terrain: Low-level walking along sandy beaches, paths, tracks and roads. The beach walk is subject to the tides, which may necessitate moving inland.

Waymarking: The beach walk is not waymarked but it is obvious to follow. The rest of the route has metal Ulster Way signposts beside the roads.

Public Transport: Ulsterbus 17, 20 and 240 serve Newcastle and Dundrum. Ulsterbus 16C serves Ballykinler from Downpatrick.

Accommodation: There is plenty of accommodation of all types around Newcastle. There are only a couple of B&Bs around Dundrum and Ballykinler.

ROUTE DESCRIPTION

Leave Newcastle by heading for the beach in front of the Slieve Donard Hotel, turning left to start plodding along the sand and shingle at the foot of a substantial concrete wall. When the tide is out, there is a chance to walk on fairly firm sands, but when the tide is in you may find the higher sand dry, loose and tiring. A very high tide might make the beach walk inadvisable, though further along there are easy options to cut inland. Timber and boulder banks help to stabilise the dunes at the start of the strand, while timber groins keep the wave-washed sands in check later. There are two ways to proceed with this walk. One is to follow the beach faithfully, which eventually entails turning at the end of the point, where the sand is decidedly softer. The other option is to cut inland from one of the prominent marker posts on the dune belt, which mark the way onto a network of paths linking up to provide a way through to Downshire Bridge. Either way, Downshire Bridge is the objective. The tree-lined road on the last stretch towards the bridge is known as The Avenue.

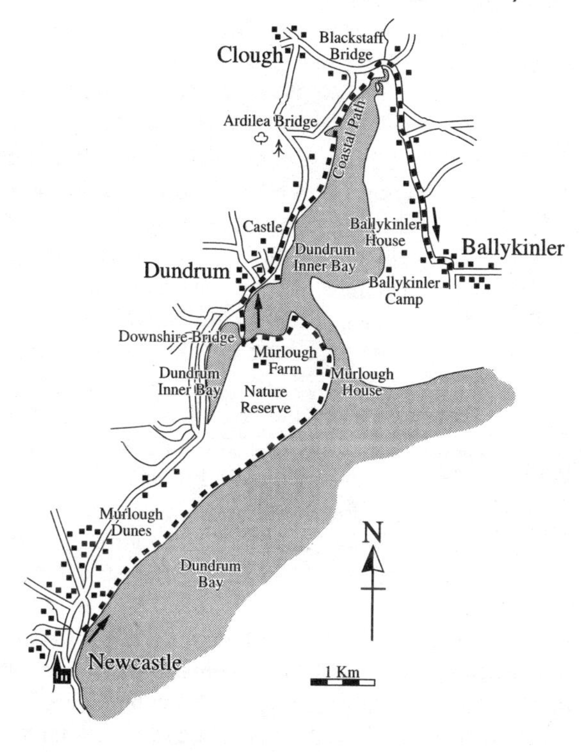

The National Trust owns the Murlough Dunes and has managed them as Ireland's first nature reserve since 1967. Stone Age settlements have been discovered beneath the sands, and some of the dunes are so well vegetated that they have become covered in thick, woody scrub. A variety of habitat types include hazel and buckthorn scrub, a flowery heath, areas of marram grass, sheltered mudflats and a sand-and-shingle foreshore. Dundrum Inner Bay is an important wintering area for brent geese, waders and ducks, while the open sea supports other ducks and divers, as well as seals. The Murlough Dunes National Nature Reserve supports varied flora, ranging from marram, heather and bracken to rare bee orchid, viper's bugloss, and more common wild pansies and bird's-foot trefoil. The reserve is home to rabbits, foxes and badgers, as well as insects such as moths and butterflies, including the rare marsh fritillary. Birds on the dunes range from skylark and meadow pipit to reed bunting and stonechat, with willow warblers, finches and thrushes also abundant. Shelduck nest in old rabbit burrows, while you may well see ringed plover on the open beach.

After passing through the Gate Lodge and crossing Downshire Bridge's lovely stone arches, turn right along a short, wooded pathway. The path, like the bridge, is part of an old railway track-bed which once led to Newcastle. The path reaches the busy A2 close to St Donard's Church in Dundrum. There are places offering food and drink on the way through the village, and there is a little accommodation and a number of bus services if the route is to be broken at this point. Walking straight through Dundrum, look out for a ruined castle on a wooded hill to the left. The current ruins are of a castle first built by John de Courcy in 1177, but the site has long been fortified and is associated with the mythic Red Branch.

The pale-bellied brent goose is the size of a mallard duck and is identified by its hoarse 'kronking' call. From August onwards, they can be seen overwintering along the coast and feeding in fields.

Pass the Dundrum boat park and recreation area, then the Gaelic football ground on the way out of Dundrum. After passing the football ground, turn right to get onto the old railway track again. The National Trust owns this stretch of path, which it has designated the Dundrum Coastal Path. There is a firm, clear path along the top of the embankment, flanked by gorse and brambles. The track-bed gradually pulls away from the busy main road, and there are fine views across the inlet of Dundrum Inner Bay, a popular site for wildfowl and waders. A reedy area is passed and later the track is flanked by a variety of trees. A small tidal lagoon is passed further on, where views are again more open and there is a chance to observe a variety of birds. The track itself is also notable for its population of badgers. Another wooded stretch leads onwards, and at one point there is a flight of steps onto a road which can be used to reach the nearby village of Clough. If you do not want to make this detour, keep following the path, then continue across fields to reach the main A2 road again at Blackstaff Bridge.

Turn right across Blackstaff Bridge and walk uphill, then right again to follow Ford Rd and Commons Rd to Ballykinler. While the map shows nothing more than a small village surrounded by fields and dunes, the reality is very different: Ballykinler Camp is a large army base, so expect to see signs of the military. There are only a couple of shops and a small number of accommodation options near by. Alternatively, you could continue along the road towards Killough.

WALK 31

BALLYKINLER TO ARDGLASS

Start: Ballykinler – 435366.

Finish: Ardglass – 559375.

Distance: 20 kilometres (12½ miles).

Map: OSNI Discoverer Sheet 21.

Terrain: Low-level, mainly along a variety of roads which can be busy, but there are options to walk along the beach in places, and the route includes a fine coastal path.

Waymarking: Mostly quite good, with metal Ulster Way signposts along the roads and wooden markers off the roads.

Public Transport: Ulsterbus 16C serves Ballykinler from Downpatrick. Ulsterbus 16A serves Killough and Ardglass from Downpatrick.

Accommodation: There are only a couple of B&Bs offering accommodation around Ballykinler, Killough and Ardglass.

ROUTE DESCRIPTION

Leave the village of Ballykinler, passing Tyrella Primary School, a shop and Ballykinler Gaelic Football Club. When the main A2 road is reached, walk straight onwards as signposted for Tyrella Beach. The main road leads past St John's Church of Ireland, which stands on an ancient church site known as Teach Riagla. Tyrella Beach is off to the right later on and offers the chance to take a break from the road; there are paths around the sand dunes, and the option of walking along the beach if the tides allow. The Ulster Way, however, stays on the road, later switching from Clanmaghery Rd to Minerstown Rd at a right bend. Pass more farms and houses, the Minerstown Tavern, Beach View House B&B and Minerstown Holiday Home Park, and further along the road turn right along a couple of minor roads signposted for St John's Point and St John's Church, whose ruins date from the 10th or 11th century.

Keep straight on to reach the rocky coast. You could turn right to have a closer look at the striking black-and-yellow banded lighthouse on the point, or you could turn left as marked by a public footpath sign

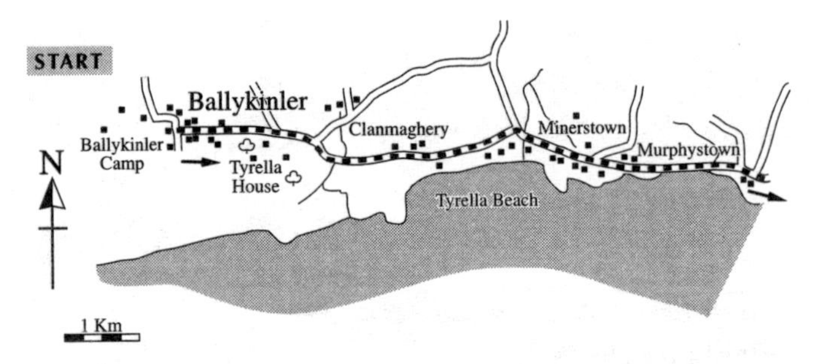

to start following the coastal path. The path crosses muddy ground at first, and it's a good idea to look ahead to spot marker posts and stiles in order to keep on course. The path is routed along a rugged coastal strip away from the cultivated fields inland, and the route is quite convoluted at times. The path runs close to a farm, then crosses a storm beach before turning round a grassy headland dominated by a stout, white-washed building. After passing this building, follow a narrow road straight towards Killough along Fisherman's Row.

The candy-striped lighthouse on the end of St John's Point.

For a while the little town of Killough was known as Port St Anne and boasted a busy harbour, windmill, limekiln and brick-works. The harbour was used by the Ward family of Castleward so they could avoid paying harbour dues in Strangford; a study of the map shows a long and suspiciously direct road running all the way from the Castleward estate to the quays at Killough. There are three interesting churches in the village, Roman Catholic, Church of Ireland and Methodist, as well as some delightful Victorian cottages and old almshouses. These buildings can be appreciated while following the main A2 road, or Castle St, out of Killough. Pass through the square and continue along the coastal road, keeping right at a road junction on the edge of town.

An old railway engine-house can be seen to the left of the road, and the course of the railway track-bed leads the eye to a series of bridge buttresses where the line once crossed a tidal inlet. The road twists and turns as it makes its way around the same inlet, passing the reedy Strand Lough and climbing uphill past the Coney Island caravan park. After passing signs for Coney Island, climb up to the right along Green Rd

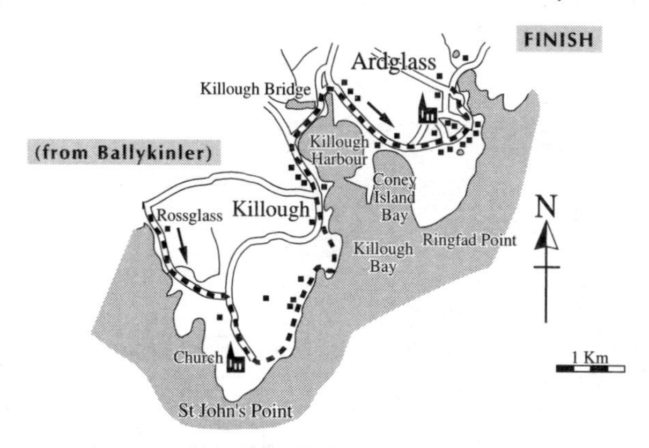

and walk down to the harbour at Ardglass. Ulster Way signposts point left to lead walkers around the harbour, passing Jordan's Castle and several other crenellated buildings. Ardglass is still an important port, but was once one of the busiest in Ulster, an era marked by the seven tower-houses and fortified storehouses around the village. After the town suffered severe damage in the 1641 Rebellion, when a resurgent native population rose against the planters of the early 1600s, much of Ardglass's trade switched to neighbouring Killough. The town has a good number of pubs, shops and restaurants, and there is some B&B accommodation available.

WALK 32

ARDGLASS TO RAHOLP

Start: Ardglass – 559375.

Finish: Raholp – 534474.

Distance: 29 kilometres (18 miles).

Map: OSNI Discoverer Sheet 21.

Terrain: Low-level coastal roads, tracks and paths. Some of the paths can be muddy. The roads can sometimes be busy, and towards the end of the day the route moves away from the coast into rolling countryside.

Waymarking: Mostly quite good, with metal Ulster Way signposts along the roads.

Public Transport: Ulsterbus 16A serves Ardglass and Ballyhornan. Ulsterbus 16B also serves Ballyhornan. Ulsterbus 16E serves Strangford and runs near Raholp. All services run to Downpatrick.

Accommodation: There is only a limited amount of accommodation available around Ardglass and Strangford, with more places located around nearby Downpatrick.

ROUTE DESCRIPTION

The main A2 road leaves Ardglass as the Strangford Rd, signposted to the right on the way out of the village. Also on the right on the outskirts of Ardglass is a short field path climbing to the ruins of Ardtole Church. This is dedicated to St Nicholas and offers a fine view of the surrounding countryside. Turn right along Sheepland Rd, which is signposted for St Patrick's Well, then turn left at the next junction to continue. Further along, to the right, another signpost for St Patrick's Well reveals a hedged, grassy track leading down towards the coast. A left turn leads straight to the site, where two small wells and a large crucifix stand in a concrete enclosure. Around St Patrick's Day, 17 March, the way to the well is bright with gorse, primroses, daisies and marsh marigolds.

Follow the shore onwards, crossing a stile, and soon a series of ruins, including an old windmill tower, are noticed around Sheepland. Later you pass by a white house sited on a headland of gorse and heather, then climb the grassy slopes to the top of Benboy Hill. Views

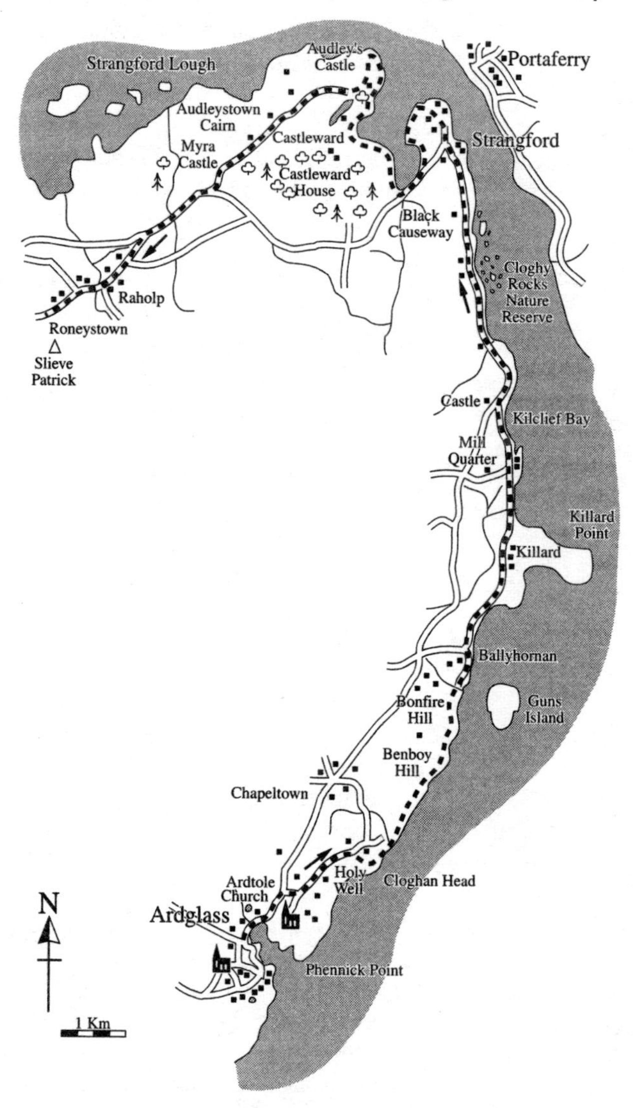

stretch along the low, rocky coast, inland to the Mountains of Mourne and Slieve Croob, with Guns Island just offshore and the Isle of Man also visible in clear weather. The path passes between high and low fields, then drops downhill to pass another low field. Carrying on close to the sea, pass a few houses along a track, then join a narrow road.

Follow the road into the village of Ballyhornan, climbing uphill towards the end to reach the Cable Bar, or follow a concrete path up to a car park.

Turn right along Killard Rd as it runs above the shore. Killard Point, a nature reserve which has an abundance of flowering plants and orchids, is off to the right. The road later becomes Shore Rd and a right turn at a junction leads past Kilclief Castle, a fine 15th-century tower-house, one of a series which you pass while following the Ulster Way. Shore Rd passes St Malachy's Park Gaelic football ground and the Strangford caravan park. Later, to the right, is the Cloghy Rocks National Nature Reserve. From a small car park by the road you can watch the rocks appear from the sea as the tide recedes. You will often see common and grey seals hauling themselves onto the rocks: these are good feeding grounds for sea creatures, as 350 million cubic metres of seawater flow in and out through the narrows of Strangford Lough twice daily. The name itself comes from the Vikings' *strang fiord*, violent inlet. Along the shore you may see brent geese, oystercatchers, curlews, shelduck and herons. The road continues into the village of Strangford, which offers food, drink and a little accommodation. There are frequent ferries across the narrows to Portaferry, where the Exploris Centre offers a glimpse into the marine life of the area.

Both the common seal and the grey seal are to be seen around the coast.

Leaving Strangford, follow Ulster Way signposts from the square along Castle St. Strangford Castle, a 16th-century tower-house, is off to the right, but keep left to continue to the gateway for Old Court, an estate dating from the 16th century which incorporates an old Customs house and chapel. Turn left at the gateway to discover the appropriately named Squeeze Cut. A flight of stone steps takes this narrow path uphill between tall walls, then it runs downhill between high brambly banks to reach a track beside Strangford Lough. Turn left along the track, noting the curious round bathing tower beside the water. Follow the track into woods, then turn right along another track signposted for the Strangford

Bay Path. Turn left and follow the path along the shore, but bear in mind that this area can be covered by water during very high tides. The path can be a bit rough underfoot but it is mostly level, passing woods and fields before turning round a pine-clad headland. A track is joined again, which is followed to the right to reach the main A2 road at Down Lodge.

Turn right to follow the road, using the footway alongside to cross the Black Causeway and reach an entrance for Castleward caravan site. Walk along a narrow road through an imposing gateway, then keep to the right to follow a woodland track onwards. The woods are dense in places, delightfully mixed, with an understorey of rhododendron, bramble and ivy. Views may be restricted, but for birdwatchers there is access to the Eagleson Hide on the shore, overlooking the Castleward Bay Refuge Area. Further along, there is a junction of tracks and a series of signposts lists various destinations and attractions on the estate. Follow the track to a tarmac road and turn right, descending past the Strangford Lough Wildlife Centre. Some wonderful buildings are reached, including Old Castle Ward and the Cornmill. Castleward House is set further inland; it is noted for having one side built in Classical style while the other is Gothic. Evidently Bernard and Anne Ward simply could not agree on which style they wanted, and their architect had to please them both!

Walk through an arched gateway after exploring the house and follow a track signposted as the Ulster Way. This runs through the woods to Strangford Sailing Club. A wooded and grassy path continues around the point crowned by Audley's Castle, and re-emerges facing the castle from the other side. Turn right along a track to reach a gate and a junction near a line of buildings called Green Row.

Keep right to follow a minor road running alongside the Castleward estate. There is a signposted right turn for Audleystown Cairn, where a detour could be made along the road and through fields to see a dual court burial cairn, retracing your steps afterwards. The road, meanwhile, has views across Strangford Lough and later passes St Tassach's Roman Catholic church. Turn right at the end of Audleystown Rd to follow the main A2 Strangford Rd. Turn left off the main road up St Patrick's Rd. The ruins of St Tassach's Church might be noticed off to the left, and there is access to them from Bannaghan Rd. St Tassach was the bishop credited with administering the last rites to the dying St Patrick, though little else is known of his life. Little is known of the history of the ancient church either, though it has been extensively altered and restored over the centuries. Cross slabs have been recorded at the site, though they have since disappeared.

St Patrick's Rd runs downhill, then climbs steeply through Raholp. The Slaney Inn and a shop are passed, while at the top of the hill is St Patrick's Primary School and the Swan Lodge B&B. Signposts for St Patrick's Way may be noticed around Raholp. This is not a long-distance waymarked route, but is actually a network of rights of way which can be used to explore the countryside further. The network brings you to St Patrick's landing place on Strangford Lough, where he began his great mission. Other places linked include Lough Money, Ballyalton and the Struell Wells near Downpatrick. You could use the St Patrick's Way path network to vary the course of the Ulster Way near Downpatrick.

WALK 33

RAHOLP TO KILLYLEAGH

Start: Raholp – 534474.

Finish: Killyleagh – 526526.

Distance: 20 kilometres (12½ miles).

Map: OSNI Discoverer Sheet 21.

Terrain: Low-level roads for the most part, which can be quite busy in places.

Waymarking: Mostly quite good, with metal Ulster Way signposts used along the roads.

Public Transport: Ulsterbus 16E runs near Raholp and links with Downpatrick. Ulsterbus 14 links Downpatrick and Killyleagh, while Ulsterbus 11 links Killyleagh with Comber and Belfast. There are also services from nearby Downpatrick to other parts of the Ulster Way.

Accommodation: There are quite a few accommodation options around Downpatrick, but there is only an inn at Killyleagh.

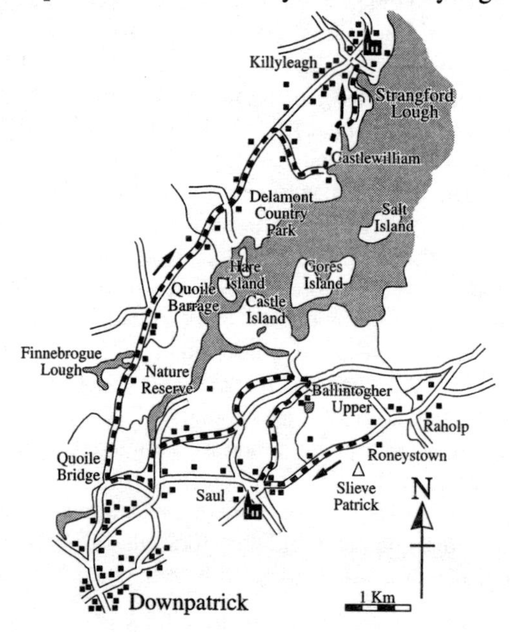

ROUTE DESCRIPTION

Leave Raholp to follow St Patrick's Rd towards Saul. On the way, there is a prominent gateway to the left, where a grassy path gives access to the summit of Slieve Patrick. This little hill bears Stations of the Cross, a Calvary scene, an open-air altar and a monumental granite statue of St Patrick inscribed with the dates '432-1932' in commemoration of the 1,500th year of his Christian mission in Ireland. The statue faces the Belfast Hills, and from here the view includes the Antrim Mountains, Scrabo Hill, Strangford Lough, the Ards Peninsula, Castleward, the Mountains of Mourne and the Isle of Man. St Patrick's Rd runs downhill, past a Roman Catholic church on the right, to the tiny village of Saul where the saint is said to have founded his first church in a local barn. Facilities are limited to Jack Robinson's bar and grill, where the Ulster Way turns right along Ballintogher Rd. It's worth making a detour to the left first, climbing Saul Brae to have a look at St Patrick's Church of Ireland, a relatively modern church built to an ancient style and incorporating a little round tower.

The rolling Ballintogher Rd passes fields and farms, then the Ulster Way turns left along the busy A2 Strangford Rd. Leave this at the next junction on the right and follow the minor Lisboy Rd uphill. The road rolls along and later runs back down to the main road. Turn right to continue, until the Quoile Countryside Centre is seen to the right, based around the ruins of Quoile Castle, which dates from around 1600. The castle was built to guard the approach to Downpatrick from Strangford Lough. Quoile Quay, built beside Strangford Lough in 1717, was a busy port serving nearby Downpatrick, and in the 1830s a paddle-steamer service ran between here and Liverpool. Flooding, however, was a common problem and floodgates were constructed near Quoile Bridge in 1745, 1802 and 1934. In 1957, after serious flooding in Downpatrick, a tidal barrier was built at Hare Island, creating the Quoile Pondage to collect floodwater for discharge into the lough. Plants and trees quickly colonised the former seashore, and in 1970 the area was declared a National Nature Reserve. The Quoile Countryside Centre was opened in 1988. Varied habitats include marshes and reed-beds, rushy grassland and willow scrub, as well as woodlands. There are abundant fish and eels, and they in turn attract herons, cormorants and grebe. The nearby Castle Island Hide facilitates birdwatchers.

The Ulster Way follows the shore of the Quoile Pondage, parallel to the main road, using paths and little footbridges. After you pass by the hefty remains of a wooden-keeled boat the path rises onto an old stone quay where there are parking spaces, toilets and picnic facilities. Walk past some bollards and follow the path parallel to the road, passing a wooden fishing stance and a substantial stone structure near the old floodgates. A footway continues beside the Quoile Rd. The Ulster Way crosses the Quoile Bridge as signposted along the main A22 Killyleagh Rd for Killyleagh and the Delamont Country Park. There is a footway on the left side of the busy road, so use it for safety's sake. (It is planned to divert the Ulster Way across the tidal barrier of the Quoile, via Castle Island and Hare Island, and take a more pleasant course to Delamont.) When the footway ends, switch to the right-hand side of the road and pass the Saltwater Mill, where water is trapped at the Finnebrogue Lough. Later, you emerge from a tree-lined stretch of the busy road and pass Pheasant's Hill B&B. Just after passing a crossroads, where Killyleagh Rd becomes Downpatrick Rd, a gate on the right reveals a path and a sign for Delamont Country Park, though the main entrance is further along the road.

Delamont Country Park is an area of open grassy spaces and patchy woodlands set in the rolling drumlin countryside beside Strangford Lough. Drumlins are rolling hillocks of ill-sorted clay and rubble dumped by melting glaciers at the end of the Ice Age. All the hills you see, and all the islands in Strangford Lough, are formed of glacial debris. Rocks were plucked and scoured from distant mountains, then ground and crushed within and beneath great ice sheets, finally being dumped in massive heaps. While the Ulster Way doesn't yet run through the park, there are a multitude of paths to explore, some of them colour-coded to provide the Mullagh Walk, Garden Walk, Strangford Walk, Corbally Walk and the Long Walk. There is a visitor centre, garden centre, bird hide, shop, café and toilets. There is a paved footway across the main road from the main entrance to Delamont Country Park, which should be followed for safety's sake. Then the Ulster Way turns right along Shore Rd and runs down to the shore of Strangford Lough. It follows the shore for a short way, then the road rises and descends, continuing as Seaview. At the end of the road, turn left along Shore St to walk into the centre of Killyleagh.

The buzzard is best identified by its large size and its wheeling, soaring flight.

Killyleagh is a mill village offering a variety of shops and pubs. Accommodation is provided at the Dufferin Arms, at the top of High St, close to Killyleagh Castle. The castle dates from at least 1610, though it has been altered considerably through the centuries. It is a remarkable edifice, often compared to a French château, with outer walls and turrets rising above the road and enclosing a grand house within. Sir Hans Sloane was born in Killyleagh in 1660 and he amassed a collection of treasures, arts and artefacts which formed the basis of the British Museum collection.

WALK 34

KILLYLEAGH TO COMBER

Start: Killyleagh – 526526.

Finish: Comber – 462688.

Distance: 27 kilometres (17 miles).

Map: OSNI Discoverer Sheet 21.

Terrain: Mostly low-level roads, which are fairly quiet, but there are some busy stretches too.

Waymarking: Metal Ulster Way signposts are used along most of the roads.

Public Transport: Ulsterbus 11 links Killyleagh with Comber and Belfast.

Accommodation: There are only a couple of B&Bs offering accommodation around Killyleagh, Killinchy and Comber.

ROUTE DESCRIPTION

Killyleagh's High St leads up to Killyleagh Castle. Keep to the right of the castle, on a brick road, passing a tower mounted with war memorials. Shrigley Rd leads away from the castle, passing Killyleagh Primary School. Shrigley is a little village with some old mills, a shop and a curious ornamental monument which looks rather surprised to find itself in the area at all! Turn left to pass the monument and mills, passing an old millpond. Walk through a crossroads and climb uphill, then walk downhill and turn left along the main A22 road. Follow the road only a short way, then turn right along Ringdufferin Rd. Turn left up a narrower road, passing a farm and continuing on a rather patchy road and track flanked by hedgerows. When the tarmac surface becomes more uniform again, follow the road to a junction and turn left. Amazingly, for all the turnings and changes along the way, you are still on Ringdufferin Rd.

Continue through the rolling drumlin country and turn right up Quarterland Rd, following it over to Quarterland Bay and passing a couple of thatched houses along the way. The road rises away from the bay and descends. Turn right along Ballymorran Rd, which turns left and runs along the shore of Ballymorran Bay. It climbs uphill later,

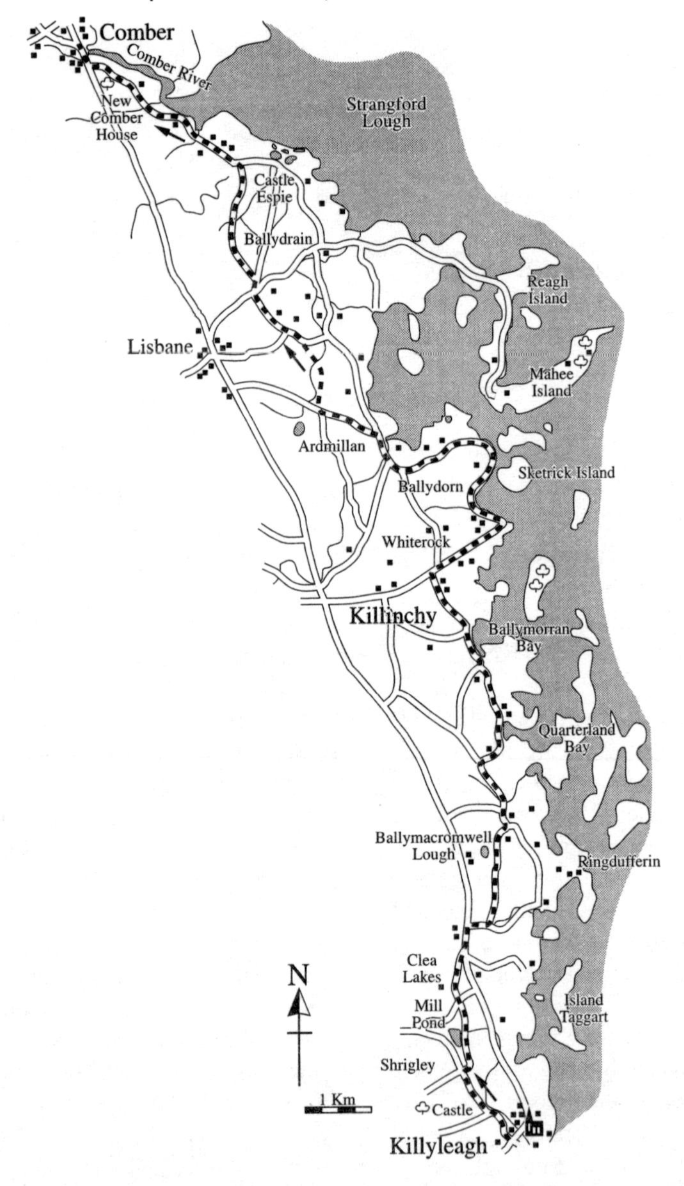

reaching a junction where a left turn will bring you to Killinchy, which has a B&B; the Ulster Way, however, turns right onto the switchback Whiterock Rd leading to Whiterock and the Tides Reach restaurant. Turn left to walk around Whiterock Bay, passing a car park and toilets on the way out of the village. A short diversion to the right across a causeway can allow a quick visit to Sketrick Island, one of fifty or so islands dotted around Strangford Lough. The ruins of Sketrick Castle face the causeway and date from at least 1470. The island is home to a sailing school and a bar and restaurant. Retrace your steps across the causeway to continue along the road.

The red-painted Ballydorn Lightship is permanently moored and is used by the Down Cruising Club. The road veers inland to the left, then you should keep right at road junctions to reach the little village of Ardmillan and its Orange Hall. After passing the hall, turn left; the road climbs uphill and there is a right turn along a grassy track at the top. The track quickly narrows to a path, which is tightly hemmed in by hedgerows. A broader track is joined and this leads down to the next tarmac road, which in turn is followed straight onwards. At the end of Lisbane Rd, turn quickly left and right and continue along Castle Espie Rd. Turn left to walk uphill and downhill along Ballyglighorn Rd, then turn left along Ballydrain Rd.

The otter, rare now, but still spotted on the quieter stretches of the Way. Watch out for otter slides in the river bank, where they slip into the water.

A right turn along Ballydrain Rd, incidentally, leads quickly to the Castle Espie Wildfowl and Wetlands Centre. Extending down to the shoreline and partly wooded, the landscape attracts swans, ducks, geese and other waders. Otters and badgers frequent the area, which also has a good cover of wildflowers. The centre includes a restaurant.

When Ballydrain Rd reaches the busy A22 road, turn right as signposted for Comber, but turn right again along the bed of an old railway track after passing a garage. If food, drink or accommodation is needed, continue into Comber. Most of its shops are arranged around a central square dominated by a column bearing a statue of Sir Robert Rollo Gillespie. His dying words, as he fell wounded in a battle in Nepal, were: 'One last shot for the honour of Down.'

WALK 35

COMBER TO HELEN'S BAY

Start: Comber – 462688.

Finish: Helen's Bay – 459830.

Distance: 23 kilometres (14 miles).

Map: OSNI Discoverer Sheet 15.

Terrain: A variety of roads, tracks and paths. Some roads can be busy. Many of the tracks and paths are in woodlands.

Waymarking: Rather patchy. Metal Ulster Way signposts are used along some of the roads. Wooden marker posts are used in some other places.

Public Transport: Ulsterbus 11 links Comber with Killyleagh and Belfast. Ulsterbus 5A links Comber and Newtownards. Newtownards has plenty of Ulsterbus services to Belfast, including 5, 7, 9 and 10. Helen's Bay has a railway service linking with Bangor and Belfast.

Accommodation: There are only a few B&Bs around Comber and Helen's Bay, but Newtownards has more accommodation options and there are plenty of places to stay off-route at Bangor or Belfast.

ROUTE DESCRIPTION

Comber is completely bypassed by the Ulster Way, which follows the route of an old railway track-bed running from the A22 road to the A21. At the end of the track, cross the A21 to reach a safe footway on the far side. Note an old railway cottage while turning right to leave Comber. A dual carriageway continues into the countryside, and this is followed straight through a crossroads. Turn left along and up a stony track running between hedgerows and passing through fields. Keep right at a couple of track junctions, passing farm buildings and an attractive whitewashed house until you reach a minor road at Killynether House. Turn left along the road, then right to enter Scrabo Country Park, where there is a car park in a mature, predominantly beech woodland.

Waymark posts and arrows indicate the course of the Ulster Way. Simply follow the clear path as it rises gently uphill from the car park, through a beech wood, bearing right later to climb steps and walk along the top side of the wood. The path leads to a car park higher up which you leave by following a clear track to Scrabo Tower. The hill bears the scant remains of an Iron Age hill fort, but the tower truly dominates the scene. There are fine views of the surrounding countryside from here, following the length of Strangford Lough to the Mountains of Mourne.

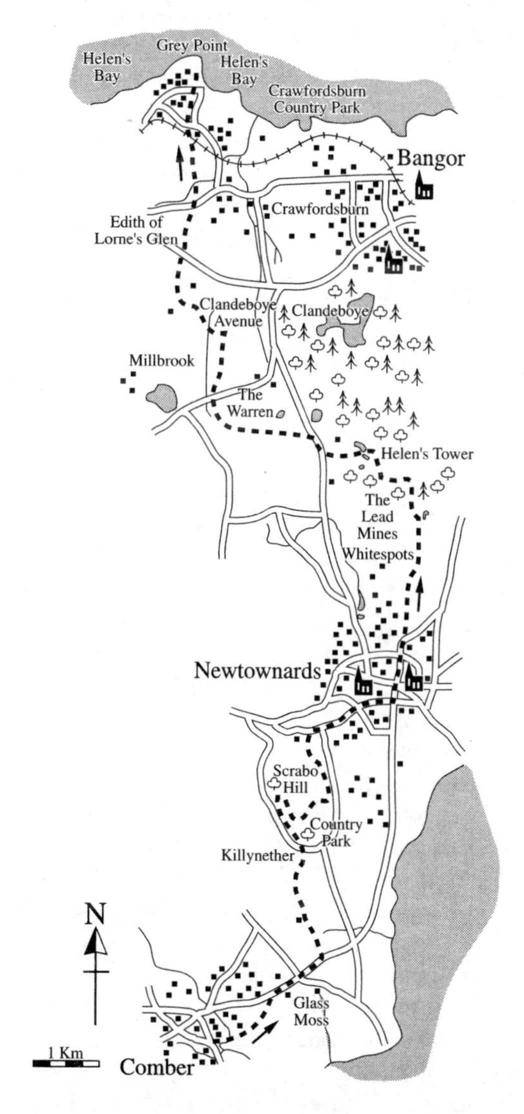

Belfast and the hills around the city can be seen off to the north. In 1683 William Montgomery mentioned 'the high hill called Scrabo ... ye stones whereof are well known in Dublin, and taken thither and elsewhere in great abundance'. Although most of Scrabo Hill is made of sandstone, the sandstone contains intrusive dykes of dolerite, which give the hill a hard cap and make it an outstanding feature in an otherwise low, rolling landscape. The tower, which is sometimes open to visitors, is properly called the Londonderry Monument and was built in memory of the 3rd Marquis of Londonderry, Charles William Stewart.

Scrabo Tower dominates the countryside around Scrabo Hill.

To leave the tower, follow a less well-defined path which cuts steeply down towards Newtownards, passing through scrub and zig-zagging down the wooded slopes. When you reach a broad, gravel path, turn left and follow it as it cuts across the side of the hill. Further along there is a turn-off to the left, where the path passes through a sheer-sided rock cutting and enters an old quarry. The North Quarry is now wonderfully overgrown, but it must have been an eyesore in its heyday. A broad, stony track leads onwards and finally descends to the Old Belfast Rd. Turn right to follow the road downhill; it soon levels out, and as you walk straight onwards it becomes Scrabo Rd and Mill St, passing a roundabout and continuing into the centre of Newtownards.

Newtownards is the 'new town' on the Ards Peninsula, a busy town with plenty of facilities. It is actually quite an old town, tracing its origins back to the founding of an abbey in the 6th century, and a ruined 13th-century friary can still be seen in town. The 'new town' was actually developed from the 17th century onwards. The well-dressed stone frontage of the Town Hall and Arts Centre faces the open space of Conway Square. To follow the Ulster Way, go round the back of the Town Hall, and follow North St due northwards. You will walk for some time before finding any Ulster Way markers. Follow the road uphill as if leaving town, reaching the entrance to a works depot. The depot is in an old quarry, and Quarry Heights is the name of the road continuing alongside the fence. It becomes rather patchy and is a rough track by the time it reaches stout blue gates. As you walk there are views along the length of Strangford Lough and back towards Scrabo Tower and the Mountains of Mourne. There are more gates to go through on the gradual ascent through fields and gorse scrub.

Away to the right is an old chimney standing in fields, but don't go near it. Instead, follow the track across the scrub-covered higher ground and aim straight towards another tall chimney. Take care, as the area is sometimes used by motorbike scramblers, and signs indicate which tracks are for scramblers and which are for walkers. The chimney is all that remains of the South Engine House which served South Mine, where shale beds covered rich lead deposits. Walk towards the stump of a derelict windmill which is quite prominent from a distance. The windmill was first used for grinding corn, then lead ore. You might like to refer to mapboards in this area, as there are potentially confusing intersections of tracks and paths, but there is a sign for the Ulster Way too.

Keep heading in roughly the same direction, following a clear track past a small pond, then pass a gateway and stile into a wood, and walk within sight of a golf course to pass another tall chimney at the edge of the wood. Waymark posts can be followed faithfully through the wood. The Ulster Way makes a sudden turn left, and later there is a prominent crossing of tracks. You could either head straight onwards, following the Ulster Way downhill, or turn right and follow another track to reach Helen's Tower at the top of the hill. The tower was completed in 1850 in honour of Helen, Lady Dufferin. If you go there, be sure to retrace your steps back to the Ulster Way afterwards. Follow the way down through the woods and turn left at another prominent crossing of tracks. The track crosses an embankment between two small ponds; the scenery here is quite charming and there may well be waterfowl about. Shortly afterwards, the route leaves the forest and follows a track which joins the busy B170 road close to the entrance to Ballyleidy sawmill.

Follow the road past the sawmill, then look out to the left for a stile and gate giving access to a woodland path. The woodland is actually a belt of trees, mostly beech and oak, threaded by a clear path. There is a view onto a golf course as the trees begin to thin out, and a couple of gates are passed before the track runs to another busy road. Cross the B170 road and pass the Old Schoolhouse, continuing along a broad, hedged track which rolls through the fields. When the track reaches gates at another belt of woodland, turn left to follow another woodland path. This is Clandeboye Avenue, which is wonderfully overgrown and a delight to follow. There is a gate along the way, then a gradual descent and exit onto the very busy A2 dual carriageway. At this point, there is no safe crossing, and a sign gives the following message:

'North Down Borough Council. Danger. Please note that this section of the Ulster Way terminates in 6 metres at the Bangor-Belfast dual carriageway. The next section commences on the opposite side of that dual carriageway. Persons who decide to continue are warned of the danger from traffic using that dual carriageway. They should exercise extreme caution crossing this busy thoroughfare. The Council accepts no responsibility for loss, death or personal injury occurring to persons crossing the dual carriageway.'

Across the road and slightly to the left you find the continuation of Clandeboye Avenue. The path leads down another belt of woodland, with double gates along the way. The path passes under a stone arch dated 1852, then a gate gives access to a narrow road. Follow the road until it turns left, then head straight on along another woodland track which runs into a cutting and passes beneath rail and road arches. There is access to Helen's Bay railway station, as well as to a couple of shops and a café. The track continues gently downhill, passing close to the back gardens of several houses and coming out in a car park. Leave the car park and cross the road: you can walk straight down to the beach at Helen's Bay or turn left to continue along the shore of Belfast Lough. There are a couple of places offering accommodation in the vicinity, while the railway line nearby offers frequent links with Belfast and Bangor, bringing many more accommodation options within easy reach.

WALK 36

HELEN'S BAY TO STORMONT

Start: Helen's Bay – 459830.

Finish: Stormont – 396740.

Distance: 18 kilometres (11 miles).

Map: OSNI Discoverer Sheet 15.

Terrain: A varied series of paths are linked to form the North Down Coastal Path; then, after following roads through Holywood, some steep woodland paths are followed at Redburn. Roads complete the day's walk.

Waymarking: There are a few marker posts along the coastal path. Metal Ulster Way signposts are used along most of the roads.

Public Transport: Helen's Bay has a railway service to Bangor and Belfast. Holywood can be reached from all railway stations. Ulsterbus services 1 and 2 link Holywood and Belfast. Fast and frequent Citybus services can be accessed throughout the suburbs of Belfast, especially along the Upper Newtownards Rd.

Accommodation: There is only one B&B at Helen's Bay, but several more options are available simply by travelling into nearby Bangor or Belfast. Holywood has a handful of B&Bs.

ROUTE DESCRIPTION

Leave Helen's Bay, following a road uphill from the bay until you reach a stile on the right bearing a sign for Crawfordsburn Country Park. There is also a blue arrow for the Coastal Walk through a woodland path which turns around Grey Point. A sign indicates a short diversion to the Grey Point Fort; built in 1904 to defend Belfast Lough, it served through both World Wars and is now occasionally open to visitors. The path continues around the point, following a low cliff-line and going through an old turnstile, and passes a boathouse at the end of a road. Keep following the path as it climbs up and down flights of concrete steps and passes through an arched gateway to regain the shore. Keep close to the shore to pass the Seahill sewage treatment works.

Scrub and bracken flank the path before it passes close to a school, then there are patches of shingle and rock at Rockport. As you walk

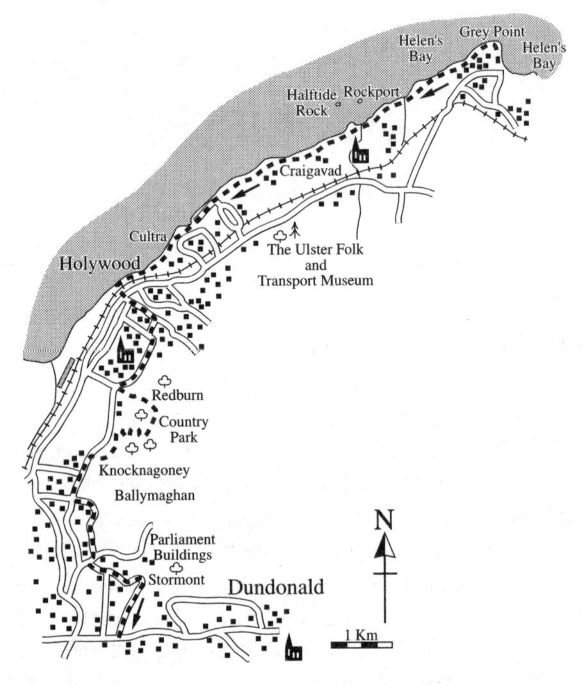

beside a tall wall, look out to the Halftide Rock, which may have seals hauled out on it, or cormorants drying their wings. After turning round a low, wooded point, the path runs beside the tall safety fence of a golf course, then continues along a narrow road beside the shore. A concrete path beside garden walls leads onto Glen Rd, then the route runs along the top of a sea wall for a while. The Ulster Folk and Transport Museum lies some distance inland, and though there is no direct access to it from the coast, it is worth making time for a visit. The easiest way to get there is to catch a train from Holywood to Cultra. The museum 'houses' a display of traditional Irish architecture, farmhouses, cottages, shops and pubs from all over Ireland which have been dismantled stone by stone and reassembled on the Cultra site. The folk park also contains a considerable collection of vintage vehicles and other artefacts. All in all, the place takes all day to explore properly.

A gravel track and Seafront Rd lead past the Royal Northern Ireland Yacht Club. After passing a small pier and slipway on Cultra Avenue, follow a path through a grassy parkland by the shore. The path gradually draws close to a railway line and eventually leads to Holywood Station, but there is a way under the railway before that point.

There is also a subway which can be used to avoid the traffic on the busy A2 dual carriageway, or you can simply cross the road and follow Shore Rd straight into the centre of Holywood. Holywood has a few B&Bs, plenty of shops, pubs and restaurants, and rapid access to Belfast.

The world's tallest permanent maypole stands at a crossroads in the centre of town, rising 20m (60ft) in the air. On a plan of the town dated 1625 something rather like a maypole is marked on the site, and it is recorded that when a Dutch ship ran aground here on May Eve, its main mast was cut down and used as the centrepiece of Holywood's May Day celebrations. The town derives its name from the Holy Wood, and although an ancient church of 620 AD is no longer in evidence, the old Priory church and graveyard date from the 13th century.

The cormorant, with wings outstretched, is a common sight around the coast and lakes.

Follow Church St uphill to pass the Church of Ireland, then turn right along Demesne Rd. This road features a left and right turn before passing Holywood Golf Course. When the road runs downhill, look out on the left for an entrance to Redburn Country Park. Redburn House no longer exists, its site now occupied by a nursing home, but it was owned by the Dunville family of Irish whiskey fame. A track known as Ardtullagh Avenue climbs uphill in Redburn Country Park, bending to the right as it climbs; then at a junction of paths the Ulster Way climbs to the top of a steep, wooded escarpment. Turn right and walk with the young trees of the New Plantation to the left and a slope of gorse bushes to the right. There are views across Holywood and Belfast Lough onward to Belfast and the Belfast Hills. Later, the path turns right and runs downhill, following waymark posts left indicating the course of the Ulster Way. A flight of steps leads out of the woods to a car park beside the Old Holywood Rd.

Turn left along the road, passing Knocknagoney Garage, then turn left up Glenmachan Rd from the Garnerville Presbyterian Church. When this leafy suburban road joins the busier Belmont Rd, turn right downhill, then left along Massey Avenue. The avenue leads to a stout set of gates giving access to the Stormont Estate. The road beyond the gates rises across a sloping parkland to the Parliament Buildings, a neo-Classical structure dating from 1932 which is the seat of government in Northern Ireland. Access is controlled and if you arrive at the gates too early or too late you will not be able to pass. (If the gates are closed, backtrack along Massey Avenue and turn left along Castlehill Road to reach the Upper Newtownards Road.) The Ulster Way turns around a statue of Lord Edward Carson, then follows the Prince of Wales Avenue downhill. You can walk through the avenues of trees which run parallel to the road if you want a break from road-walking. The lower sets of gates give way to the busy Upper Newtownards Rd. The Stormont Hotel stands to the left, but the Ulster Way turns right. There are frequent buses in and out of Belfast if lodgings or other facilities need to be reached.

WALK 37

STORMONT TO DUNMURRY

Start: Stormont – 396740.

Finish: Dunmurry Station – 293691.

Distance: 24 kilometres (15 miles).

Maps: OSNI Discoverer Sheet 15. The Greater Belfast Street Map is also useful.

Terrain: Roads, tracks and paths over the Castlereagh Hills, followed by woodland walking through the Lagan valley.

Waymarking: Metal Ulster Way signposts are used along most of the roads, with wooden marker posts in forests.

Public Transport: There are frequent Citybus services around the suburbs of Belfast, as well as a railway station at Dunmurry. There are also frequent City Stopper services around Dunmurry.

Accommodation: While some hotels and B&Bs occur quite close to the walk around the suburbs of Belfast, rapid public transport services bring most places in the city within reach.

ROUTE DESCRIPTION

Turning right after passing through the Stormont gates, the Ulster Way runs beside the busy Upper Newtownards Rd which can be crossed safely at the traffic lights beside the Stormont Presbyterian Church, after which you continue along the road called Thornhill Park. Turn right along Barnett's Rd, which runs beside the bed of an old railway track. Further along, but off-route, this old line becomes the Beersbridge Nature Walk and Bloomfield Walkway. Turn left along the busy King's Rd, then turn right at the traffic lights to follow Gilnahirk Rd, passing a row of shops. Follow the road uphill and pass St Dorothea's Church of Ireland to reach Gilnahirk Presbyterian Church. Turn right up the track known as the Rocky Rd, which climbs between hedgerows high above the city, running through fields and becoming a concrete lane later. It reaches a road junction near Gilnahirk Golf Course, where a right turn leads along Upper Braniel Rd. This road passes the Hillmount Nursery Centre, which has a café. Continue along and downhill, reaching a crossroads with the busier Ballygowan Rd. Cross over and walk up Manse Rd. Turn left along Lisnabreeny Rd, though you could detour right first to admire Castlereagh Presbyterian Church. Lisnabreeny Rd dips downhill, then climbs over a crest.

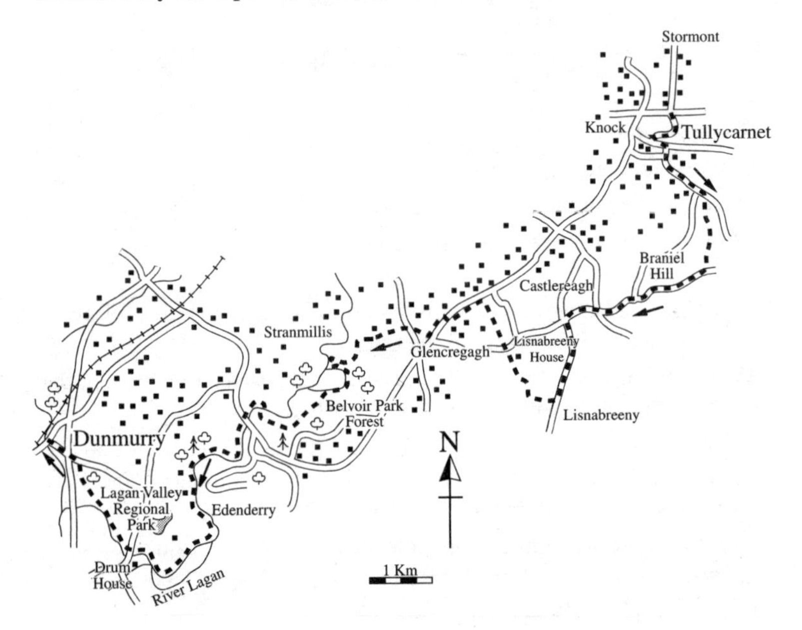

Off to the right is a car park, where the National Trust has improved the Lisnabreeny Path. This path passes an ancient rath, or ring fort, surrounded by trees planted in the 19th century. The path enjoys a fine view over Belfast and the Belfast Hills as it descends through fields alongside a golf course and passes close to Lisnabreeny House, which is now home to Lagan College's music department. The college, which opened in 1981, was the first integrated school in Northern Ireland. A tunnel with a wooden walkway passes under Glencregagh Rd to reach the top of Cregagh Glen. This is a fine, wooded ravine owned by the National Trust, featuring a well constructed pathway equipped with flights of steps and a series of footbridges. There is no mistaking the way down through the glen, though it is also possible to explore the glen's other paths, which you bring you higher over the city. Cregagh Glen changes with the seasons, covered with foliage throughout the summer months, while in autumn the golden hues can be breathtaking. The path zig-zags down through the glen and finally debouches onto the busy dual carriageway, Upper Knockbreda Rd. The contrast between the quiet glen and the busy city could not be more complete.

Turn left on leaving the glen, walking along the footway beside the road or, better still, along the residential Beechgrove Drive which runs at a slightly higher level parallel to the main road. When Beechgrove Drive leads back to the main road, cross over safely using a prominent footbridge, then continue along the main road, passing Knockbreda High School. Turn right down Upper Galwally, between the shopping developments of the Drumkeen Complex and Forestside. Cross Saintfield Rd at the traffic lights and continue straight onwards down a quiet residential road. Turn quickly right and left to continue down Galwally Avenue, where things become much quieter.

Towards the end of the avenue, after passing a small pool managed as a bird reserve, watch for a woodland path starting from a set of bollards. Two stout stiles are passed, then the Ulster Way is marked along a woodland path to the right in Belvoir Park Forest. The path descends to follow the River Lagan, and while you could continue beside the river, another path takes you up to a car park and the Forest Education Centre, based in a fine courtyard building. The Belvoir estate dates from Plantation times and was first enclosed by the Hills of Hillsborough. After many changes of ownership it became a naval arms depot, before becoming a public amenity in 1961. Colour-coded walks around Belvoir Park Forest include the Lagan Trail, Breda Trail and Garden Trail; information about them can be obtained from the Education Centre or from noticeboards. The RSPB (Royal Society for the Protection of Birds) also has an office in the building.

The Ulster Way keeps to the right to pass the Education Centre and follows another path going down through the woods again. Walk through a crossing of paths and drift uphill, turning right at the next path junction and walking downhill again. Cross a stone step-stile to leave the woods and walk across a humpbacked bridge over the weed-filled Lagan Canal. The River Lagan was made navigable piecemeal; side-canals with locks were built to open the waterway as far as Lisburn by the 1760s. Turn left and walk along a narrow tarmac road beside the canal, then cross a broad wooden bridge over the river. Walk past a car park to the left and continue into Clement Wilson Park, following a tarmac path set on a raised embankment – the embankment was made from demolished air-raid shelters and is known as the Burma Rd. The path can be followed between lines of young trees to the River Lagan, then under a busy road bridge to reach the stone arches of Shaw's

Bridge. Shaw's Bridge was originally a wooden structure which allowed Cromwell to get his big guns across the river in 1655. The stone-arched bridge dates from 1709, but now carries only pedestrian traffic.

From a car park at Shaw's Bridge, the Ulster Way is signposted along the Lagan Canal Towpath. There are gates at the start, another gate further along the tarmac path, then the wooden arch of Gilchrist Bridge. The bridge leads over to Edenderry, and if you cross to explore this old mill village you must make your way back to this point. The towpath leaves the River Lagan and follows a spur canal past the Eel Weir picnic site. An old lock is passed further along, and later a rickety bridge (which isn't used) spans the old canal. The towpath runs alongside the River Lagan later, then goes through a gate and beneath a busy road at Drum Bridge. The little village of Drumbeg, with its fine church and a pub, is just a short way along the road, on the other side of the river; many of the people who founded the city of Belfast are buried in the village churchyard. The path drifts away from the river and enters Sir Thomas and Lady Dixon Park. The Stables coffee house can be visited at this point, or you could explore the City of Belfast International Rose Gardens which spread out near by.

Instead of stopping at the coffee house, you could keep left and stay on the rugged, wooded margins of the park, passing a fenced compound and picking up a narrow path. The path can be muddy in places later, and there are glimpses of the Lagan alongside. After crossing an inflowing stream, the path climbs up a grassy slope planted with an interesting variety of young trees, with views back across the park. Pick up and follow a path through more mature woodland, gradually drifting down towards a busy road. The path moves away from the road, then leaves the woodlands and joins a quiet suburban road, Dunmurry Lane. Turn left and follow it uphill, then downhill, and cross the road at a bridge. Pass the Beechlawn Hotel and continue through a set of traffic lights to reach the railway station at Dunmurry.

DONEGAL SECTION

County Donegal

Distance: 111 kilometres (69 miles)

When the Ulster Way was being developed in a huge circuit around Northern Ireland, a spur was also routed through Co. Donegal. The driving force behind the trail was Gaye Moynihan, and she was visited on occasion by Wilfrid Capper, who showed a great interest in the development of the route. This stretch of the Ulster Way runs northwards from Pettigo to Falcarragh by way of Lough Eske, Fintown and Dunlewy. It is more of a wilderness walk than the rest of the Ulster Way, passing through empty forests and across bogs and mountains. It is rough and tough underfoot in many places and often there are no paths. The route calls for careful navigation with a map and compass in poor visibility. Unlike the rest of the Ulster Way, this trail has 'nondirectional' marker posts, rather than arrows or signposts. The posts indicate that you are still on course, but unless you can spot the next one in line, you will have to do your own trail-finding.

I was once asked to play the role of go-between at a time when Cospóir (The National Sports Council) wanted to upgrade the route with the co-operation of Donegal County Council. Although an offer was made to secure funding for the route, it was quickly rejected. It was felt that too many waymarks would be an intrusion and footbridges over rivers in remote areas would reduce the wild quality of the region. What today's walker will find, therefore, is a very sparsely marked route, without paths in places, with a number of rivers to ford and no markers at all on the northern stretches. This section of the Ulster Way is for capable navigators only; for those who can look after themselves in the mountains; for those who are adequately prepared for a walk on the wild side.

A great measure of self-sufficiency is required on this walk, as there are no towns and only a couple of small villages along the way, and very few shops and pubs. There are long walks between places offering food, drink and accommodation. Wise walkers will book their beds in advance or ensure that someone will meet them at agreed stages of the route. If anything brings progress to a halt in the more remote parts of the mountains, then walkers may need to spend the night in the wilds. The terrain can be energy-sapping and you may need more food and drink than you imagine. On the bleak and exposed mountainsides, bad weather can be debilitating, and you need to be ready for any eventuality.

Be warned before setting out that conditions can be very bad in wet weather. Bogs can be very soft after heavy rain and rivers can swell to the point where they become impassable. The main circuit of the Ulster Way around Northern Ireland is a challenging walk in itself, but one might well regard it as a preparation for the spur through the Donegal highlands!

WALK 38

PETTIGO TO LOUGH ESKE

Start: Pettigo – 109668.

Finish: Ardeevin, Lough Eske – 987828.

Distance: 29 kilometres (18 miles).

Map: OSI Discovery Sheet 11.

Terrain: Mostly roads and tracks through farmland, forest and bog, but there is a wet and muddy forest ride in the middle of the day's walk.

Waymarking: Sparse non-directional marker posts are used and careful map-reading is essential.

Public Transport: Ulsterbus 194 links Pettigo with Enniskillen, with some services extending to Belleek. Bus Éireann 31 and 68 offer summer services to Pettigo, linking with Enniskillen and Sligo respectively. Bus Éireann 64, 69 and 480 run along the main road towards the end of the day, offering services to and from Donegal Town.

Accommodation: There are a few B&Bs around Pettigo. A few B&Bs can also be found on the roads around Lough Eske.

ROUTE DESCRIPTION

Think carefully about your needs before leaving Pettigo. There are no shops or pubs on this day's walk, and if the Ulster Way is followed faithfully there will be no shops or pubs until Fintown is reached. There are, however, bus services on the main road at the end of the day, linking with Donegal Town and Letterkenny. You should book your night's accommodation in advance if you want to stay near Lough Eske, or make other arrangements to be collected at the end of the day if you are staying elsewhere.

Before leaving Pettigo, a visit to the Lough Derg Journey Heritage Centre offers walkers an insight into the famous Lough Derg pilgrimage prior to setting off on their own journey. The centre offers a highly colourful interpretation of the ancient pilgrimage, using everything from candles to ultra-violet lighting, mirrors and music, with quotes from Irish writers such as Heaney, Kavanagh and Yeats supported by Shakespeare and Dante. The idea, evidently, is to illustrate the pilgrimage's Celtic origins.

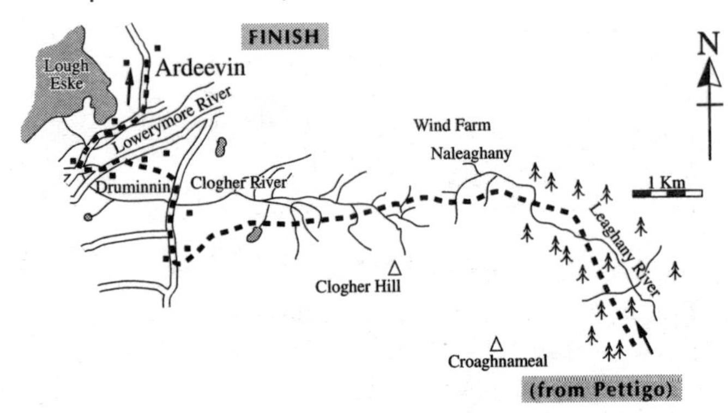

Leave Pettigo by following the Lough Derg road, or R233, which is signposted from a monument in the middle of the village. Continue straight onwards, passing a turning signposted for Lettercran, rising and falling through fertile farmland, then passing another turning for Lettercran. When the road descends gently and bends right, continue straight onwards up a narrow road. There is a signpost pointing left for Carn Graveyard. Although off the course of the Ulster Way, Carn was often visited by pilgrims on their journey to Lough Derg. The road rises alongside a small forest and passes a couple of farms, then comes down to a crossroads. Walk straight through and uphill, rising from fields to broad bogland, with a view of Lough Derg to the left. The sight of St Patrick's Purgatory, which looks as if it were sailing on the waters of the lake like a spiritual battleship, has a certain surreal quality which stands in complete contrast to the wilderness all around.

Myths and legends, mystery and history have gathered round Lough Derg for centuries. It is said that after Fionn Mac Cumhail killed a witch on the shores of the lough, the warrior Conan chanced upon her bones. He was warned that the thigh bone contained a worm which would grow into a ravenous monster once it touched the lough; nonetheless he broke the bone and cast the worm into the water. Sure enough, the worm became a monster devouring sheep, cattle and people: some two hundred cattle a day eventually had to be driven onto the nearby hill of Crocknacunny to feed him. Conan resolved to put an end to the beast and, hiding among the cattle, allowed himself to be swallowed whole, then proceeded to hack his way out, wounding the creature grievously. St Patrick, however, is credited with dealing the final death-blow. The monster's blood stained the water red, hence the name Lough Derg or *dearg*.

Another legend holds that when St Patrick had difficulty explaining hell and purgatory to the Irish, he retired to a cave on a small island in the lough where God granted him a fearful vision of the afterlife to help him give a convincing account to the pagan natives. For centuries afterwards, pilgrims from all over Europe made their way to Lough Derg in search of a similar vision, despite being exhorted not to attempt the experience: a 12th-century knight called Owen was besieged by demons for several days during his visit. Today's pilgrims are expected to fast for twelve hours before reaching Lough Derg, where they make

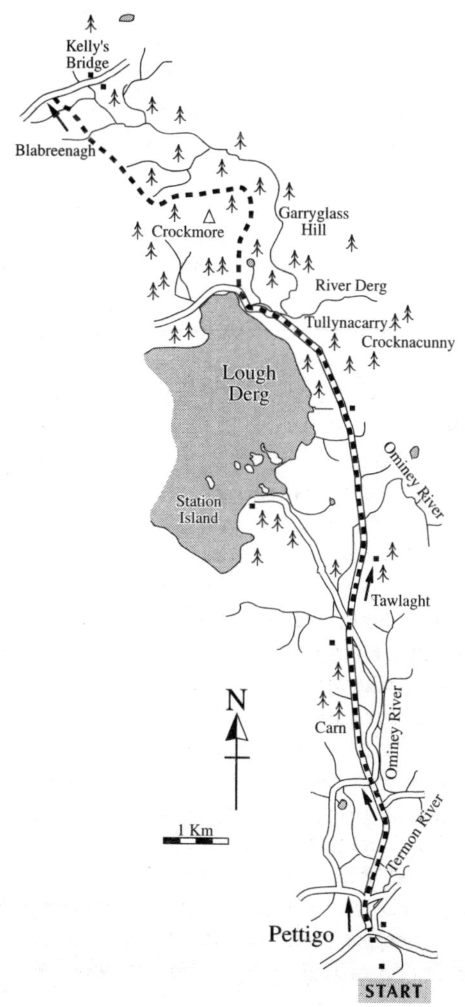

rounds of the island in their bare feet, praying and performing other rituals for three days while subsisting on black tea or coffee with only biscuits to eat, and fast for a further twelve hours after leaving the island. If the truth be told, the Donegal section of the Ulster Way is a much tougher trial than St Patrick's Purgatory!

The road enters an extensive tract of forestry on the slopes of Crocknacunny. Turn left at a road junction to touch the shore of Lough Derg briefly, crossing the outflowing River Derg. There is a building off to the right along an access road, but continue further into the forest and turn right along the next forest track, passing a barrier gate. Follow the track uphill, then turn left further uphill. The track bends to the right, then another left turn leads up past another barrier gate. Marker posts tend to look rather like old tree stumps and are not really obvious, but traces of white paint may help to identify them. The track reaches a high right bend, then runs downhill to cross a stream on the slopes of Binna Hill. Ahead, on a distant mountain, is a whirling wind farm. The Ulster Way runs fairly close to it, so keep it in your sights if the day is clear. If the day is misty, then take special care with map-reading.

The Ulster Way heads off to the right, leaving the track to follow a grassy forest ride. The marker posts are quite obvious, but the ride is tussocky and boggy and proves quite difficult to traverse on foot. The ride leads back onto the forest track later, so if you want to stay on the track and enjoy an easier walk, then do so. The track continues on an undulating course until it reaches a narrow tarmac road. This road doesn't feature on most maps, but in its broadest sense it could be said to provide a new cross-Border link between Donegal Town and Castlederg. There are few habitations along its course and it carries very little traffic.

Turn left up the road, then turn right down another forest track. Keep straight onwards and walk uphill at a junction, then look out for a grassy ride drifting slightly to the right of the track. This ride has to be followed, as the stony track ends abruptly further along. Cross a stream and follow the ride uphill. There are marker posts, but the ground is very wet and boggy. Although a drainage ditch has been cut, heavy machinery has left the ground in a perilously soft state so tread carefully and expect to sink in places. Eventually, the Leaghany River cuts across the ride and has to be forded, which can be difficult in wet weather. Continue uphill to a point where two forest rides cross, and turn left. Walk straight through another intersection of rides to reach the edge of the forest. A line of marker posts leads across a boggy moorland, and the turbines of the upland wind farm are seen at close quarters across Lough Naleaghany.

The marker posts show the way onto a bog road, which later joins the broad access track leading down from the wind farm. This track is an intrusion in the wilderness and has obliterated the old bog road for most of its length. However, it provides a way down that is easy, dry and obvious to follow. There are views across Lough Eske to the Blue Stack Mountains, through the Barnesmore Gap and round to Donegal Bay. Continue straight onto a tarmac road and walk downhill through farmland. Turn right at a junction, then keep right along a road signposted for Ballybofey which brings you across Clogher Bridge. The road climbs and there are two narrow roads off to the left; take the second one, which leads past a few houses to drop suddenly down to the busy N15 road at Druminnin. There is a telephone box beside the road, which may prove useful. There are a couple of B&Bs in the direction of Donegal Town and a few more on the road around Lough Eske, which is signposted near by as the Lough Eske Drive. To lessen the next day's distance, turn right along the Lough Eske road, then right again, then left to find one of the B&Bs situated along the road.

WALK 39

LOUGH ESKE TO FINTOWN

Start: Ardeevin, Lough Eske – 987828

Finish: Fintown – 924023.

Distance: 35 kilometres (22 miles).

Map: OSI Discovery Sheet 11.

Terrain: A few roads and tracks, but mostly rugged bogland and mountainsides, which may be pathless in places. The Owendoo River may prove impassable after heavy rain.

Waymarking: Sparse non-directional marker posts are used and careful map-reading is essential.

Public Transport: Bus Éireann 64, 69 and 480 run along the main road near Lough Eske, offering services to and from Donegal Town. McGeehan's Coaches operate a local service around Fintown, linking with Glenties and Letterkenny.

Accommodation: A few B&Bs are located in the countryside around Lough Eske. Fintown has only very limited B&B accommodation.

ROUTE DESCRIPTION

Continue along the Lough Eske Drive, following the road roughly parallel to the eastern shore, though there is only an occasional glimpse of the water. The winding road passes several houses, crosses Corabber Bridge and climbs uphill in a sweeping zig-zag. Turn right along a narrower tarmac road, crossing Greenan Bridge and Edergole Bridge, then follow a stony track beyond the last farm buildings. The track passes a small forest and fords a river, then zig-zags up a rugged slope to reach Doonan Waterfall. Although a fine little waterfall can be seen on the Corabber River, the Doonan Waterfall is tucked out of sight in a rocky gorge, but can seen by making a short diversion to the right. The track ends at a small water intake.

Follow a boggy path roughly parallel to the Corabber River. There are marker posts and, as this is a popular access point for the Blue Stack Mountains, the path is well trodden. Further up the valley, after crossing a couple of streams and passing some rough knolls, the route needs more care. Do not overshoot the broad gap at the head of the valley, but drift gradually to the left up and across a rugged slope to reach a higher gap at 400m (1,300ft). In mist this is a tricky move, but if successfully accomplished a line of marker posts leads down the far side towards the Owendoo River. There is a boggy, stony path across the mountainside which leads down to a ruined stone sheepfold. Cross the floor of the valley to reach the Owendoo River and look for a safe ford. After heavy rain, the river may be impassable, a bad trap for hapless wanderers because you do have to cross it.

The Ulster Way leads downstream, but tends away from the river and climbs over a broad and boggy shoulder to reach Letterkillew. A straggly row of farms can be seen on the far side of the glen, and there is a farm access road which can be gained if this day is to be cut short for any reason. The nearby settlement of Commeen is well off-route downstream and has only basic services. The farm access road also extends left up through the forest, offering an easier alternative route to the next high gap. To stick to the Ulster Way, however, turn left and walk roughly parallel to the Owengarve River, tracing it upstream. The ground here is often wet and muddy. Only one farm building stands on the southern side of the Poldoo Glen, while the head of the glen is under forest. Keep to the left of the forest, in the shadow of the bouldery Glascarns Hill, picking a way up towards the gap at the head of the glen. Marker posts show the way across the gap at around 300m (985ft) and down the far side towards an isolated farm at Crolack.

Follow the track away from Crolack, crossing a bridge over the Reelan River and climbing uphill. Turn left on a tarmac road to pass an old school and a young forest, as well as a couple of old farmsteads. This sparsely settled area is known as The Croaghs. After passing a more modern house, look out for a sketchy track on the right which leads onto a boggy slope. Follow this track a short way and cross a fence, then aim for an obvious gap between Croveenananta and a subsidiary summit called Lacroagh. Marker posts need to be searched for with care on the way across a moorland; the route is like a switchback, running roughly northwards across hummocky bogland and streams. A fence needs to be crossed first near Lacroagh, while later it is best to keep to the right of a fence until a stream in a rocky gorge can be safely crossed. There is a fine view westwards towards Lough Ea before a minor road is reached.

Turn right along the road and pass a turning to the left. Go through a gate on the left afterwards and follow a grassy track down to a con-

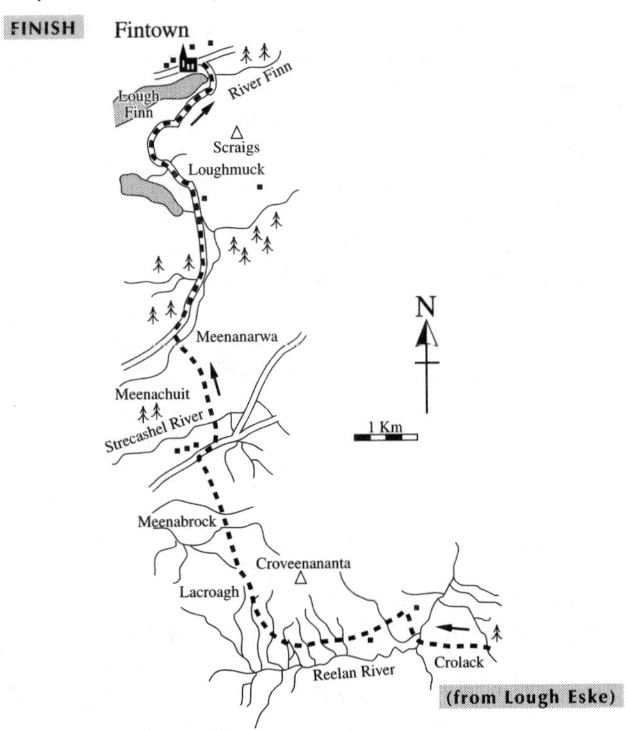

crete bridge over the Strecashel River. Walk uphill and cross a stony track on a newly forested slope. Continue over the crest of the hill and walk down to cross another bridge. A short ascent leads to another minor road. Turn right to follow this road through young forest, passing into fields and climbing to the little hillside settlement of Loughmuck. There are good views over Lough Muck as the road crosses a high shoulder and passes a water tank. On the way downhill, the road cuts across the lower slopes of a rugged hill called Scraigs, overlooking Lough Finn and Fintown.

When the minor road crosses the outflowing River Finn it climbs to join the R252 road. The Ulster Way turns right at this point, but weary wayfarers will doubtless turn left into the village of Fintown. Walk past St Colmcille's Roman Catholic church to the village, which has a couple of shops, a pub and a café. There is the little Fintown Railway to visit at An Mhuc Dhubh Station, but the only real transport service in the valley is provided by McGeehan's Coaches. Accommodation is quite limited and if a bed cannot be secured then you may need to travel on towards Glenties. McGeehan's offer local services both ways along the road from Fintown.

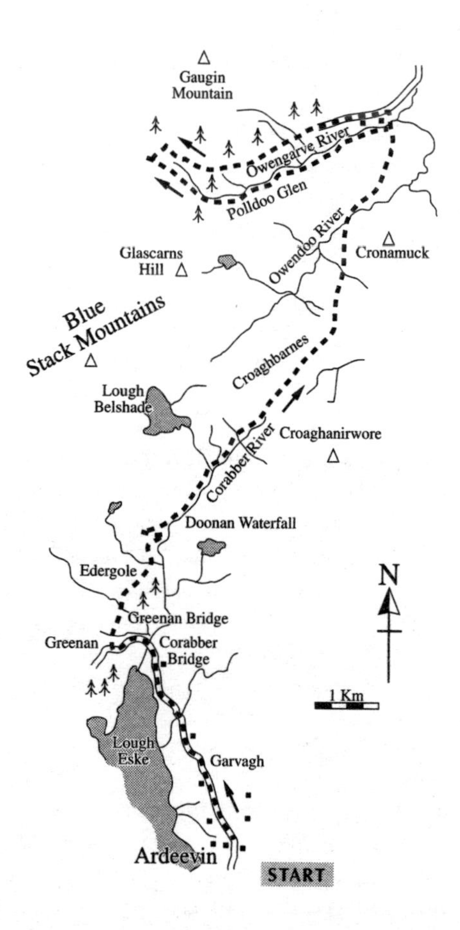

WALK 40

FINTOWN TO DUNLEWY

Start: Fintown – 924023.

Finish: Dunlewy – 923197.

Distance: 29 kilometres (18 miles).

Maps: OSI Discovery Sheets 1, 6 and 11.

Terrain: A few roads and tracks, but mostly rugged bogland and mountainsides, which may be pathless in places.

Waymarking: Sparse non-directional marker posts are used and careful map-reading is essential.

Public Transport: McGeehan's Coaches operate a service around Fintown, linking with Glenties and Letterkenny. There is no public transport around Dunlewy.

Accommodation: Fintown has only very limited B&B accommodation. There are a couple of B&Bs and hostels at Dunlewy.

ROUTE DESCRIPTION

Leave Fintown by following the R250 road in the direction of Letterkenny. After leaving the village the road enters a forest, where you turn left along a narrower road. Emerging from the forest, the road leads into the quiet Glenaboghil, past a handful of small farms and into an area of young forest. At the end of the road a prominent track turns down to the left, but keep walking straight on from a gate along a less clear rushy track. This continues through young forest, passing a few old ruins. After crossing a dip in the track, climb over to a ruined farmstead in a clump of sycamores. A grassy track runs downhill to the left, crossing a newly forested valley. Step over a small log bridge and follow the track uphill and across a fence.

Look carefully for marker posts as Lough Muck cannot be seen at first on this broad barren moorland. When it is seen, keep to the left-hand side to reach the gap at its head. The gap is spattered with little pools and you should aim to reach the firmer ground beyond before picking your way around the steep slopes of Crockastoller. Again, look carefully for marker posts, which show the way round into a valley

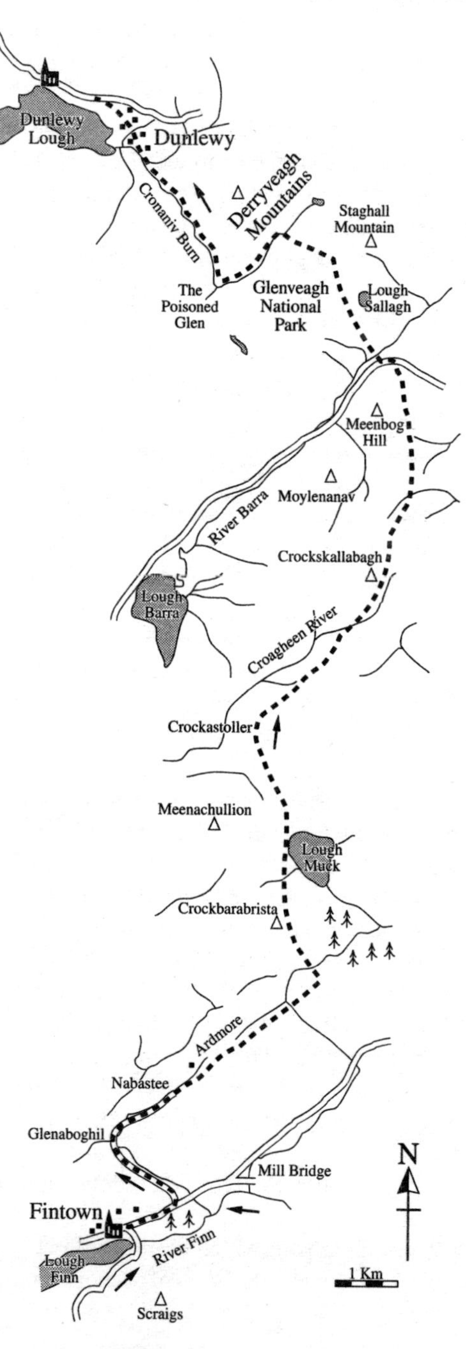
Dunlewy Lough
Dunlewy
Derryveagh Mountains
Cronaniv Burn
Staghall Mountain
The Poisoned Glen
Glenveagh National Park
Lough Sallagh
Meenbog Hill
Moylenanav
River Barra
Crockskallabagh
Lough Barra
Croagheen River
Crockastoller
Meenachullion
Lough Muck
Crockbarabrista
Ardmore
Nabastee
Glenaboghil
Mill Bridge
N
Fintown
Lough Finn
River Finn
Scraigs
1 Km

drained by the Croagheen River. Pick any course towards the head of the valley, but don't climb too high on the boulder-strewn slopes of Crockastoller, and don't walk too close to the river either. Cross the river towards the head of the valley and follow the marker posts across the shoulder of Crockskallabagh at around 450m (1,475ft). Keen hill-walkers might like to make a bid for the nearby summit of Moylenanav.

Take care on the descent, which is roughly northwards and involves crossing a stream and a boggy gap while heading for the shoulder of Meenbog Hill. There are no paths and in mist you need to navigate with map and compass. A final marker post stands near a broad bend on the R254 road. The rest of the Ulster Way through Donegal is unmarked. It hardly matters: anyone who has managed to get this far is obviously a competent navigator and should have no trouble with the rest of the route. Turn left to follow the road, but keep an eye peeled to the right, as there is a fine view along the length of Glenveagh, taking in Lough Veagh and Glenveagh Castle. Ahead are the rugged Derryveagh Mountains which form part of the Glenveagh National Park.

St Colmcille, Ireland's greatest missionary saint and founder of monastic settlements from Donegal around to Scotland, was born at Lough Gartan near Glenveagh in the year 521 AD. Little more is heard of Glenveagh for a thousand years, when in 1608, Caher O'Doherty retired to 'the unknown and inaccessible fastnesses of Glyn-Lough Vagh' to evade the English forces. In the 19th century Glenveagh was purchased by John George Adair, a man remembered as a particularly harsh landlord. He was in constant dispute with his tenants, eventually evicting them in a shameful manner. Glenveagh Castle, which was built from 1868, lends a certain Scottish air to the glen. Adair died in 1885, but his wife Cornelia continued to develop the estate, stocking it with red deer. She is remembered as a gracious hostess, throwing parties and taking in Belgian refugees in the First World War. The castle was caught up in the Troubles of the 1920s, and in later years was bought by Henry McIlhenny of Philadelphia, who enhanced the castle and its gardens. He sold the estate to the Office of Public Works, which was keen to obtain a property in Co. Donegal to develop as a national park, and shortly before he died in 1986 he gave Glenveagh Castle as a gift to the State. In effect, the State obtained a wild, remote landscape already tailor-made as a national park. This is the only national park on the Ulster Way.

Look for a stalking path which climbs to the top of a tumbling watercourse on the mountainside. While it cannot be joined easily on its ascent from the head of Glenveagh, it is possible to walk uphill and join it at the top. Leave the R254 road and cross a dip to reach a tall deer fence. There is no gate and the national park authorities do not recommend climbing the fence: the accepted method is to squeeze through at waist level, taking care not to strain the wires. Once through the fence, follow the stream to the top of the slope and maybe use the path for a short stretch. There is a tract of rock and bog to be negotiated where special care is needed.

The idea is to cross the rugged Ballaghgeeha Gap and find a way down into the Poisoned Glen. Spend some time scouting around to locate a relatively short and not-too-steep initial descent. The upper part of the glen bears plenty of bog asphodel, brightening the tussocky grass and heather, and in the near distance the splendid pyramid of Errigal pierces the sky. While tracing a small river downstream the deer fence has to be negotiated again. The lower part of the Poisoned Glen is very boggy, with tussocks of grass and bog myrtle, while massive boilerplate slabs of granite rise towards the head of the glen and to the domed summit of Slieve Snaght.

Ireland hosts three types of deer: red deer, fallow deer and sika deer. Pictured here is the red deer, the largest of the deer still to be found in the Donegal and Wicklow Mountains.

There are a vague series of squelchy paths through the Poisoned Glen, and it is best to stay on the eastern side of the river throughout. The settlement of Dunlewy can be seen ahead; a ruined church is also prominent. A stone arch brings you across another river and the track eventually leads you out of the glen. When a road bend is reached, keep to the right and walk uphill, passing the ruined Church of Ireland building. A few farms and houses are passed, and a couple of B&Bs. When the road joins the R251, the Ulster Way turns right. Anyone wishing to reach a larger range of facilities, however, should turn left. The road leads to a couple of shops and B&Bs, as well as a pub and hostels. If you have time to spare in the area you could visit the Dunlewy Centre, which has a café and craft centre.

WALK 41

DUNLEWY TO FALCARRAGH

Start: Dunlewy – 923197.

Finish: Falcarragh – 934322.

Distance: 18 kilometres (11 miles).

Map: OSI Discovery Sheet 1.

Terrain: Upland tracks and paths can be rough, wet and boggy. The final stretch to Falcarragh is on minor roads.

Waymarking: The stretch from Dunlewy to Falcarragh has never been waymarked.

Public Transport: There is no public transport around Dunlewy. Lough Swilly Buses serve Falcarragh, linking with Derry. O'Donnell's Coaches run to Belfast, while McGinley's Coaches run to Dublin.

Accommodation: There are a couple of B&Bs and hostels at Dunlewy. Falcarragh has a few B&Bs and a hostel.

ROUTE DESCRIPTION

Follow the R251 road uphill from Dunlewy, passing a car park offering a fine view of the Poisoned Glen and Derryveagh Mountains. The road rises gradually around the lower slopes of Errigal. As the road begins to level out on a broad moorland, you will find a number of places from where you could start on an ascent of Errigal; one is at a small parking place where a boggy pathway brings you onto a steep and stony ridge leading to the summit. It's an optional detour and one which is worth considering on a clear day. To continue along the course of the Ulster Way, follow the road further and look out for an old track running off to the left. A solitary gate pier is all that marks this point.

The track climbs gently uphill, opening up views of the surrounding mountains of Errigal, Slieve Snaght and Dooish. Squelchy bog has overwhelmed the track in places, but the line is always clear. A sweeping zig-zag brings you round a rugged hump off to the left known as the Chrystal Rock, which is embedded with clusters of quartz crystals. The track crosses a shoulder and starts to descend in sweeping loops towards Altan Lough. On a clear day, this is one of the great scenic

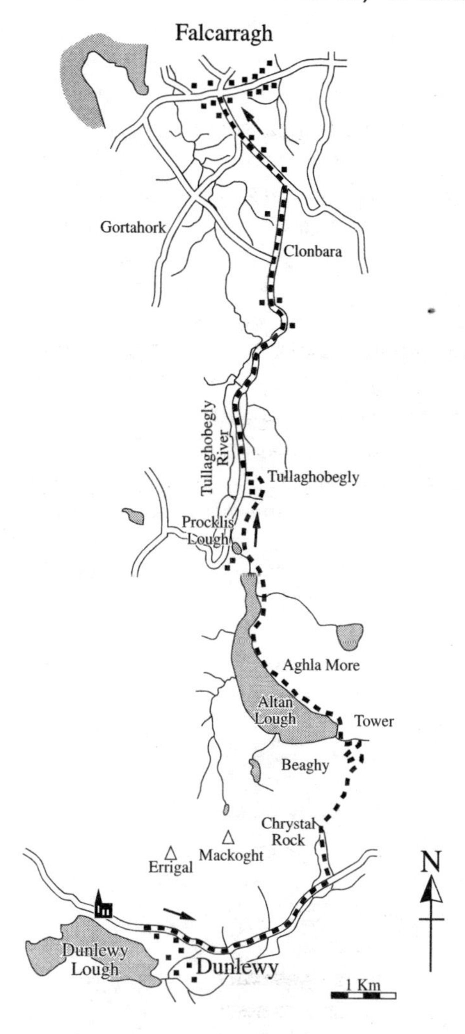

highlights of the Ulster Way. A ruined tower-house stands at the head of the lough, with Aghla More towering overhead. A little beach by the lough-side gives way to a greensward which is sometimes enlivened with wild iris.

Walk along a narrow sheep-path beside the lough, around the foot of Aghla More. The steep slope is covered in bracken at first, becoming rocky, then later there is heather and scree. Towards the foot of the lough the slope is gentler, but more heathery and boggy. While it is possible to ford the outflowing Tullaghobegly River, it is likely to leave walkers with wet feet. Instead, head onwards across a broad, gently sloping moorland hump. When clumps of trees are seen on the far side, keep well to the right, crossing a couple of fences. This part of Tullaghobegly is mostly in ruins, and once the last of the trees and ruins are passed, it is possible to join a minor road running northwards.

The road winds through the countryside past a number of farms and ruins, then later crosses the course of an old railway line. A stretch of the road runs across a broad bogland, leaving behind a mountainous panorama which reaches from Muckish to Errigal; the course of the arduous Glover Highland Walk, or simply 'the marathon'. The village of Falcarragh and the profile of Tory Island can be seen ahead. Although there is a road leading off to the left, keep straight onwards and turn left at the next road junction. A feature of interest off to the left later is the 13th-century Tullaghobegly church and graveyard. The road runs directly into Falcarragh, ending at a crossroads where all the services of the village are readily to hand. Food, drink and accommodation are all available, and when the time comes to leave, a variety of buses and coaches run as far afield as Derry, Belfast, Dublin, and even Glasgow.

On the wetlands, wild iris (*Iris pseudacorus*) produces its vivid yellow flowers in May and June.

USEFUL INFORMATION

TRANSPORT

Ulsterbus timetables and information, Belfast (028) 9033 3000.

Citybus timetables and information, Belfast (028)) 9024 6485.

Northern Ireland Railway timetables and information, Belfast (028) 9089 9411.

Bus Éireann timetables and information, Dublin (01) 8366111.

Lough Swilly Bus timetables and information, Derry (028) 7126 2017.

EMERGENCIES

In case of emergency – police (RUC or Garda), ambulance, fire brigade, lifeboat or mountain rescue – the number to dial wherever you are on the Ulster Way is 999. Be ready to give full details of the emergency and do exactly as you are told.

ACCOMMODATION AND TOURIST INFORMATION

Useful guides include *Where to Stay in Northern Ireland* and *An Information Guide to the Ulster Way: Accommodation for Walkers,* published by the Northern Ireland Tourist Board. Donegal Tourism publishes a *Donegal Accommodation Guide.*

The Northern Ireland Tourist Board and Donegal Tourism can handle bookings through either their head offices or any of their networked offices.

Northern Ireland Tourist Board, 59 North Street, Belfast, BT1 1NB. Telephone (028) 9024 6609.

Donegal County Tourism, Derry Road, Letterkenny, Co. Donegal. Telephone (074) 21160.

ULSTER WAY VISITOR ATTRACTIONS

Colin Glen Forest Park, Belfast (028) 9061 4115.

Cave Hill Heritage Centre, Belfast Castle (028) 9077 6925.

Belfast Zoo, Belfast (028) 9077 6277.

Glenariff Forest Park, Glenariff.

Giant's Causeway Centre, Causeway Head (028) 7073 1855.

Portrush Countryside Centre, Portrush (028) 7082 3600.

Plantation of Ulster Centre, Draperstown (028) 7962 7800.

Sperrin Heritage Centre, Glenelly (028) 8264 8142.

Gortin Glen Forest Park, Gortin.

Ulster History Park, Cullion (028) 8264 8188.
Ulster American Folk Park, Mountjoy (028) 9045 2250
Lough Derg Journey, Pettigo.
Marble Arch Caves, Florence Court (028) 6634 8855.
Florence Court House (028) 6634 8249.
Benburb Heritage Centre, Milltown (028) 3754 9752.
The Argory, Derrycaw (028) 8778 4753.
Peatlands Park, Church Hill (028) 3885 1102.
Scarva Visitors Centre, Scarva (028) 3883 2163.
Mourne Heritage Trust, Newcastle (028) 4372 4059.
Tyrella Beach, Tyrella (028) 4485 1228.
Exploris Centre, Portaferry (028) 4272 8062.
Castleward, Strangford (028) 4488 1204.
Quoile Countryside Centre, Downpatrick (028) 4461 5520.
Delamont Country Park, Delamont (028) 4482 8333.
Castle Espie Wildfowl & Wetlands Centre (028) 9187 4146.
Crawfordsburn Country Park (028) 9185 3621.
Ulster Folk & Transport Museum, Cultra (028) 9042 8428.
Belvoir Park Forest, Belfast (028) 9049 1264.

BIBLIOGRAPHY

Paddy Dillon, *Exploring the North of Ireland,* Ward Lock (192pp colour). A large-format book containing thirty-one lavishly illustrated one-day walking routes, taking in classic stretches of the Ulster Way. Also includes an overview of the Ulster Way.

Paddy Dillon, *25 Walks in and around Belfast*, The Stationery Office (106pp colour). From the centre of Belfast to the suburbs and surrounding countryside, including the Ulster Way near the city.

Rosemary Evans, *The Visitor's Guide to Northern Ireland*, Blackstaff Press (216pp colour). Useful for first-time visitors. Plenty of descriptions of places and attractions, with historical notes and events mentioned along the way.

Richard Rogers, *Ulster Walk Guide,* Gill & Macmillan (96pp b/w). Nearly fifty walks, many of them taking in areas of the countryside covered by the Ulster Way. This little book was one of the first to offer a good selection of walks around Northern Ireland.

Alan Warner, *Walking the Ulster Way,* Appletree Press (184pp b/w). The story of the first long walk around the route before it was fully agreed or waymarked. The route has since changed in many places, but the kindliness of the people remains the same.

Peter Wright, *Ulster Rambles,* Greystone Books (97pp b/w). Subtitled 'Fourteen Great Walks on the Ulster Way', picking off some of the best parts of the route. Summaries of the walks were published in a colour leaflet by the Northern Ireland Tourist Board.

ACCOMMODATION

NORTH-EASTERN SECTION

COUNTY ANTRIM – 190 KM (118 MILES)

BELFAST (Dunmurry)

Beechlawn House Hotel, 4 Dunmurry Lane, Dunmurry. (028) 9061 2974.

Mrs M Hughes, Warren House, 10 Thornhill Rd, Dunmurry. (028) 9061 1702.

Balmoral Hotel, Blacks Rd, near Dunmurry. (028) 9030 1234.

Forte Posthouse, 300 Kingsway, Dunmurry. (028) 9061 2101.

BELFAST (Fortwilliam)

Mrs S Cooper, Drumragh, 647 Antrim Rd. (028) 9077 3063.

BELFAST (Newtownabbey)

Mrs D Robinson, Perpetua House, 57 Collinbridge Park, Newtownabbey. (028) 9083 3041.

Mrs P Kelly, Iona, 161 Antrim Rd, Newtownabbey. (028) 9084 2256.

Glenavna House Hotel, 588 Shore Rd, Newtownabbey. (028) 9086 4461.

Mrs G McCabe, 109 Jordanstown Rd, Newtownabbey. (028) 9086 4702.

University of Ulster, Shore Rd, Jordanstown. (028) 9036 6394.

Glendun Court, Glenville Rd, Whiteabbey. (028) 9085 3005.

Loughshore Caravan Park, Shore Rd, Jordanstown. (028) 9086 8751.

BALLYNURE

Mrs M Crawford, Woodbine Farm, 98 Carrickfergus Rd, near Ballynure. (028) 9335 2092.

Mrs H Park, Rockbank, 40 Belfast Rd, Ballynure. (028) 9335 2261.

Mrs B McKay, Beechcroft, 43 Belfast Rd, Ballynure. (028) 9335 2334.

Mrs R McAskie, Brackenview, 42 Larne Rd, Ballynure. (028) 9332 3820.

GLENARM

Mr & Mrs Palmer, Burnside Country House, 37 Dickeystown Rd, Glenarm. (028) 288 41331.

Mrs E McAllister, Black Bush Cottage, 34 Dickeystown Rd, Glenarm. (028) 2884 1559.

Mrs M McAllister, Town Brae House, 6 Town Brae Rd, Glenarm. (028) 2884 1043.

Mrs M Morrow, Margaret's House, 10 Altmore St, Glenarm. (028) 288 41307.

Mr D McLoughlin, Nine Glens, 16 Toberwine St, Glenarm. (028) 2884 1590.

Mrs E Boyle, Riverside House, 13 Toberwine St, Glenarm. (028) 2884 1474.

Mrs I Boyle, 4 Toberwine St, Glenarm. (028) 2884 1219.

Mrs M Dempsey, 35 The Cloney, Glenarm. (028) 2884 1640.

CARNLOUGH

Londonderry Arms Hotel, 20 Harbour Rd, Carnlough. (028) 2888 5255.

Bridge Inn, 2 Bridge St, Carnlough. (028) 2888 5669.

Bethany Guesthouse, 5 Bay Rd, Carnlough. (028) 2888 5667.

Mrs P McKay, Glenview, 124 Ballymena Rd, Carnlough. (028) 2888 5546.

Mrs M McMullan, Harbour View, 50 Harbour Rd, Carnlough. (028) 2888 5335.

Mr J Rowan, 7 Shingle Cove, Carnlough. (028) 2888 5638.

Ruby Hill Caravan Park, 46 Largy Rd, Carnlough. (028) 2888 5692.

Bay View Caravan Park, 89 Largy Rd, Carnlough. (028) 2888 5685.

GLENARIFF

Glenariff Forest Park Caravan Site, 98 Glenariff Rd, Glenariff. (028) 2175 8232.

Mrs K McHenry, Dieskirt Farm, 104 Glen Rd, Glenariff. (028) 2177 1308.

Mrs M McHenry, Alt an Cogaid, 109 Glen Rd, Glenariff. (028) 2177 2064.

Mrs E O'Loan, Sanda, 29 Kilmore Rd, Glenariff. (028) 2177 1785.

Mrs M McAllister, Wilmar House, 26 Kilmore Rd, Glenariff. (028) 2177 1653.

Mr & Mrs Colligan, The Bay, 204 Coast Rd, Glenariff. (028) 2177 1858.

Mrs B Leech, Lasata, 72 Glen Rd, Glenariff. (028) 2177 1578.

Mrs R Ward, Lurig View, 4 Lurig View, Glenariff. (028) 2177 1618.

CUSHENDALL

Mrs N McAuley, The Burn, 63 Ballyeamon Rd, Cushendall. (028) 2177 1733.

Mrs K Quinn, Shramore, 27 Chapel Rd, Cushendall. (028) 2177 1610.

Mrs O McAuley, Cullentra House, 16 Cloghs Rd, Cushendall. (028) 2177 1762.

Mrs J McAuley, Garron View, 14 Cloghs Rd, Cushendall. (028) 2177 1018.

Thornlea Hotel, 6 Coast Rd, Cushendall. (028) 2177 1223.

Tros-Ben-Villa, 8 Coast Rd, Cushendall. (028) 2177 1130.

Mrs M O'Neill, Glendale, 46 Coast Rd, Cushendall. (028) 2177 1495.

Ms A Carey, The Meadows, 81 Coast Rd, Cushendall. (028) 2177 2020.

Mrs B O'Neill, Mountain View, 1 Kilnadore Rd, Cushendall. (028) 2177 1246.

Mrs A McKeegan, Riverside, 14 Mill St, Cushendall. (028) 2177 1655.

Mrs R Hamill, Culbidagh House, 115 Middlepark Rd, Cushendall. (028) 2177 1312.

Mrs M McCurry, Ashlea, 2 Tromra Rd, Cushendall. (028) 2177 1651.

Mrs A Wilkinson, Irene, 8 Kilnadore Rd, Cushendall. (028) 2177 1898.

Mrs N Mitchell, Carn Neill, 21 Glenariff Rd, Cushendall. (028) 2177 1392.

Central Bar, 7 Bridge St, Cushendall. (028) 2177 1730.

Cushendall Youth Hostel, Moneyvart House, 42 Layde Rd, Cushendall. (028) 2177 1344.

Cushendall Caravan Park, 62 Coast Rd, Cushendall. (028) 2177 1699.

Glenville Caravan Park, 20 Layde Rd, Cushendall. (028) 2177 1520.

CUSHENDUN

Mrs W McKay, Sleepy Hollow, 107 Knocknacarry Rd, Cushendun. (028) 2176 1513.

Cushendun, 10 Strandview Park, Cushendun. (028) 2176 1266.

Mrs M McAuley, 125 Tromra Rd, Cushendun. (028) 2176 1214.

Villa Farmhouse, 185 Torr Rd, Cushendun. (028) 2176 1252.

Mrs A McKendry, The Burns, 116 Torr Rd, Cushendun. (028) 2176 1285.

Mrs A McCormick, Cloneymore, 103 Knocknacarry Rd, Cushendun. (028) 2176 1443.

Mrs M McFadden, Drumkeerin, 201a Torr Rd, Cushendun. (028) 2176 1554.

Cushendun Caravan Park, 14 Glendun Rd, Cushendun. (028) 2176 1254.

BALLYCASTLE

Mrs O McHenry, Torr Brae, 77 Torr Rd, Ballycastle. (028) 2076 9625.

Mrs M McCarry, Colliers Hall, 50 Cushendall Rd, near Ballycastle. (028) 2076 2531.

Mrs D McKay, Tara House, 49a Ann St, Ballycastle. (028) 2076 2282.

Mrs A Gormley, Glenhaven, 10 Beechwood Ave, Ballycastle. (028) 2076 3612.

Ms A McHenry, Beechwood, 9 Beechwood Ave, Ballycastle. (028) 2076 3631.

Mrs E McAlister, Willeen, 1 Church Rd, Ballycastle. (028) 2076 3560.

Mrs A Hill, Broughanlea House, 59 Cushendall Rd, Ballycastle. (028) 2076 2842.

Mrs A Christie, Glenfarg, 4a Moyarget Rd, Ballycastle. (028) 2076 2018.

Mrs B McIlroy, Braemar, 72 Moyle Rd, Ballycastle. (028) 2076 2529.

Marine Hotel, 1 North St, Ballycastle. (028) 2076 2222.

Mrs K Delargy, Fair Head View, 26 North St, Ballycastle. (028) 2076 9376.

Mrs G McLernon, Ardaghmore, 35 North St, Ballycastle. (028) 2076 3329.

Mr E Shannon, Kenmara House, 45 North St, Ballycastle. (028) 2076 2600.

Mr M Jameson, Hilsea, 28 Quay Hill, Ballycastle. (028) 2076 2385.

Mrs M Mulholland, Silversprings, 20 Quay Rd, Ballycastle. (028) 2076 2080.

Mrs M Crawford, Ammiroy House, 24 Quay Rd, Ballycastle. (028) 2076 2621.

Mrs A McHenry, Cushleake House, 32 Quay Rd, Ballycastle. (028) 2076 3798.

Mrs V Greene, Fragrens, 34 Quay Rd, Ballycastle. (028) 2076 2168.

Glenluce Guest House, 42 Quay Rd, Ballycastle. (028) 2076 2914.

Ms M McMahon, Cuchulain House, 56 Quay Rd, Ballycastle. (028) 2076 2252.

Mrs J Lynn, Rathushard House, 3 Rathlin Rd, Ballycastle. (028) 2076 2237.

Mrs F Chambers, Broughgammon, 56 Straid Rd, Ballycastle. (028) 2076 3260.

Antrim Arms, 75 Castle St, Ballycastle. (028) 2076 2284.

Mrs Bartlett, Sunningdale, 28 Clare Rd, Ballycastle. (028) 2076 3859.

Mr A McKiernan, Bushbane House, 28 Whitepark Rd, Ballycastle. (028) 2076 3789.

Mrs P Black, Clare House, 33 Whitepark Rd, Ballycastle. (028) 2076 3889.

Castle Hostel, 62 Quay Rd, Ballycastle. (028) 2076 2337.

Ballycastle Backpackers, 4 North St, Ballycastle. (028) 2076 3612.

Watertop Open Farm, 118 Cushendall Rd, Ballycastle. (028) 2076 2576.

Silvercliffs Holiday Village, 21 Clare Rd, Ballycastle. (028) 2076 2550.

Fair Head Caravan Park, 13 Whitepark Rd, Ballycastle. (028) 2076 2077.

Maguire's Strand Caravan Park, 32 Carrickmore Rd, Ballycastle. (028) 2076 3294.

CARNDUFF

Mrs H Smyth, Gortconney Farm House, 52 Whitepark Rd, Carnduff, near Ballycastle. (028) 2076 2283.

BALLINTOY

Mrs F Jamieson, Carrick-A-Rede House, 109 Whitepark Rd, near Ballintoy. (028) 2076 2274.

Mrs Kane, Kilmean Farm, 4 Glenstaughey Rd, near Ballintoy. (028) 2076 3305.

Mrs J McCaw, Knocksaughey House, 122 Whitepark Rd, Ballintoy. (028) 2076 2967.

Mrs R McFall, Ballintoy House, 9 Main St, Ballintoy. (028) 2076 2317.

Fullerton Arms, 22 Main St, Ballintoy. (028) 2076 9613.

Mrs V Brown, Glenmore House, 94 Whitepark Rd, near Ballintoy. (028) 2076 3584.

Mr & Mrs Isles, Whitepark House, Whitepark Bay, near Ballintoy. (028) 2073 1482.

Larrybane Campsite, Larrybane, near Ballintoy. (028) 2076 2178.

Sheep Island View Hostel & Campsite, 42 Main St, Ballintoy. (028) 2076 9391.

Whitepark Bay Youth Hostel, Whitepark Bay, near Ballintoy. (028) 2073 1745.

DUNSEVERICK

Mrs O Rutherford, Danescroft, 171 Whitepark Rd, Portbraddan. (028) 2073 1586.

Mrs H McConaghy, Greenacres, 3 Isle Rd, Dunseverick. (028) 2073 2084.

Mrs A Kerr, Spring Farm, 15 Isle Rd, Dunseverick. (028) 2073 1780.

GIANT'S CAUSEWAY

Causeway Hotel, 40 Causeway Rd, next to Giant's Causeway Centre. (028) 2073 1226.

Mr J Smyth, Hillcrest Country House, 306 Whitepark Rd, near Bushmills. (028) 2073 1577.

Mrs F Lynch, Carnside Farmhouse, 23 Causeway Rd, near Bushmills. (028) 2073 1337.

Mrs M Mitchell, Kal-Mar, 64a Causeway Rd, near Bushmills. (028) 2073 1101.

Mrs R Ramage, 28 Lochaber, 107 Causeway Rd, near Bushmills. (028) 2073 1385.

Mrs L Ramage, North Winds, 299 Whitepark Rd, near Bushmills. (028) 7073 1374.

PORTBALLINTRAE

Mr J Wishart, Larkfield, 18 Ballaghmore Rd, Portballintrae. (028) 2073 1726.

Mrs M Wilson, Cedar Lodge, 44 Ballaghmore Rd, Portballintrae. (028) 2073 1763.

Mrs H Wilkinson, Keeve-Na, 62 Ballaghmore Rd, Portballintrae. (028) 2073 2184.

Bayview Hotel, 2 Bayhead Rd, Portballintrae. (028) 2073 1453.

Mrs B Cooke, Bayhead House, 8 Bayhead Rd, Portballintrae. (028) 2073 1441.

Beach House Hotel, 61 Beach Rd, Portballintrae. (028) 2073 1214.

Portballintrae Caravan Park, 60 Ballaghmore Rd, Portballintrae. (028) 2073 1478.

PORTRUSH

Magherabuoy House Hotel, 41 Magheraboy Rd, near Portrush. (028) 7082 3507.

Mrs J Adams, Loguestown Farm House, 58 Loguestown Rd, near Portrush. (028) 7082 2742.

Causeway Coast Hotel, 36 Ballyreagh Rd, Portrush. (028) 7082 2435.

Mrs A Ebbitt, Aghalun, 2 Caldwell Park, Portrush. (028) 7082 3166.

Mrs R Anderson, Beulah House, 16 Causeway St, Portrush. (028) 7082 2413.

Royal Court Hotel, 233 Ballybogey Rd, Portrush. (028) 7082 2236.

Mrs A Armstrong, Summer Island House, 14 Coleraine Rd, Portrush. (028) 7082 4640.

Abercorn, 57 Coleraine Rd, Portrush. (028) 7082 5014.

Glenkeen, 59 Coleraine Rd, Portrush. (028) 7082 2279.

Brookvale, 61 Coleraine Rd, Portrush. (028) 7082 3678.

Glencroft, 95 Coleraine Rd, Portrush. (028) 7082 2902.

Mrs L Hoy, Mount Royal, 2 Eglinton St, Portrush. (028) 7082 3342.

Eglinton Hotel, 49 Eglinton St, Portrush. (028) 7082 2371.

Mrs M Mair, An Uladh, 73 Eglinton St, Portrush. (028) 7082 2221.

Ma-Ring Guest House, 17 Kerr St, Portrush. (028) 7082 2765.

West Strand Guest House, 18 Kerr St, Portrush. (028) 7082 2270.

Casa-A-La-Mar, 21 Kerr St, Portrush. (028) 7082 2617.

Mrs J Collins, Oakdene, 6 Lansdowne Crescent, Portrush. (028) 7082 4629.

Alexandra, 11 Lansdowne Crescent, Portrush. (028) 7082 2284.

Prospect House, 20 Lansdowne Crescent, Portrush. (028) 7082 2299.

Old Manse Guest House, 3 Main St, Portrush. (028) 7082 4118.

West Bay View, 48 Mark St, Portrush. (028) 7082 3375.

Mrs R Torrens, Drumlee, 50 Mark St, Portrush. (028) 7082 3133.

Hayesbank/Kantara, 5/6 Ramore Avenue, Portrush. (028) 7082 3823.

Mr N Torrens, Atlantis, 10 Ramore Avenue, Portrush. (028) 7082 4583.

Metropole House Hostel, 70 Eglinton St, Portrush. (028) 7082 3511.

Portrush Independent Hostel, 5 Causeway View Terrace, Portrush. (028) 7082 4845.

Hilltop Holiday Park, 60 Loguestown Rd, Portrush. (028) 7082 3537.

Carrick Dhu Caravan Park, 12 Ballyreagh Rd, Portrush. (028) 7082 3712.

Blair's Caravan Park, 29 Dhu Varren, Portstewart Rd, Portrush. (028) 7082 2760.

Skerries Holiday Park, 126 Dunluce Rd, Portrush. (028) 7082 2531.

NORTH-WESTERN SECTION

COUNTIES DERRY & TYRONE – 179 KM (111 MILES)

PORTSTEWART

Mr R Perry, Mulroy House, 8 Atlantic Circle, Portstewart. (028) 7083 2293.

Mrs M Lutton, Hebron, 37 Coleraine Rd, Portstewart. (028) 7083 2225.

Mrs E Robinson, Wanderin' Heights, 12 High Rd, Portstewart. (028) 7083 3250.

Rockhaven, 17 Portrush Rd, Portstewart. (028) 7083 3846.

Windsor Hotel, 8 The Promenade, Portstewart. (028) 7083 2523.

Mrs J Kelly, Craigmore House, 26 The Promenade, Portstewart. (028) 7083 2120.

Mrs B Laughlin, Mount Oriel, 74 The Promenade, Portstewart. (028) 7083 2556.

Mrs D McGarry, Akaroa, 75 The Promenade, Portstewart. (028) 7083 2067.

Mrs M Austin, Gorse Bank House, 36 Station Rd, Portstewart. (028) 7083 3347.

Ashleigh House, 164 Station Rd, Portstewart. (028) 7083 4452.

Oregon, 168 Station Rd, Portstewart. (028) 7083 2826.

Mrs E Caskey, Strandeen, 63 Strand Rd, Portstewart. (028) 7083 3159.

Edgewater Hotel, 88 Strand Rd, Portstewart. (028) 7083 3314.

Mr & Mrs Nichol, Chez Nous, 1 Victoria Terrace, Portstewart. (028) 7083 2608.

Lis-Na-Rhin Guesthouse, 6 Victoria Terrace, Portstewart. (028) 7083 3522.

Causeway Coast Hostel, 4 Victoria Terrace, Portstewart. (028) 7083 3789.

Juniper Hill Caravan Park, 70 Ballyreagh Rd, Portstewart. (028) 7083 2023.

Portstewart Holiday Park, 80 Mill Rd, Portstewart. (028) 7083 3308.

COLERAINE

Lodge Hotel, Lodge Rd, Coleraine. (028) 7034 4848.

Mrs S Wells, Beth-a-Bara, 1 University Park, Coleraine. (028) 7032 9279.

Mrs K Gurney, 40 Avonbrook Gardens, Coleraine. (028) 7035 7286.

Mrs J Doak, Tramalis, 5 Ballindreen Rd, Coleraine. (028) 7035 5204.

Mr M Pollock, Milesric, 12 The Boulevard, Coleraine. (028) 7035 5674.

Mr Eyre, Cairndhu, 4 Cairn Court, Coleraine. (028) 7034 2854.

Mrs M Barbour, Mizpah, 44 Carthall Rd, Coleraine. (028) 7034 3288.

Ms C McWilliam, Clanwilliam Lodge, 21 Curragh Rd, Coleraine. (028) 7035 6582.

Mrs J King, Camus House, 27 Curragh Rd, Curragh Rd, Coleraine. (028) 7034 2982.

Mrs D Chandler, Coolbeg, 2e Grange Rd, Coleraine. (028) 7034 4961.

Mrs G McConnaghie, Karjul, 32 Lower Captain St, Coleraine. (028) 7035 2038.

Mrs M Kerr, Carnadoon, 41a Portstewart Rd, Coleraine. (028) 7035 7492.

Mrs D McClelland, Tullan's Farm, 46 Newmills Rd, Coleraine. (028) 7034 2309.

Mrs L Neely, Hillview Farm, 40 Gateside Rd, Coleraine. (028) 7034 3992.

Mrs S Neely, 52a Gateside Rd, Coleraine. (028) 7035 7185.

Ms D Cuthbert, Town House, 45 Millburn Rd, Coleraine. (028) 7034 4869.

Mrs C Harbison, Manicore, 69 Millburn Rd, Coleraine. (028) 7035 1884.

Mr H Guy, The Laurels, 26 Mountsandel Rd, Coleraine. (028) 7035 1441.

Mrs R Acheson, Cherith, 9 Waterford Drive, Coleraine. (028) 7035 5228.

Mr W Wallace, Breezemount House, 26 Castlerock Rd, Coleraine. (028) 7034 4615.

Mrs H Roulston, Manor Cottage, 44 Cranagh Rd, Coleraine. (028) 7034 4001.

Mrs W Gribbon, Cranagh Lodge, 50 Cranagh Rd, Coleraine. (028) 7034 4621.

Mrs A Jack, Cranagh Hill, 52 Cranagh Rd, Coleraine. (028) 7035 1138.

Tullan's Farm Caravan Park, 46 Newmills Rd, Coleraine. (028) 7034 2309.

CASTLEROCK

Mrs J McConkey, Craighead House, 8 Circular Rd, Castlerock. (028) 7084 8273.

Mrs M Carr, Cranford House, 11 Circular Rd, Castlerock. (028) 7084 8669.

Mrs L Burke, Liskinbwee, 10 Exorna Lane, Castlerock. (028) 7084 8909.

Mrs M Henry, Bannview, 14 Exorna Lane, Castlerock. (028) 7084 8033.

Golf Hotel, 17 Main St, Castlerock. (028) 7084 8204.

Marine Inn, 9 Main St, Castlerock. (028) 7084 8456.

Mrs C Henry, Carneety House, 120 Mussenden Rd, Castlerock. (028) 7084 8640.

Mrs E Norwell, Kenmuir House, 10 Sea Rd, Castlerock. (028) 7084 8345.

Mrs L Tosh, Shandon, 41 Sea Rd, Castlerock. (028) 7084 8262.

Castlerock Holiday Park, 24 Sea Rd, Castlerock. (028) 7084 8381.

Guysmere Centre, Sea Rd, Castlerock. (028) 7084 8672.

DOWNHILL

Downhill Hostel, 12 Mussenden Rd, Downhill. (028) 7084 9077.

Downhill Campsite, Downhill. (028) 7084 8728.

BELLARENA

Mrs M McGinn, Carraig Mór House, 17 Duncrun Rd, Bellarena. (028) 7775 0250.

Mrs D Copeland, Old Rectory, 4 Duncrun Rd, Bellarena. (028) 7775 0477.

FORMOYLE

Mrs G Neely, Bratwell Farm, 23 Knocknougher Rd, near Formoyle. (028) 7084 9088.

Mrs J Kerr, Rockmount, 241 Windyhill Rd, Ballinrees. (028) 7034 2914.

DRUMSURN

Mrs J Foster, Cloghan Farm House, 8 Cloghan Rd, Drumsurn. (028) 7776 2405.

GLENULLIN

Mrs C Mullan, Bealach Speirin, 75 Glen Rd, Glenullin. (028) 2955 8696.

DUNGIVEN

Mrs M McCloskey, Edenroe, 5 Lackagh Park, Dungiven. (028) 7774 2029.

Mrs J Haslett, Cherryview, 297 Drumrane Rd, Dungiven. (028) 7774 1471.

Mrs M McMacken, Bradagh, 132 Main St, Dungiven. (028) 7774 1346.

Mrs M McCloskey, Edenroe, 5 Lackagh Park, Dungiven. (028) 7774 2029.

Mr J Sweeney, Sliabh Na Mon, 918 Glenside Rd, Carn. (028) 7774 1210.

DRAPERSTOWN

Mrs H Kelly, Rural College, Derrynoid Forest, near Draperstown. (028) 7962 9100.

Mrs M Kelly, Neilly's, 19 Moneyneany Rd, Draperstown. (028) 7962 8313.

Mrs P Flanagan, Moyola View, 35 Tobermore Rd, Draperstown. (028) 7962 8495.

GORTIN

Mrs F McCrory, Lenamore Lodge, 19 Crockanboy Rd, Gortin. (028) 8164 8460.

Gortin Outdoor Centre, 198 Glenpark Rd, Gortin. (028) 8264 8083.

GORTIN GLEN

Gortin Glen Caravan Park, Lisnaharney Rd, Gortin Glen. (028) 8164 8108.

GLENHORDIAL

Omagh Hostel, 9a Waterworks Rd, Glenhordial, near Omagh. (028) 8224 1973.

MOUNTJOY

Mrs W Sterritt, Killynure, 95 Castletown Rd, Mountjoy. (028) 8266 1482.

Mr & Mrs McAuley, Derrylynn, 13 Beltany Rd, Mountjoy. (028) 8224 4256.

Mr E Mc Farland, Dunmore House, Mountjoy West. (028) 8224 2126.

Ulster American Folk Park, Residential Centre, Camphill Rd, near Mountjoy. (028) 8224 0918.

BARONSCOURT

Hunting Lodge Hotel, Letterbin, Baronscourt. (028) 8166 1679.

SOUTH-WESTERN SECTION

COUNTY FERMANAGH – 199 KM (123½ MILES)

GORTNAGULLION

Mr R Loane, Montaugh Farm, Drumskinny. (028) 6663 1385.

PETTIGO

Mrs H O Shea, Hill Top View, Billary, Pettigo. (072) 61535.

Mrs K McVeigh, The Willows, Donegal Rd, Pettigo, (072) 61565.

Mrs M Leonard, Avondale, Lough Derg Rd, Pettigo. (072) 61520.

ROSSCOR

Riverside House, 601 Loughshore Rd, Drumbadreevagh. (028) 6665 8649.

BELLEEK

Hotel Carlton, 2 Main St, Belleek. (028) 6658 282.

The Fiddlestone, 15 Main St, Belleek. (028) 6665 8008.

Mrs C Mullin, 190 Garrison Rd, Corry, Belleek. (028) 6865 8588.

DERRYGONNELLY

Mr R Pierce, Pierces Folly, Dresternan, near Derrygonnelly. (028) 6664 1735.

Mrs J Elliott, Drumary Farm House, Glenasheevar Rd, Derrygonnelly. (028) 6864 1420.

Mrs J Wray, Meadow View, Sandhill, Derrygonnelly. (028) 6864 1233.

Navar Guest House, Derryvarey, Derrygonnelly. (028) 6864 1384.

Tir Navar Holiday Village, Creamery St, Derrygonnelly. (028) 6664 1673.

BELCOO

Corralea Lodge, Corralea, near Belcoo. (028) 6638 6325.

Mr G Rasdale, Riverside, Holywell, Belcoo. (028) 6638 6471.

Ms T McGovern, Bush Cottage, Belcoo. (028) 6638 6242.

Mrs B McGovern, Glann-N House, Carrontreemall, Belcoo. (028) 6638 6471.

Mr R Doherty, Bella Vista, Cottage Drive, Belcoo. (028) 6638 6469.

Mrs K Sweeney, Belcoo House, 31 Main St, Belcoo. (028) 6638 6304.

ABOCURRAGH

Abocurragh Farm, Abocurragh, Letterbreen. (028) 6634 8484.

FLORENCECOURT

Tullyhona House, 59 Marble Arch Rd, Florencecourt. (028) 6634 8452.

Mrs E Fraser, Lanmore Lodge, Florencecourt. (028) 6634 8642.

KINAWLEY

Mrs K Cassidy, Corrakelly House, 14 Drumroosk Rd, near Kinawley (028) 6774 8705.

DERRYLIN

Mrs J Whittendale, Hollytree Farm, Drumanybeg, Knockaraven PO, near Derrylin. (028) 6774 8319.

LOWER LOUGH ERNE

Share Holiday Village, Smith's Strand, Shanaghy, near Lisnaskea. (028) 6772 2122.

LISNASKEA

Ortine Hotel, Main St, Lisnaskea. (028) 6772 1206.

Colorado Guesthouse, 102 Lisnagole Rd, near Lisnaskea. (028) 6772 1486.

PORTS

Mr K Mewes, Ports House, Ports, near Newtownbutler. (028) 6773 8528.

NEWTOWNBUTLER

Lanesborough Arms, 6 High St, Newtownbu tler. (028) 6773 8488.

SOUTHERN SECTION

COOUNTIES TYRONE & ARMAGH – 158 KM (98½ MILES)

FIVEMILETOWN

Valley Hotel, 60 Main St, Fivemiletown. (028) 6652 1505.

Fourways Hotel, 41 Main St, Fivemiletown. (028) 6652 1260.

Mrs G Malone, Ashlone House, 76 Colebrooke Rd, Fivemiletown. (028) 6652 1553.

Mr A Malone, Valley Villa, 92 Colebrooke Rd, Corcreevy. (028) 6652 1553.

Mrs E Fitzgerald, Church View, 2 Murley Rd, Fivemiletown. (028) 6652 2059.

Mrs D McManus, Station House, Fivemiletown. (028) 6652 8124.

Mrs R Lowry, Blessingbourne, Fivemiletown. (028) 6652 1221.

Round Lake Caravan Park, Murley Rd, Fivemiletown. (028) 8776 7259.

Mrs M McFarland, Timpany Manor, 53 Ballagh Rd, near Fivemiletown. (028) 6652 1285.

FARDROSS

Clogher Valley Country Caravan Park, Fardross Forest. (028) 8554 8932.

CLOGHER

Mrs M Kelly, River Furey House, 24 Monaghan Rd, Lisbane, near Clogher. (028) 8254 8843.

Corick House, 20 Corick Rd, Clogher. (028) 8554 8216.

BALLYGAWLEY

Mrs E Lyttle, The Grange, 15 Grange Rd, Ballygawley. (028) 8166 8053.

AUGHNACLOY

Mrs I McClements, Garvey Lodge, 62 Favour Royal Rd, near Aughnacloy. (028) 8555 7239.

Mr & Mrs Liggett, Rehaghy Lodge, 35 Rehaghy Rd, near Aughnacloy. (028) 8555 7693.

CALEDON

Mrs C Agnew, Model Farm, 70 Derrycourtney Rd, Ramakitt, near Caledon. (028) 3756 8210.

Mrs E Reid, Tannaghlane House, 15 Tannaghlane Rd, near Caledon. (028) 3756 8247.

BENBURB

Benburb Valley Youth Hostel, 89 Milltown Rd, Tullymore Etra, Benburb. (028) 3754 9752.

MOY

Muleany House, 86 Gorestown Rd, Moy. (028) 8778 4183.

Mrs L McNeice, Charlemont House, 4 The Square, Moy. (028) 8778 4755.

MAGHERY

Maghery Caravan Park, Maghery. (028) 3832 2205.

PORTADOWN

Mrs M Stephenson, Redbrick Country House, Corbrackey Lane, near Portadown. (028) 3833 5268.

Mrs A O'Neill, Drumcree House, 38 Ashgrove Rd, Portadown. (028) 3833 8655.

Carngrove Hotel, 2 Charlestown Rd, Portadown. (028) 3833 9222.

Mrs P McKeever, 113 Charlestown New Rd, Portadown. (028) 3833 3391.

Mrs R Turkington, 17 Gallrock Rd, Portadown. (028) 3885 2189.

Seagoe Hotel, Upper Church Lane, Portadown. (028) 3833 3076.

Mr G Black, Bannview, 60 Portmore St, Portadown. (028) 3833 6666.

Mrs M Hughes, Avonbawn, 140 Thomas St, Portadown. (028) 3833 9030.

Mrs M Blevins, Sirron, 157 Charles St, Portadown. (028) 38 354980.

GILFORD

Mrs M Buller, Mount Pleasant, 38 Banbridge Rd, Gilford. (028) 3883 1522.

DRUMBANAGHER

Mrs E Thompson, Deer Park, 177 Tandragee Rd, Drumbanagher. (028) 3082 1409.

NEWRY

Canal Court Hotel, Merchants Quay, Newry. (028) 3025 1234.

Mrs P O'Hare, Marymount, Windsor Avenue, Newry. (028) 3026 1099.

Mrs S Doolan, Ashdene House, 28 Windsor Avenue, Newry. (028) 3026 7530.

Mrs T Guthrie, Green Acre, 8 Church Ave, Newry. (028) 3025 1479.

Ms E Baxter, Woodcroft, 8 Warren Hill, Newry. (028) 3026 7133.

Mrs C Farrell, Millvale House, 8 Millvale Rd, Newry. (028) 3026 3789.

Mrs L Magee, Cara House, 22 Laurel Grove, Newry. (028) 3025 0587.

Hillside Guest House, 1 Rock Rd, Newry. (028) 3026 5484.

Ashton House, 37 Omeath Rd, near Newry. (028) 3026 2120.

SOUTH-EASTERN SECTION

COUNTY DOWN – 234 KM (145 MILES)

BURREN

Mrs M Ryan, Ryans, 19 Milltown St, Burren. (028) 4177 2506.

ROSTREVOR

Mrs E Henshaw, Forestbrook House, 11 Forestbrook Rd, Rostrevor. (028) 4173 8105.

Mrs M Gavaghan, An Tobar, 2 Cherry Hill, Rostrevor. (028) 4173 8712.

Knockbarragh Hostel, Knockbarragh Rd, Rostrevor. (028) 4173 9716.

Rostrevor Youth Centre, Warrenpoint Rd, Rostrevor. (028) 4173 9716.

Kilbroney Caravan Park, Shore Rd, Rostrevor. (028) 4173 8134.

KILLOWEN

Mrs P Donnan, Fir Trees, 16 Killowen Rd, Killowen. (028) 4173 8602.

Mrs M Murphy, Hillcrest Farmhouse, 12 Kilfeaghan Rd, Killowen. (028) 4173 8114.

ATTICAL

Mrs M Trainor, Hill View House, 18 Bog Rd, Attical. (028) 4176 4269.

NEWCASTLE

Mrs G Keown, Cherry Villa, 12 Bryansford Gardens, Newcastle. (028) 4372 4128.

Mr & Mrs Biggerstaff, Ashmount, 19 Bryansford Rd, Newcastle. (028) 4372 5074.

Brook Cottage Hotel, Bryansford Rd, Newcastle. (028) 4372 2204.

Enniskeen House Hotel, 98 Bryansford Rd, Newcastle. (028) 4372 2392.

Burrendale Hotel & Country Club, 51 Castlewellan Rd, Newcastle. (028) 4372 2599.

Slieve Donard Hotel, Downs Rd, Newcastle. (028) 4372 3681.

Mr & Mrs G Keogh, Savoy House, 20 Downs Rd, Newcastle. (028) 4372 2513.

Mrs M Macauley, Beach House, 22 Downs Rd, Newcastle. (028) 4372 2345.

Mrs M Dornan, Innisfree House, 7 Dundrum Rd, Newcastle. (028) 4372 3303.

Mrs M Lavery, 12 Linkside Park, Newcastle. (028) 4372 3638.

Donard Hotel, 27 Main St, Newcastle. (028) 4372 2203.

Avoca Hotel, 93 Central Promenade, Newcastle. (028) 4372 2253.

Briers Country House, 39 Middle Tollymore Rd, Newcastle. (028) 4372 4347.

Mrs M McBride, Homeleigh, 7 Slievemoyne Park, Newcastle. (028) 4372 2305.

Harbour House Inn, 4 South Promenade, Newcastle. (028) 4372 3445.

Mrs M Murray, Glenside Farmhouse, 136 Tullybrannigan Rd, Newcastle. (028) 4372 2628.

Newcastle Youth Hostel, 30 Downs Rd, Newcastle. (028) 4372 2133.

Tollymore Forest Park Campsite, 176 Tullybrannigan Rd, near Newcastle. (028) 4372 2428.

DUNDRUM

Mrs S McKeating, Mourne View House, 16 Main St, Dundrum. (028) 4375 1457.

The Road House Inn, 157 Bay Rd, Dundrum. (028) 4375 1209.

BALLYKINLER

Mr & Mrs Corbett, Tyrella House, Clanmaghery Rd, Tyrella. (028) 4485 1422.

Mrs M Macauley, Havine Farm, 51 Ballydonnell Rd, Tyrella. (028) 4485 1242.

MINERSTOWN

Mrs M Mackey, Beachview House, 66b Minerstown Rd, Minerstown. (028) 4485 1923.

ARDGLASS

Mrs M Donnan, Strand Farm, 231 Ardglass Rd, near Ardglass. (028) 4484 1446.

Burford Lodge, 30 Quay St, Ardglass. (028) 4484 1141.

Mr & Mrs Convery, Ardglass Bungalow, 11 High Green, Ardglass. (028) 4484 1721.

Ms B O'Shea, The Cottage, 9 Castle Place, Ardglass. (028) 4484 1080.

Mr R O'Conboirne, Mariner's Rest, 9 Downpatrick Rd, Ardglass. (028) 4484 1543.

Coney Island Caravan Park, 74 Killough Rd, near Ardglass. (028) 4484 1448/1210.

STRANGFORD

Mrs M Thornton, Strangford Cottage, 41 Castle St, Strangford. (028) 4488 1208.

Strangford Caravan Park, 87 Shore Rd, Strangford. (028) 4488 1888.

Castle Ward Caravan Park, Castle Ward, near Strangford. (028) 4488 1680.

PORTAFERRY (off-route via ferry)

Portaferry Hotel, 10 The Strand, Portaferry. (028) 4272 8231.

Mrs M Adair, Adairs, 22 The Square, Portaferry. (028) 4272 8412.

Mrs M Ritchie, St Clare's, 8 Marian Way, Portaferry. (028) 4272 8719.

The Narrows, 8 Shore Road, Portaferry. (028) 4272 8148.

Barholm Hostel, 11 The Strand, Portaferry. (028) 4272 9598.

SAUL

Mrs E McMorris, Swan Lodge, 30 St Patrick's Rd, Saul. (028) 4461 5542.

DOWNPATRICK

Abbey Lodge Hotel, 38 Belfast Rd, Downpatrick. (028) 4461 4511.

Mrs J Fitzsimons, Hillcrest, 157 Strangford Rd, Downpatrick. (028) 4461 2583.

Mrs B Kerr, Dunleath House, 33 St Patrick's Drive, Downpatrick. (028) 4461 3221.

Mrs J Murray, Hillside, 62 Scotch St, Downpatrick. (028) 4461 3134.

Mrs E Coburn, Arolsen, 47 Roughal Park, Downpatrick. (028) 4461 2656.

Mrs R Wright, Troutbeck, 38 Cargagh Rd, Downpatrick. (028) 4483 0894.

Mrs J Bailey, Pheasant's Hill, 37 Killyleagh Rd, near Downpatrick. (028) 4461 7246.

KILLYLEAGH

Dufferin Arms Coaching Inn, 35 High St, Killyleagh. (028) 4482 8229.

KILLINCHY

Mrs P Gordon, Burren Cottage, 19 Main St, Killinchy. (028) 9754 1475.

Mrs D Crawford, Barnageeha, 90 Ardmillan Rd, Killinchy. (028) 9754 1011.

Ms P Jackson, Craigeden, 33 Craigarusky Rd, Killinchy. (028) 9754 1005.

COMBER

Old Schoolhouse Inn, 100 Ballydrain Rd, near Comber. (028) 9754 1182.

Mrs M Hamilton, Trench Farm, 35 Ringcreevy Rd, Comber.
(028) 9187 2558.

Mrs M Walker, Long Reach, 140 Belfast Rd, Comber. (028) 9187 1903.

NEWTOWNARDS

Mrs A McKibbin, 17 Ballyrogan Rd, Newtownards. (028) 9181 1693.

Strangford Arms Hotel, 92 Church St, Newtownards. (028) 9181 4141.

Mrs V Kerr, Ard Cuan, 3 Manse Rd, Newtownards. (028) 9181 1302.

Greenacres, 5 Manse Rd, Newtownards. (028) 9181 6193.

Mrs W Cochrane, Cuan Chalet, 41 Milecross Rd, Newtownards. (028) 9181 2302.

Mrs D White, Edenvale House, 130 Portaferry Rd, Newtownards. (028) 9181 4881.

Mrs J Lindsay, Rockhaven, 79 Mountain Rd, Newtownards. (028) 9182 3987

CLANDEBOYE

Clandeboye Lodge Hotel, 10 Estate Rd, Clandeboye. (028) 9185 2500.

BANGOR

There are many accommodation addresses in Bangor between 2 and 4 miles off-route to the east.

HELEN'S BAY

Mrs E Eves, Carrig-Gorm, 27 Bridge Rd, Helen's Bay. (028) 9185 3680.

HOLYWOOD

Ardshane Country Guesthouse, 5 Bangor Rd, Holywood. (028) 9042 2044.

Rayanne Guesthouse, 60 Demesne Rd, Holywood. (028) 9042 5859.

Culloden Hotel, 142 Bangor Rd, Holywood. (028) 9042 5223.

Mr & Mrs Donaldson, Altona House, 69 Church Rd, Holywood. (028) 9042 1179.

Mrs J Foster, Carnwood House, 85 Victoria Rd, Holywood. (028) 9047 1745.

Number Two, 2 Victoria Rd, Holywood. (028) 9042 2662.

BELFAST

Stormont Hotel, 587 Upper Newtownards Rd, Belfast. (028) 9065 8621.

Lismore Lodge, 410 Ormeau Rd, Belfast. (028) 9064 1205.

Ravenhill Guest House, 690 Ravenhill Rd, Belfast. (028) 9020 7444.

Oakdene Lodge, 16 Annadale Ave, Belfast. (028) 9049 2626.

Roseleigh Guesthouse, 19 Rosetta Park, Belfast. (028) 9064 4414.

Laburnum Lodge, 16 Deramore Park, Belfast. (028) 9066 5183.

Kilnamar, 174 Finaghy Rd South, Belfast. (028) 9061 1564.

Mr P Cormacain, Failte, 11 Finaghy Park North, Belfast. (028) 9061 9610.

DONEGAL SECTION

COUNTY DONEGAL – 111KM (69 MILES)

PETTIGO

Mrs H O' Shea, Hill Top View, Billary, Pettigo. (072) 61535.

Mrs K McVeigh, The Willows, Donegal Rd, Pettigo. (072) 61565.

Mrs M Leonard, Avondale, Lough Derg Rd, Pettigo. (072) 61520.

LOUGH ESKE

Mrs M McHugh, Lakeland, Birchill, Ballybofey Rd, Lough Eske. (073) 22481.

Ms G McGettigan, Rhu Gorse, Lough Eske. (073) 21685.

Mr K Clarke, Ard na Mona, Lough Eske. (073) 22650.

Mrs M McGinty, Ardeevin, Lough Eske. (073) 21790.

Mrs N McGinty, The Arches, Lough Eske. (073) 22029.

FINTOWN

The nearest listed accommodation is at Glenties, 7 to 10 miles off-route.

DUNLEWY

Ms N O Donnell, Radharc an Ghleanna, Dunlewy. (075) 31835.

Dunlewy Youth Hostel, Dunlewy. (075) 31180.

FALCARRAGH

Mrs C Cannon, Cuan na Mara, Ballyness, Falcarragh. (074) 35327.

Mr S Gallagher, Ballyconnell House, Falcarragh. (074) 35363.

Mrs M Murphy, Ferndale, Falcarragh. (074) 65506.

Shamrock Lodge Hostel, Falcarragh. (074) 35859.

*The Northern Ireland telephone codes are valid from June 1999